Josephine Pollard

Young Folks' Life of Jesus Christ

Josephine Pollard

Young Folks' Life of Jesus Christ

ISBN/EAN: 9783744783583

Printed in Europe, USA, Canada, Australia, Japan

Cover: Foto ©Lupo / pixelio.de

More available books at **www.hansebooks.com**

JESUS CARRYING THE CROSS.

YOUNG FOLKS'

LIFE OF

JESUS CHRIST

BY

JOSEPHINE POLLARD

AUTHOR OF "THE HISTORY OF THE NEW TESTAMENT IN WORDS OF ONE SYLLABLE;"
"HISTORY OF THE OLD TESTAMENT IN WORDS OF ONE SYLLABLE;"
"BATTLES OF AMERICA IN WORDS OF ONE SYLLABLE;"
"THE BIBLE AND ITS STORY;" ETC.

GEORGE ROUTLEDGE AND SONS, LIMITED
NEW YORK: 9 LAFAYETTE PLACE
LONDON, GLASGOW AND MANCHESTER

The Caxton Press
171, 173 Macdougal Street, New York

CONTENTS.

Chapter I.
The Birth of Jesus.. 1

Chapter II.
The Boyhood of Jesus.. 22

Chapter III.
Jesus Comes Out of Nazareth—His Baptism and Temptation...... 45

Chapter IV.
The First Disciples—The Miracle at Cana—The Passover Feast—Driving out the Money-Changers—Nicodemus.............. 57

Chapter V.
The Woman of Samaria—Jesus in Galilee—Healing of the Nobleman's Son—Rejected at Nazareth............................ 73

Chapter VI.
Jesus in Galilee—He Preaches from a Boat—The Calling of Matthew—Choosing the Twelve—The Sermon on the Mount...... 87

Chapter VII.
The Sermon on the Mount (Continued)—The House Built Upon a Rock.. 104

Chapter VIII.
Healing the Leper—The Centurion's Servant—The Widow of Nain—Mary Magdalene.. 113

Chapter IX.
Jesus at the Seaside—He Teaches in Parables—The Sower—The Wheat and the Tares—Grain of Mustard Seed—Hidden Leaven—Hidden Treasure—The Pearl of Price—The Drag Net—The Storm on the Lake—The Herd of Swine........................ 128

Chapter X.
Healing of the Paralytic—Matthew's Feast—The Raising of Jairus's Daughter—Two Blind Men—The Dumb Demoniac—Jesus Sends Out the Twelve Apostles........................ 141

Chapter XI.

The Pool of Bethesda—Healing of the Helpless Cripple—The Discourse that Followed—Jesus Returns to Galilee—Twelve Apostles Sent Out—The Murder of John the Baptist 156

Chapter XII.

Five Thousand Fed—Jesus Walks on the Sea—The Discourse at Capernaum about Eating with Unwashed Hands 169

Chapter XIII.

In the Cornfield—The Lord's Prayer—The Blind and Dumb Demoniac—The Pharisees Ask for a Sign—Jesus Dines with Scribes and Pharisees—Unwashed Hands—Anger of His Enemies—The Parable of the Rich Fool—Be Ye Also Ready 183

Chapter XIV.

Jesus Leaves Capernaum—The Syro-Phœnician Woman—The Deaf-and-Dumb Man—Four Thousand Fed—Cæsarea Philippi—Peter's Confession 198

Chapter XV.

The Transfiguration—Healing the Lunatic Boy—Which Shall Be Greatest?—The Tribute Money—The Ninety and Nine—Jesus Rejected by the Samaritans—"I Go Not Up Yet to the Feast" 206

Chapter XVI.

The Feast of Tabernacles—The Speech Near the Treasury—The Jews Pick Up Stones to Throw at Him 223

Chapter XVII.

The Man Born Blind—The Parable of the Sheep-fold—Jesus Says "I am the Door"—He Leaves Galilee 236

Chapter XVIII.

In Perea—Who is my Neighbor?—Parable of the Good Samaritan—The Man with the Dropsy—The Great Supper—The Lost Sheep—The Lost Piece of Money—The Lost Son 248

Chapter XIX.

Parable of the Unjust Steward—Dives and Lazarus—The Coming of the Kingdom—Is it Lawful? Suffer Little Ones to Come Unto Me—The Unmerciful Servant 260

Chapter XX.

Bethany—Martha and Mary—"The Good Part"—Jesus Goes Again to Perea—The Master Calleth Thee—Lazarus is Raised from the Dead—The High-Priest Prophesies—Jesus Retires to the City of Ephraim 273

CHAPTER XXI.

On the Way to Jerusalem—The Ten Lepers—The Sons of Zebedee—Jericho—Zaccheus—Blind Bartimacs—Parable of the Ten Pounds—The Feast at Bethany—Mary's Offering—The Rage of Judas 287

CHAPTER XXII.

Bethpage—The Entry into Jerusalem, Palm Sunday—Hosanna—The Boys in the Temple—The Barren Fig-tree—Who Gave Them Authority?—The Two Sons—The Wicked Husbandmen—The Chief Corner Stone—"Shall We Pay Tribute to Cæsar?"—Jesus Near the Treasury—The Poor Widow—The Sadducees Ask Questions—Jesus Bids Farewell to the Temple 298

CHAPTER XXIII.

Parable of the Ten Virgins—Ten Talents—Picture of the Last Day—"Inasmuch as Ye Did it not to Me"—The Paschal Feast—"Lord, Is it I?"—The Traitor Made Known 319

CHAPTER XXIV.

The Last Supper—Jesus Prays With and For His Disciples—The Promise of the Comforter 334

CHAPTER XXV.

In the Upper Room—Gethsemane—The Judas Kiss—Jesus on Trial—He is Sent to Pilate—Condemned to Death—Cruelty of the Soldiers 344

CHAPTER XXVI.

The Way to the Cross—The Crucifixion—The Burial—The Ascension—"He is Risen" 364

CHAPTER XXVII.

Easter Sunday—The Women at the Tomb—Peter and John—Why Weepest Thou?—The Walk to Emmaus—Jesus Shows Himself to His Disciples—Doubting Thomas—The Heavy Net—"Feed My Lambs"—The Day of Pentecost 384

LIST OF ILLUSTRATIONS.

	PAGE
Jesus Carrying His Cross (*Frontispiece*).	
The Star of the East	1
Plan of Jerusalem at the Time of King Herod	2
The Angel Appearing to Mary	3
Houses in Bethlehem	7
The Shepherds at Night	9
The Birth of Jesus	11
Simeon in the Temple	13
The Child Jesus	15
Nazareth	18
The Magi Before Herod	19
Houses in Nazareth	21
The Wise Men Before Herod	23
Roll of the Pentateuch	26
The Flight into Egypt	27
Cylinder Holding the Pentateuch	29
View of Jerusalem	31
Walls of Jerusalem	33
The Jaffa Gate, Jerusalem	34
Restitution of the Temple	35
Interior of St. Stephen's Gate, Jerusalem	37
Passover Cake	38
Portion of the Temple Wall	39
Representation of the Face of Our Lord	42
Jesus in the Temple	43
General View of the Tabernacle	47
John the Baptist	49
Son, Why hast Thou thus Dealt with Us?	51
Jesus in His Youth	55
The Temptation	59
John the Baptist Preaching	63
Driving the Sellers from the Temple	66
The Marriage at Cana	67
The Woman of Samaria	75
The High Priest	80
Colossal Lamp	82
The Ark	83

LIST OF ILLUSTRATIONS.

	PAGE
A Levite	84
Table of Shew-bread	85
Eastern Lamps	86
Phylacteries	87
South End of the Sea of Galilee	88
On the Sea of Galilee	89
Jesus and Peter	92
Jesus Curing the Sick	93
Shepherd and the Lamb	97
The Sermon on the Mount	101
The House Built Upon a Rock	111
Christ, and the Centurion	115
Eastern Bier	116
The Widow's Son Brought to Life	117
Sidon at the Present Day	121
Magdalene, Anointing the Feet of Jesus	125
The Sower	129
The Enemy Sowing Tares	131
Leaven	133
Seeking Great Pearls	134
Parable of the Net	136
Stilling the Tempest	137
Jesus and the Demoniac	139
The Paralytic Cured	143
Cured by Touching His Garment	145
The Raising of Jairus's Daughter	149
The Pool of Bethesda	157
Salome Before Herod	165
Herodias With the Head of John the Baptist	168
Feeding the Multitude	171
Jesus Walking on the Sea	173
Christ the Consolator	179
In the Cornfields	184
The Withered Hand	185
Jesus and the Syro-Phœnician Woman	199
Jesus Blesses the Children	211
Peter and the Tribute-Money	215
The Sending Out of the Seventy	217
Sidon	220
Waving the Branches at the Feast of the Tabernacles	227
The Pool of Siloam	237
The Unfruitful Tree	246
The Great Feast	251
The Lost Sheep	255

LIST OF ILLUSTRATIONS.

	PAGE
The Prodigal's Return	258
The Unjust Steward	261
The Rich Man and the Beggar	265
He Put His Hands Upon Them	271
Mary and Martha	274
Bethany	275
Resurrection of Lazarus	285
Jesus and Zaccheus	291
Mount of Olives	299
The Entry into Jerusalem	301
Moonlight on the Mount of Olives	305
Give to Cæsar that which is Cæsar's	311
The Widow's Mite	313
Jesus Weeping Over Jerusalem	317
The Foolish Virgins	321
The Talents	324
Judas Bargaining to Betray Jesus	329
The Last Supper	335
In the Garden of Gethsemane	345
Judas Betrays Christ	349
Christ Before Pilate	359
The Whipping Post	362
Scourge	363
Jesus Crowned With Thorns	365
Carrying the Cross	366
The Crucifixion	367
Aceldama, or The Field of Blood	371
The Descent from the Cross	375
Laying Jesus in the Tomb	377
"He is Risen"	379
Jesus Appearing to Mary Magdalene	381
The Incredulity of Thomas	387
Jesus Shows Himself to his Disciples	389
The Coming of the Holy Ghost	393
The Ascension	397

PREFACE.

THE Life of our Lord Jesus Christ is so woven through the Old and New Testaments, that one must read from Genesis to Revelation in order to gain a correct knowledge of his wonderful history. Moses, Abraham, Isaac, Jacob, Joseph, Joshua, Samuel, David, and others knew him by faith. He was to them a present help in time of trouble. The Prophets foretold the coming of One who was to be mightier than any king upon the throne, wiser and holier than any priest or prophet, and more kind and faithful than any friend and brother man had ever known. This God-man was sent into the world to make peace between God and men. He was born among them, lived among them, saw their sinful ways, and knew the wickedness of their hearts. Now there is no power on earth so strong as love. It will conquer when all else fails. The reason why men had fallen away from God was because they were afraid of him. They bowed their heads and prostrated their bodies, and pretended to be good, but their hearts were hard, and they did evil all their days. Jesus came to teach them and us to lead better lives, to love God, and to do his will like children, and not like slaves; and he was an example to them and to us in his life and in his death.

As we follow him from Bethlehem to Calvary—from the Cradle to the Grave—and witness his sorrow in the Garden of Gethsemane, we realize somewhat the depth of a Saviour's love, and are amazed at his mercy and forgiveness. The author of this simplified story of Jesus has been greatly helped in her work by Canon Farrer's "Life of Christ," and Edersheim's "Life and Times of Jesus the Messiah," and yet in spite of her efforts she is deeply conscious that "the half has not been told." J. P.

THE LIFE OF JESUS CHRIST.

CHAPTER I.

THE BIRTH OF JESUS.

The Jewish race had long been slaves, and were compelled to pay taxes to other nations. For a time, they had had kings of their own; but their reign came to an end. The Twelve tribes were scattered, and those that had kept together were under the dominion of the Emperor of Rome, with Herod as their governor.

But the Jews had great faith in the Word of God, as contained in the Books of the Old Testament, and in several there was mention made of a star that was to rise in the East and flood with light the whole Jewish nation.

There were magicians in those days who studied the stars, and read the open page of the sky as if it were the Book of Fate. Certain stars foretold great wars or a long term of peace, and were consulted in regard to business affairs, or the taking of a journey.

The houses in the East had flat roofs, and it was easy for men to gather there at night to talk over the affairs of the day, and to watch the stars come out one

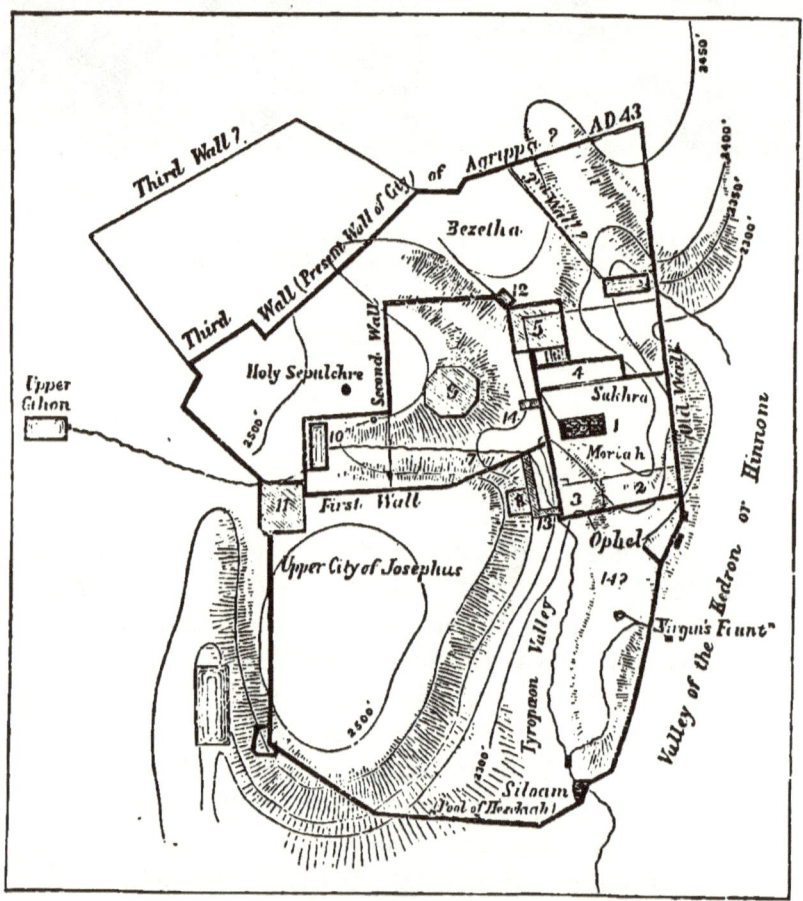

PLAN OF JERUSALEM AT THE TIME OF KING HEROD.

1. Temple of Solomon. ⎫
2. Palace of Solomon. ⎬ Herod's Temple.
3. Added by Herod. ⎭
4. Exhedra.
5. Antonia.
6. Cloisters joining Antonia to Temple.
7. Xystus.
8. Agrippa's Palace.
9. Zion.
10. Lower Pool of Gihon.
11. Herod's Palace.
12. Bethesda.
13. Bridge built by Herod.
14. The Lower City.

by one in the clear, blue sky above. They faced the East always at prayer time, and at night directed their gaze to this quarter, from whence a star was to rise

THE ANGEL APPEARING TO MARY.

that would be like no other star that the eye of man had ever seen.

Night after night, for years and years, the Jews had watched the scroll outspread above them, and had faith to believe that, although they might die without the sight, there was still some good in store for the children of Israel, God's chosen people.

In order that he might know whether the Jews were dying out or increasing, the Emperor Augustus had a census, or count, taken of them once a year. This was not done at their own homes, as was the case in Rome, but the Jews were allowed to keep up their old custom—of each tribe meeting at the town where its family originally belonged.

As the Jews were scattered all over the land of Judea, and not a few of them dwelt in Roman towns and villages, the journey they had to take once a year was long and distasteful to them. Palestine, or the Holy Land, was divided into two parts by the river Jordan, and on either side of the deep valley rose the limestone rocks that formed the hill country. The northern part was called the land of Galilee, and the southern the land of Judea, after Judah, one of the twelve sons of Jacob.

In a cleft of the Galilean hills lay the little village of Nazareth, mostly inhabited by poor Jews who led simple lives, and attended diligently to their various trades. Among these people was one, Joseph, a carpenter, and his wife, Mary.

Some months before an angel had come to Mary, and told her that she would give birth to a child, who should be called Jesus, because he was to save the people from their sins. Mary could not understand just what was meant, but she put her trust in God, and waited patiently.

Both Joseph and Mary were of the house of David; and when the time came for the roll to be called, they had to go from their home in Nazareth to Bethlehem of Judea, a small town about six miles south of Jerusalem. The name, Bethlehem, means House of Bread, and was probably given because of its fertile fields that bore rich crops of grain.

Tired out with the long, slow journey, there was still quite a steep hill for Mary to climb before she reached Bethlehem, and the inn where she hoped to rest. Many had passed them on the road, bent on the same errand, and as "first come, first served" is the rule in all inns, the rooms were all taken by the time that Joseph and Mary arrived.

It was a winter's night, and the air was chill, and a nice room and soft bed would have been most welcome to the weary travelers. But they were crowded out; there was no room for them at the inn. Outside were sheds where the cattle were fed and put up for the night, and into one of these Mary and Joseph went and made themselves as comfortable as they could.

That same night, Jesus was born, and Mary, with her own hands, wrapped the child in swaddling clothes, as the loose bands of cloth were called, and no one at the inn knew of what had taken place.

So it is in the world at all times. Jesus comes to a heart and asks to be taken in. There is no room for him. He is crowded out. But away from the gay halls of pride and wealth there is a poor soul who feels very humble and unworthy. She has nothing to offer in return for the honor but a warm welcome, and that is enough. Here Jesus is born, and the whole place illumined; and the heart which was once full of dust and chaff is now swept and garnished as the palace of a King.

Off on one of the hills of Judea a group of shepherds kept watch of their flocks, lest they should be carried off by the thieves or robbers that infested those regions. All through the calm, still hours of the night

HOUSES IN BETHLEHEM.

they remained on guard, while the stars twinkled on high, and gave no sign of what was near at hand.

All at once a great light shone around them, so dazzling they were sore afraid. And in the midst of this light was an angel, who drew near them and said: "Fear not; for I bring you glad tidings of great joy. For unto you is born this day, in the city of David, a Saviour, who is Christ the Lord. And this shall be a sign to you: Ye shall find a babe wrapped in swaddling clothes lying in a manger."

THE SHEPHERDS AT NIGHT.

And, suddenly, there stood near the angel a multitude of the heavenly host, praising God and saying: "Glory to God in the highest, and on earth peace, good-will toward men!"

When the angels had gone back into heaven, the shepherds said to one another: "Let us go at once to Bethlehem and see this thing which the Lord hath made known to us." With the simple faith of little children, glad and willing to obey, they set out in great haste, and found Mary and Joseph and the babe lying in a manger.

This was the sign they sought; and when they had seen it they made known abroad the words the angels had spoken to them concerning this child, and those who heard, wondered at the story the shepherds told, and talked much about this, the first gospel message. They might go their ways and forget, but Mary remembered all that was said, and pondered over them in her heart. And the shepherds went back to their flock, giving thanks and praise to God for all that they had seen and heard.

At the end of forty days, Mary took Jesus in her arms and went with him to the Temple to present him to the Lord. It was customary, on such an occasion, to offer a young lamb as a burnt-offering, and a young pigeon, or turtle-dove, as a sin-offering. Mary was too poor to provide herself with a lamb—she needed it not, for in her arms she bore the Lamb of God, who was to take away the sins of the world—and so took instead two young pigeons, and in a humble and devout manner she presented herself before the priest.

There was at this time in Jerusalem a holy man named Simeon. He was very old, but the spirit of God had made known to him that he should not die until he had seen the Messiah.

On a certain day a sudden impulse led him to the Temple, and when Joseph and Mary brought in the child Jesus, Simeon recognized him at once as the Light that was to shine in the world. Then he took the child in his arms, and blessed God, and said: "Lord, now lettest thou thy servant depart in peace, according to thy word; for mine eyes have seen thy salvation, which thou hast prepared before the face of all people; a light to lighten the Gentiles, and the glory of thy people Israel."

And the child's father and mother wondered at the things which were spoken concerning him. And Simeon blessed them, and said unto Mary his mother:

THE BIRTH OF JESUS.

"Behold, this child is set for the falling and rising of many in Israel, and for a sign which shall be spoken against. Yea, a sword shall pierce through thy own

SIMEON IN THE TEMPLE.

soul, that the thoughts of many hearts may be revealed."

This referred to the death of Jesus on the shameful cross—the grief that would be like a sword in Mary's heart—and the hatred that would be shown by the foes of Jesus.

There was living in Jerusalem one Anna, a prophetess, who had now reached the age of eighty-four years. She had been a widow for the greater part of her life, and now devoted all her time to religious exercises, spending many hours of each day in the Temple. She came in at the very moment when Simeon took the young child in his arms, and gave thanks to God, and spoke of Jesus to all those who waited for the redemption of Jerusalem. And when all these things were done, Joseph and Mary returned to Bethlehem, and made their home there for some little time.

Now there were in the East three wise men, who, having seen the strange star in the sky, determined to take it as their guide and follow where it lead them. The Greek name for those scholars was MAGI, and even kings were wont to consult them in regard to their affairs. They first bent their steps towards Jerusalem, and when they reached the city they asked of this one and that one, "where is he that is born King of the Jews? for we saw his star in the East and have come to worship him." We are not told that these three men came from the same place. It is not likely that they knew each other at all, but having seen the same new star, and come to Jerusalem on the same errand, they were naturally drawn together and became great friends. And this is the case with all those who set out to find Jesus.

Now Herod had been made Governor of all Judea, and his word was law among the Jews. He had ruled them with a rod of iron the better to please his own master, the Roman Emperor Cæsar Augustus, from whom he hoped to receive some great reward.

When Herod, the King, heard of the wise men, and the question they asked, he was greatly troubled, for

THE CHILD JESUS BROUGHT TO THE TEMPLE.

he feared he was about to lose his power and position. The Jews in Jerusalem were likewise in a great state of alarm, lest Herod, because of his jealousy, should be driven to great acts of cruelty. Gathering together all the chief priests and scribes, Herod inquired of them where the Christ they believed in was to be born. They told him, "In Bethlehem of Judea," for so it had been written by the prophet Micah.

Then Herod privately called the wise men, and learned of them exactly when the star appeared. And he sent them to Bethlehem, and said: "Go and search diligently for the young child, and when ye have found him, bring me word that I also may come and worship him."

When they had heard the King, they went their way; and lo, the star which they saw in the East went on before them till it came and stood over the place where the young child was. And when they saw the star they rejoiced with exceeding great joy. And coming into the house they saw the young child with Mary, his mother; and they fell down and worshiped him, and opening their treasures presented him costly gifts of gold, frankincense and myrrh. And being warned of God in a dream that they should not return to Herod, they went by another way into their own country.

After the departure of the wise men, an angel of the Lord appeared to Joseph in a dream, saying: "Arise, and take the young child and his mother, and flee into Egypt, and stay there until I tell thee what to do: for Herod will seek the young child to destroy him."

Egypt was near, and, though a Roman province, was not under Herod's control. Many Jews resided there, and it was an easy and convenient place of refuge.

Joseph did not delay, but rose the same night, and

took the young child and his mother, and departed into Egypt.

Herod was very angry, indeed, at the way in which he had been trifled with by the wise men, and therefore sent forth officers to put to death all the male children in Bethlehem and the borders thereof, from two years old and under. So dreadful were his crimes that it is easy to believe that only for this rea-

NAZARETH.

son did he inquire so particularly when the star was first seen, for in that way could he reckon the age of the young child Jesus.

We may imagine the grief and sorrow there was in and around Bethlehem at this time: Mothers weeping for the little ones that were torn from their arms and put to death in the most cruel manner. Vain were tears and prayers. The tyrant's will was law. Those

THE MAGI BEFORE HEROD.

who heard the wild wail of anguish, may well have imagined that Rachel, the beloved wife of Jacob, who was regarded as the mother of the Jewish race, mingled her tears with those so cruelly bereaved.

But a greater tyrant than himself laid low the wicked Herod, and put an end to his fiendish crimes. And when Herod was dead, behold an angel of the Lord appeared in a dream to Joseph, in Egypt, saying:

HOUSES IN NAZARETH.

"Arise, and take the young child and his mother, and go into the land of Israel, for they are dead who sought the young child's life." And Joseph arose and took the young child and his mother, and came towards the land of Judea.

But when he heard that Archelaus—the worst one of Herod's four sons—reigned in his father's stead, he was afraid to return to Bethlehem.

So seeking council of God in prayer, he was led to return to Galilee, and took up his abode there in a city called Nazareth.

The name Nazareth meant a shoot or twig; the city was called "the town of shrubs," and those who dwelt there were looked down upon and despised by the better class of Israelites.

This was the will of God, that he who was to be the Light of the World, should be born in an humble manger, and dwell in a lowly city, among those who were despised by their fellow-men.

CHAPTER II.

THE BOYHOOD OF JESUS.

How little the Bible tells us of the boyhood of Jesus; and how much we would like to know of those early days over which there hangs so deep a veil. Each one can picture for himself how the Holy Child appeared, and what were his youthful sports and pastimes. Nothing is told us, except that he grew in wisdom and in stature; and the inference is that he was much like other little boys— only better behaved. He was a Holy Child from the beginning, and Satan had no power over him.

Joseph was a carpenter and had to work industriously at his trade, while Mary found her time fully occupied in household duties, and in the care of her children. Jesus early became familiar with the routine of home-life, the making of bread, the filling of the evening lamp, the preparation for the regular meals, and also for the Sabbath observances.

THE WISE MEN BEFORE HEROD.

On each door-post was a folded bit of parchment inscribed with the name of the Most High, and this was reverently touched by each one who went in or out, and then the fingers kissed that had come in contact with this sacred name. This the young child could do, even before he had learned to lisp a single word, and what light it throws upon many passages of Scripture. This name on the door-post was a symbol of God's watchful care over the homes of Israel, and put into words it meant: "The Lord shall preserve thy going out and thy coming in, from this time forth, and even for evermore."

There were many things the Jewish mother could do to entertain her young children, and to assist in their proper training. She could tell them stories of the past, the history of the Jews, and heroic deeds of some member of her own tribe; and teach them the hymns of the church, and the meaning of various symbols made use of in their domestic and public worship.

She taught them to use their eyes and ears, and all that they saw and heard made a lasting impression upon their minds.

As soon as the boy learned to speak, the father took him in hand to train him in the knowledge of the law and of the Scriptures, certain verses of which he had to commit to memory. While still very young the boy was taught a birthday-text, some verse of Scripture beginning or ending with or at least containing the same letters as his Hebrew name.

Then he must learn the Psalms for the days of the week, or festive Psalms, or those connected with the festive pilgrimages to Zion.

When the child was between five and six years old he was sent to school, and this was considered such an important event, that it was deemed unlawful to live in a place where there was no school. For a long time it was not uncommon to teach in the open air; but, after a while synagogues and schools were built, where at first the pupils and teachers

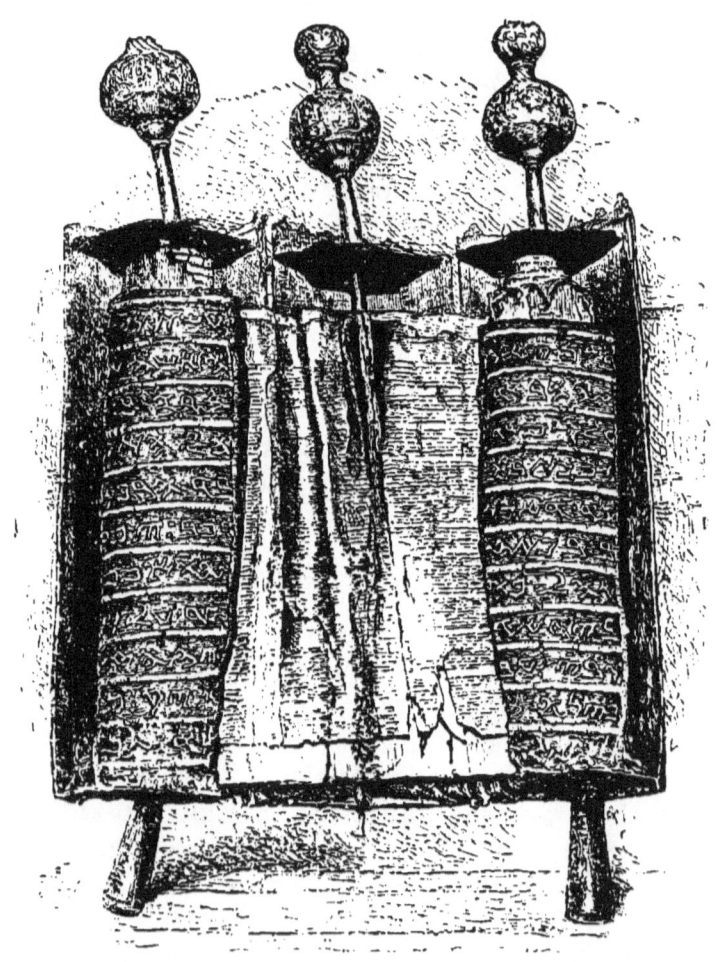

ROLL OF THE PENTATEUCH.

stood, or else sat on the ground in a semicircle, the children facing their teachers.

Up to ten years of age, the Bible was the only text-book, the study of it beginning with the Books

THE FLIGHT INTO EGYPT.

of Leviticus. Thence it passed to other parts of the Pentateuch, as the first five books of the Bible are called; then to the Prophets, and, finally, to the remaining history of the Jews, and all the traditions of the race.

Care was taken not to send a boy too early to school, nor to overwork him when there. If, after three or five years of tuition, he showed no aptitude for books or study, it was decided that he would not become a learned man, or qualify himself to enter the academy.

We are told that there were no learned Rabbis at Nazareth at any time. We do not know quite certainly whether there were any schools there, but if so we may be sure that the Child Jesus was faithful in his attendance, and obedient to all the rules. All male Jews were required to appear in Jerusalem at the three yearly feasts, but women were only commanded to be present at the Passover feast, which celebrated the leading of the Israelites out of Egyptian bondage. A boy of twelve years of age

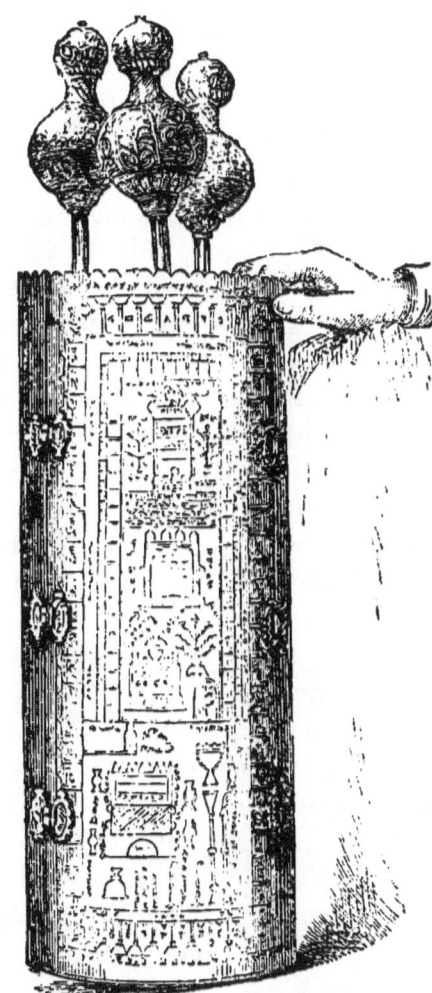

CYLINDER HOLDING THE PENTATEUCH.

became a Son of the Law, and was henceforth bound to obey the law in all that it required.

It was in the spring of the year that Jesus, for the first time, went up with his parents to the Paschal feast at Jerusalem. It was a long journey, and full of danger, for robbers frequented the roads, and lay in wait for all travelers. Therefore, merchants and Pilgrims united together in large bands, the women, aged men, and young children riding on camels or mules, while the men and youths went mostly on foot, occasionally getting a lift from their fellow-travelers who were glad of a change of exercise. The way was beguiled with music and song, relatives visited with each other, and the pilgrimage became a gala occasion and the chief social event of the year.

As they drew near to Jerusalem, the festive company from Nazareth was increased by other bands, and all joined in singing to the accompaniment of the flute, those Psalms of Ascent* which would kindle in their hearts a spiritual flame, and prepare them for the solemn yet joyous services.

We may imagine with what emotions Jesus gazed for the first time on these scenes: the City of Jerusalem, the wonderful Temple on Mount Moriah, and the vast crowds gathering there for one purpose. The houses, built of white marble, and decorated profusely with gold, shone with dazzling magnificence under the rays of the noonday sun; but, above all, rising terrace upon terrace, was the Temple itself which attracted all eyes, and was an object of admiration and pride to every Israelite.

David made preparations for building the Temple on a royal scale of magnitude and magnificence, but did not live to carry them out. The work fell into the hands of his son, King Solomon, who was ably

---

* Ps. cxx–cxxxiv.

VIEW OF JERUSALEM.

assisted by Hiram, King of Tyre, who furnished cedar-trees and fir-trees, and sent men to aid in the work, for the love that he bore to King David. The Temple was begun B.C. 1012, and was seven years in building. The stone was made ready before it was brought there, so that there was neither hammer nor ax nor any tool of iron heard in the house while it was building.

The design of the Temple was suggested by that of

WALLS OF JERUSALEM.

the tabernacle, although everything was on a much larger scale. Herod made many additions, but the Temple of our Lord's time was no less true to the plan given to Moses than was the tabernacle itself.

Solomen's Temple was destroyed by fire, and a new one was built on the same site by Zerubbabel, after the return of the Jews to the Holy Land. But it was far inferior to Solomon's Temple. Herod the Great, who was fond of fine buildings, and wished to add to his own glory as well as to the splendor of Jerusalem,

THE JAFFA GATE, JERUSALEM.

began rebuilding the Temple in a magnificent style, but it was not completed until long after his death. Around the main building was a wall of great

RESTITUTION OF THE TEMPLE.

strength, magnificently adorned with columns, porticoes, and ten entrance gateways of extraordinary splendor were on the east, north and south sides.

Beyond this inner enclosure was the outer, leaving an open space or court between the two buildings. The outer enclosure was, indeed, a spacious colonnade, the columns carrying arches along the entire length of the east, west and north sides of the square. This

INTERIOR OF ST. STEPHEN'S GATE, JERUSALEM.

grand arcade led along the south side of the Temple and its courts, and communicating with the city on the west, and on the east with the east walk of the outer enclosure, it formed the approach to the great east entrance to the Temple itself, and was called the ROYAL PORCH.

The east walk of the colonnade of the outer enclosure, which was opposite to the entrance front of the Temple, was distinguished as SOLOMON'S PORCH, and enriched with architectural embellishments. The outer wall had seven gates, of which the principal are the Jaffa Gate, the Damascus Gate, the Stephen's Gate and the Zion Gate. North of the outer wall stood the Tower of Antonia, which was built by Herod, and named after Mark Antony, and communicated directly with the Temple by an underground passage way.

The Passover feast brought many people into Jerusalem, and throngs filled the Temple at all of the services. At the end of the seven days, the caravans

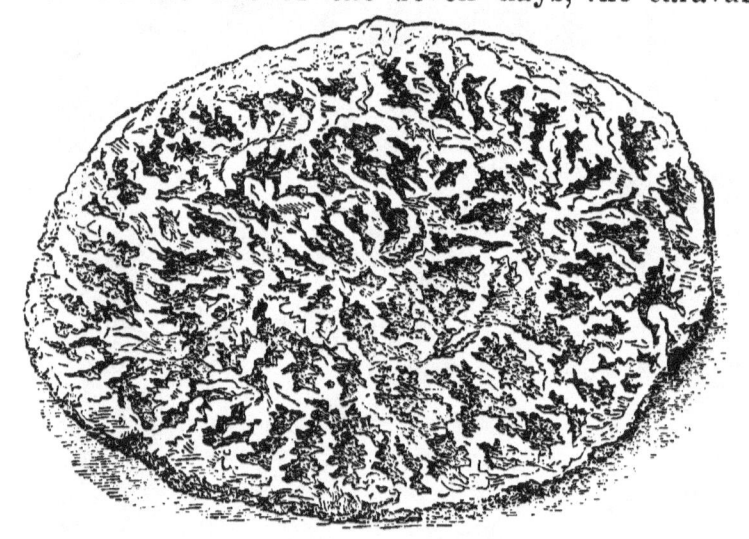

PASSOVER CAKE.

were again made up and started off on the homeward journey. Jesus was not with Joseph and Mary; but they, supposing he was somewhere in the company and would join them at nightfall, gave themselves no great uneasiness. But when he failed to appear on that day or the next, they began to be anxious and sought for him among their kinsfolk and acquaintances; and, not finding him, they turned back and kept looking for him all along the road to Jerusalem.

They found Jesus at last in the Temple—in one of the porches of the court—sitting in the midst of the

PORTION OF THE TEMPLE WALL. "THE JEWS'" WAILING PLACE.

learned Rabbis, hearing them and asking them questions. And all those who heard him were amazed at his understanding and his answers. When his parents saw him they were astonished, and his mother said to him: "Child, why hast thou treated us in this way? Behold, thy father and I have sought thee sorrowing." He had never given them any trouble before, and they were grieved and distressed by his strange behavior.

Jesus said to them: "Why did ye go about seeking me? Did ye not know that I must be about my Father's business?" They had dedicated him to the service of God, and ought to have known where to find him. But they understood not the meaning of his words; and Jesus went back with them to Nazareth, and was in subjection to them, a dutiful and obedient child. And he grew in wisdom and in stature, and in favor with God and men.

Among the Jews it was deemed a religious duty to learn some trade, and as Joseph was a carpenter it is but natural to suppose that Jesus made himself familiar with the tools, and assisted in his father's workshop.

Jesus had no intimate companion of his own age— no one with whom he could talk of the future, and of his work in the world. In his lonely walks, however, he held communion with Nature, and learned the ways of the birds of the air and the lilies of the field. He watched the plowman, the sower, the reaper and the vine-dresser, and read the lesson of the tares and the wheat, and knew the time of grapes and of figs.

He saw how the shepherd led, and fed and watched his flock, called the sheep with well-known voice, and brought them to the fold, following after those that had strayed, and tenderly carrying them back, ever ready to defend them at the cost of his life.

He knew the habits of the fox, and had tracked him to his secret lair. He knew how and where the eagle built its nest, and how the young ones were fed. He observed the joys and sorrows and wants of the people, the self-indulgence of the rich, the exactions of the tax-gatherer, and the oppression of the widow by unjust judges, and all these things made a deep impression on his mind.

Even in the synagogue he found wrongs that needed correcting; for, although the outward observance of the law was correct, the inward and spiritual meaning seemed altogether lost sight of.

How little we know of Jesus during the thirty years that he spent in Nazareth! And this was part of God's plan. We are not to think too much of him as a man. What his bodily appearance was, we can scarcely imagine. We are to dwell more upon his work

REPRESENTATION OF THE FACE OF OUR LORD.—(*From an Early Print.*)

and his character, and to pattern after him that we may be Christ-like in all our ways. Jesus manifested his love for home and the family circle, and taught a beautiful lesson to the young of self-denial, of gentle obedience and divine patience. He longed to be out in the world, to be doing a more glorious work; but his lot was cast with the poor and lowly people of Nazareth, and there he must stay until God's good time.

JESUS DISPUTING WITH THE DOCTORS IN THE TEMPLE.

CHAPTER III.

JESUS COMES OUT OF NAZARETH—HIS BAPTISM AND TEMPTATION.

In the days of King Herod, there was a certain priest named Zachariah. His wife's name was Elizabeth, and they were a pious and praiseworthy couple. The one grief of their heart was that they were childless, and had no son or daughter to comfort them and care for them in their old age.

It was the custom to portion out the work for the priests, each one being taken in his turn, and serving but once during the entire week.

The inner temple, where the ark was kept, was called the "holy of holies," and no one but the High Priest was permitted to enter the place. All the outside service was done by the lower order of priests, who had been trained for the work, and whose ancestors were priests of the tribe of Levi. Hence they were often called Levites.

The day came for Zachariah to serve in the temple, or tabernacle, and his lot was to burn incense on the altar set apart for that purpose. While this was being done, the multitude outside were on their faces praying to God after the fashion of the East. They thought that their prayers and supplications would be born heavenward on the smoke that arose from the altar of incense, the priest standing between them and God to intercede in their behalf.

While Zachariah was thus occupied in the temple, an angel came and stood at the right side of the altar. And Zachariah was troubled when he saw him, and in great fear. But the angel said to him: "Fear not, Zachariah, for thy prayer is heard, and thy wife shall bear thee a son, and his name shall be called John. And thou shalt have joy and gladness, and many shall rejoice at his birth. For he shall be great in the sight of the Lord, and shall drink neither wine nor strong drink; and he shall be filled with the Holy Ghost from the hour of his birth, and many of the children of Israel shall he turn to the Lord their God. And he shall go before Him, in the spirit and power of Elijah, to prepare the people for the coming of the Lord."

Zachariah said to the angel, "By what sign shall I know this? for I am an old man, and my wife is well advanced in years." The angel said: "I am Gabriel—one of the chief angels nearest to God—and I am sent to bring these glad tidings. And behold thou shalt be dumb and not able to speak, until the day that these things take place, because thou didst not have faith to believe in the message I brought."

The people outside waited for Zachariah, and wondered why he remained so long a time inside the temple; and when he came out he could not speak to them; and they knew that he had seen a vision, for he made signs unto them and remained speechless.

In due season God gave Elizabeth a son, and her neighbors and relations rejoiced with her at this great proof of God's mercy. On the eighth day they all came together, and called the child Zachariah, after his father.

But the mother said, "Not so; but he shall be called John." They said to her, "There is none of thy kindred that is called by that name;" and they asked Zachariah by signs what he would have the child called. He asked for a writing tablet and wrote, "His name is John." And they all marvelled. And immediately Zachariah opened his mouth, his tongue was loosed, and he spoke and gave thanks and praise to God. And fear came upon all that dwelt round

GENERAL VIEW OF THE TABERNACLE.

about them, and the story was told throughout all the hill-country of Judea. And those who heard of the strange things that had taken place, laid them up in their hearts, saying, "What then will this child be?" For the hand of the Lord was with him.

The child grew in size and strength, and early in his young manhood John took up his abode in the wilderness of Judea, which was not far from where his parents lived. Here in solitude, by privation and discipline, he was to fit himself for his life-work.

JOHN THE BAPTIST.

He wore a dress of camel's hair—a coarse cloth woven of the hair that it shed each year—and around his waist a leather girdle. His food was locusts and wild honey, locusts being eaten by the poorer classes in the East, in place of the meat they were unable to buy.

John was a few months older than Jesus, and when he was thirty years of age he began preaching the gospel in the wilderness of Judea. His cry was: "Repent; for the kingdom of heaven is at hand. For this is He that was spoken of through the prophet Isaiah, saying, The voice of one crying in the wilderness, Prepare ye the way of the Lord, make his path straight."

People thronged to hear him from Jerusalem, and all Judea, and all the region round about the Jordan, and many confessed their sins and were baptized. But when John saw the Pharisees and Sadducees coming to be baptized, he said to them: "O generation of vipers, who hath warned you to flee from the wrath to come? Bring forth fruit worthy of repentance."

John knew they were not fit subjects for baptism until their hearts were purified and they led better lives. They were simply attracted towards the new teacher, and regarded him at first as a great prophet; but when he rebuked their sins, and pointed to Christ as their Messiah, they turned from him with hate, and refused to listen to him.

The fame of the new preacher—who claimed to be a messenger from God—soon reached the hill-country of Galilee, and Jesus left his home in Nazareth, and came down to the Jordan to be baptized by him. But John would have hindered him, saying, "I have need to be baptized by thee, and comest thou to me?" Jesus said, "Let it be so for this time, that we may fulfil the law of righteousness." The Jews were commanded to bathe frequently. It was part of their religion, and Jesus wished to conform to all the requirements of the law. Baptism is merely a sign, or symbol, that as water cleanses the outer man, so will repentance and faith in Jesus Christ cleanse the inner man, and take away all traces of sin.

When Jesus himself ordered the baptism, John hesitated no longer, but led him into the water and performed the solemn rite. And as Jesus went up out of the water, lo, the heavens were opened and the spirit of God taking the form of a dove rested upon him. And a voice from out of the heavens said, "This is my beloved Son in whom I am well pleased."

From the waters of Jordan, Jesus was led by the

SON, WHY HAST THOU THUS DEALT WITH US?

Spirit into the wilderness : that is, the voice of God within him told him to go there. Forty days and nights he spent in that lonely place, and though wild beasts were plenty they did him no harm. During all this time he had eaten nothing ; he had been fed with spiritual food and was unconscious of hunger ; but after it was over he became very weak, and had a great desire for food.

Then Satan, who always comes to us in our weakest moments, appeared before Jesus and said unto him, "If thou art the Son of God, command that this stone be made into bread." Jesus answered him, "It is written that man shall not live by bread alone, but by every word that proceedeth out of the mouth of God." Severe though his sufferings were, he fought against this temptation of the evil one. As Son of God he might have had power to perform a miracle, to prove himself equal with God. But this he would not do. His trust was in God, who would supply all his needs.

When Satan found that he could not tempt him to do wrong in that direction, he led him into the holy city of Jerusalem, and to the highest pinnacle of the temple. From this great height one could not look down without becoming dizzy; yet Satan said to Jesus: "If thou art the Son of God cast thyself down; for it is written, He shall give His angels charge concerning thee, lest haply thou dash thy foot against a stone." Jesus said unto him, "It is likewise written, thou shalt not tempt the Lord thy God."

When we are in a dangerous place, we must still trust in God to show us the way of escape, and to keep us in safety.

Foiled at this point, Satan took Jesus up to a high mountain, and showing him "all the kingdoms of the world and the glory of them, said to him, All these things will I give thee, if thou wilt fall down and worship me." Jesus said unto him: "Get thee behind me, Satan; for it is written, Thou shalt worship the Lord thy God, and him only shalt thou serve." Then the devil left him; and behold angels came and ministered unto him.

These three temptations of Jesus are to teach us how to resist the evil one who is always watching for a chance to overcome our good resolutions. There are times when we are weak and sad, and Satan comes and urges us to enter into worldly pleasures, and to "eat, drink and be merry." He would convince us that in these things true happiness may be found; but it is not so. If God has afflicted us in any way, we may be sure it is for some wise purpose, and the soul that puts its trust in God, will have strength given to it at all times.

We must not, however, be lifted up, or feel that God will do more for us than he will for the rest of our fellow-creatures, because we have always kept his commandments, and avoided the company of sinners. "Let him that thinketh he standeth, take heed lest he fall." Beware of pride and self-righteousness.

Let not the riches of the world tempt you to forsake the higher life, and become a prince among the powers of darkness. Better be poor, and a Christian, than the wicked owner of vast estates, or a miser who worships gold as if it were his God.

The greatest victory any one can gain, is the victory over Satan, and this can only be obtained by earnest and frequent prayer. We need not go in the wilderness to escape him; for he will find us there. He assails the minister in his pulpit, as well as the poor creature whose home is a wretched hovel. One may say, "I was hard pressed and driven into sin." That is no excuse. If the devil gets between us and our duty to God we have but to say, "Get thee behind me, Satan!" and the victory is more than half won.

JESUS IN HIS YOUTH.

Trust in God is the staff on which we lean, and happy is he under all circumstances who can say, as David did, "Though he slay me, yet will I trust in him."

CHAPTER IV.

THE FIRST DISCIPLES—THE MIRACLE AT CANA—THE PASSOVER-FEAST — DRIVING OUT THE MONEY-CHANGERS—NICODEMUS.

AFTER his triumph over the temptations of Satan, Jesus returned to the fords of the Jordan, where John still continued preaching and baptizing. One and another had said of John: "He is really worth hearing. He is not like the teachers we have been accustomed to listen to. His words burn, and the heart is stirred to its inmost depths. He is not afraid to tell men the truth about themselves. He has nothing to gain or to lose." Hearing these things, the Jews sent priests and Levites from Jerusalem to ask him, "Who art thou?" He confessed who he was, and denied nothing. And he said, "I am not the Christ." They asked him, "What then? Art thou Elijah?" He said, "I am not." "Art thou the prophet Isaiah?" He answered, "No."

Then said they unto him, "Who art thou? that we may give an answer to those that sent us. What sayest thou of thyself?" He said, "I am the voice of one crying in the wilderness, Make straight the way of the Lord."

Some from among the Pharisees had been sent, and they were very strict in their observances of the outward forms of religion, and held themselves up as patterns for all the rest of the world. They were fond of asking questions, and, therefore, said to John,

"Why baptizest thou then, if thou be not the Christ, nor Elijah, nor Isaiah?"

John answered them, saying, "I baptize with water, but in the midst of you is one whom ye know not, coming after me, whose sandals I am not worthy to unloose."

The next day, John saw Jesus coming towards him, and said: "Behold the Lamb of God, which taketh away the sin of the world. This is he of whom I spoke. And I knew him not; but that he might be made manifest to Israel, therefore come I baptizing with water." And John bare witness, saying: "I beheld the Spirit descending as a dove out of heaven, and it rested upon him. And I knew him not; but he that sent me to baptize with water, said unto me, Upon whomsoever thou shalt see the Spirit descending and abiding upon, the same is he which baptizeth with the Holy Spirit. And I have seen and borne witness that this is the Son of God."

The next day John was standing with two of his disciples, and as Jesus walked near them he said, "Behold the Lamb of God!" and the two disciples heard him speak, and they followed Jesus. And Jesus turned and beheld them following, and said unto them, "What seek ye?" They said unto him, "Rabbi,"—which is the Hebrew word for Master or Teacher—"where dost thou dwell?"

He saith unto them, "Come, and ye shall see." They came, therefore, and saw where he abode, and remained with him all that day; for this was early in the morning. One of the two who followed Jesus was named Andrew, Simon Peter's brother. And he first findeth his brother Simon, and saith unto him, "We have found the Messiah," which is, being interpreted, the Christ. And he brought him to Jesus. Jesus, looking upon him, said, "Thou art Simon the son of Jonas: thou shalt be called Cephas." This

THE TEMPTATION.

name signifies a stone or rock, and in the Greek is called Petros, and in our language Peter. So, from that time, this disciple was known as Simon Peter. The other one of the two disciples who followed was named John, and he sought his brother James and brought him to Jesus.

The next day Jesus set out for Galilee, and on the way he found a man named Philip, and said unto him, "Follow me." Now Philip was from Bethsaida, the birthplace of Andrew and Peter. And Philip went out in search of his friend Nathaniel, and said unto him, "We have found him of whom Moses, in the law and the prophets, did write, Jesus of Nazareth, the son of Joseph." Nathaniel said unto him, "Can any good thing come out of Nazareth?" Philip saith unto him, "Come and see."

Now Nathaniel was a good man, and had often prayed for the coming of the Messiah, his favorite place of prayer being under a fig-tree in his own garden. And when Philip came for him he made no delay, but went at once to see Jesus. If we really desire to see Jesus, we do not need a second call.

Jesus saw Nathaniel coming, and saith, "Behold, an Israelite indeed, in whom is no guile." Nathaniel was surprised that Jesus had any knowledge of him, and he asked, "Who has been telling thee about me?"

Jesus said unto him, "Before Philip called thee, when thou wast under the fig-tree, I saw thee." Nathaniel answered him, "Rabbi, Master, thou art the Son of God; thou art the King of Israel." Jesus said unto him, "Because I said unto thee, I saw thee under the fig-tree, believest thou? thou shalt see greater things than these." And speaking to all the disciples, he said, "Verily, verily, I say unto you ye shall see heaven open, and the angels of God ascending and descending upon the Son of Man."

As Jesus and his disciples continued their journey they came to a small town in Galilee, named Cana, where a marriage-feast was being held. These feasts lasted from seven to fourteen days, and were occasions of great rejoicing. The mother of Jesus was there, and Jesus and his disciples were also invited. When the supply of wine was exhausted, the mother of Jesus said unto him: "They have no wine." And Jesus said unto her, "Woman, what have I to do with thee? mine hour is not yet come."

Jesus meant that he was no longer under the control of his mother, but must do God's will, and wait for the hour or the moment when He should direct him. His mother said to the servants, "Whatsoever he tells you to do, that do."

In the court, near the entrance to the house, were six stone water-pots, each one of which would hold at least twenty gallons. Jesus saith to the servants, "Fill the water-pots with water." And they brought water from the spring and filled them to the brim. And he said, "Draw now, and bear to the ruler of the feast." And they bare it. When the ruler of the feast, the chief guest, had tasted the wine—none but the servants knowing whence it came—he calleth the bridegroom, and saith to him: "Every man first setteth on the good wine, and when men are drunken, then that which is worse, but thou hast kept the good wine until now." This did Jesus, as the beginning of his signs, in Cana of Galilee, and his disciples believed in him.

After this he went down to Capernaum, accompanied by his mother, his brethren and his disciples, and stayed there for a few days. And the Passover of the Jews was at hand, and Jesus went up to Jerusalem with the other pilgrims that wended their way thither. The temple-courts were filled with the buyers and sellers of oxen, sheep and doves to be used in the

JOHN THE BAPTIST PREACHING.

daily sacrifices, and close up to Solomon's Porch, were the shops of the merchants, and the tables of the money-changers.

Every man of Israel had to pay a certain sum each year into the Temple treasury, and this Temple-tribute, or tax, could only be paid in half-shekels. A shekel was worth about sixty-two and a half cents of our money, and those who came from a distance and had not the right kind of coin could easily get it changed at the money-changers.

The Passover took place in April, and preparations for the feast were made at least a month before. The bridges and the roads were put in repair, and even the sepulchres whitened, so that no sickness might break out among the pilgrims. In every country town the money-changers opened their stalls, or banks, thus allowing plenty of time for all the Jews to get their money changed, for which, of course, a charge would be made.

By the last of March, the pilgrims began to arrive in Jerusalem, and then the stalls in the country were closed, and the money-changers sat in the Temple-courts. A great many foreign Jews took advantage of this opportunity to change their foreign money at the tables before they made their purchases of the dealers. The money had to be weighed; and there was much disputing and bargaining, and the sound of loud talking and the clink of money penetrated even to the inner Temple.

When Jesus entered the Temple and found it turned into a market for the sale of oxen, sheep and doves, and saw the money-changers sitting at their tables, he took a whip of small cords and drove out the cattle and those who traded in that sacred place. He poured out the money, and overturned the tables on which the bankers had heaped their change, and said to them that sold doves "Take these things hence;

make not my Father's house a house of merchandise."

His disciples, noticing his indignation, remembered

DRIVING THE SELLERS FROM THE TEMPLE.

that David had written in one of his Psalms: "The zeal of thine house hath eaten me up." The Jews therefore answered and said unto him, "What sign

THE MARRIAGE IN CANA.

shewest thou that thou hast the right to do these things?"

Jesus said unto them, "Destroy this Temple, and in three days will I raise it up." The Jews said, "Forty and six years was this Temple in building, and wilt thou raise it up in three days?" But he spake of the temple of his body. When, therefore he was raised from the dead his disciples remembered that he said this: and they believed the Scripture, and the word which Jesus had said.

Many of the Jews questioned his right to do these things, or to exercise any authority over them, and, looking upon the Temple merely as a building, gave no thought to the spiritual meaning of his words. But there were those who believed in him, and partly understood what he meant. And one of these, a Pharisee named Nicodemus, a ruler of the Jews, came to Jesus by night, and said to him: "Rabbi, we know that thou art a teacher come from God, for no one can do these signs that thou doest except God be with him."

Jesus said, "Verily, verily, I say unto thee, except a man be born anew, he cannot see the kingdom of God." Nicodemus saith unto him, "How can a man be born when he is old?"

Jesus answered: "Except a man be born of water and of the Spirit he cannot enter into the Kingdom of God. That which is born of the flesh is flesh; and that which is born of the Spirit is spirit. Marvel not that I said to thee, Ye must be born again. The wind bloweth where it listeth, and thou hearest the sound thereof, but canst not tell whence it cometh and whither it goeth: so is every one that is born of the Spirit."

Nicodemus said unto him, "How can these things be?" Jesus said, "Art thou a teacher of Israel, and knowest not these things?" Nicodemus was a member of the Sanhedrim, the great court of law, which was composed of 71 members, before whom criminals were brought, and who were regarded as the wisest teachers in the land. In the opinion of this body of men Jesus was guilty of a great crime; and Nicodemus needed to be cautious in going out to see him.

Jesus said the wind was an emblem of the Spirit. We cannot tell how our hearts are made over, and how the old man, full of sin and wickedness, becomes the new man full of grace and good works. Nicodemus had failed in his teachings and in his knowledge of the Scripture, if he had not made it plain that a man, to have favor with God, must have a new heart and lead a holy life.

Jesus said, "We speak that which we know, and testify of that which we have seen: and ye receive not our witness." Jesus knew that Nicodemus only half believed in him, and he said: "If I tell you of earthly things and ye believe not, how shall ye believe if I tell you of heavenly things. And no one hath ascended up into heaven but he that came down from heaven—the Son of Man. And as Moses lifted up on high the serpent in the wilderness, even so must the Son of Man be lifted up; that every one that believeth in him may not perish but have eternal life. For God so loved the world that he gave his only-begotten Son, that every one that believeth in him may not perish but have eternal life. For God sent not the Son unto the world that he may judge the world, but that the world through him may be saved. He that believeth in him is not judged; but he that believeth not is judged already; because he hath not believed in the name of the only-begotten Son of God. And this is the judgment, because the light is come into the world, and men loved the darkness rather than the light, for their works were wicked. For every one that doeth evil hateth the light, and he cometh not to the light lest his sins be discovered. But he who is faithful to the truth cometh to the light, that it may be shown what great works God hath wrought in him."

Jesus himself was the light that God sent into the world, not to show sinners how bad they were, and to bring them to judgment, but to arouse them from their sins, and to show them how to be forgiven.

We know ourselves that wicked people prowl around in the night to hide their crimes under cover of the darkness. They think they will not be found out, but though they escape the eye of man, they cannot hide from God. He sees and remembers. But he is also ready to forgive; and when the wicked one says, "I am sorry," and tries to lead a better life, and asks God for Christ's sake to cleanse his heart and to blot out his iniquities, the poor sinner is forgiven and sent on his way rejoicing.

After these things Jesus and his disciples came into the land of Judea, and there he tarried with them and baptized. And John also was at Ænon near to Salem, because there were many waters there; and those who came to him were baptized. For John was not yet cast into prison. But there was a falling off in the number of his followers, and John's disciples were jealous of the power manifested by Jesus and his disciples. There arose, therefore, a questioning on the part of John's disciples with a Jew about purifying. A certain Jew had said that the baptism of Jesus was far more cleansing than that of John. So they came to John, and said unto him, "Rabbi, he that was with thee beyond the Jordon, to whom thou hast borne witness, behold, the same baptizeth, and all men come to him." They did not tell the exact truth, for they wished to make out a good story, and arouse John to a sense of his danger from such a rival.

John answered and said: "A man can receive nothing except it have been given him out of heaven. Ye yourselves bear me witness that I said, I am not the Christ, but I am sent before him. He that hath the bride is the bridegroom; but the friend of the bridegroom, who standeth and heareth him, rejoiceth greatly because of the bridegroom's voice: this my joy therefore hath been fulfilled."

The figure of the bride and the bridegroom is frequently made use of in the Old and New Testaments. It is a holy relation. Jesus is the bridegroom. He is leading home his bride—His people—the church established in His name. John laid no claim to the name of the bridegroom, but he listened to His voice at the marriage-feast and was a sharer in His joy. John was simply a messenger, a forerunner, and now that the Master had come, there was nothing further for him to do. "He must increase," said John to his disciples, "but I must decrease. For he whom God hath sent speaketh the words of God: for not by measure giveth he the spirit. The Father loveth the Son, and hath given all things into his hand. He that believeth in the Son hath eternal life; but he that believeth not the Son shall not see life; but the wrath of God abideth on him."

We cannot say that we love God, and yet refuse to acknowledge Jesus as our Saviour. Our faith in Him is proof of our obedience to God. Sin keeps us out of heaven. There is no happiness in wrongdoing. But when we join hands with Christ, and put our trust in Him we have a foretaste of heaven on earth and a pledge of everlasting bliss to come.

CHAPTER V.

THE WOMAN OF SAMARIA—JESUS IN GALILEE—HEALING OF THE NOBLEMAN'S SON—REJECTED AT NAZARETH.

Our Lord knew what was in the minds of the Pharisees, and of the comparisons they made between his teaching and that of John. And the news spread about that Jesus was making more disciples than John ever had made, and this, of course, aroused a great deal of ill-feeling. For this reason, and that John's work might not be hindered, Jesus decided to leave the land of Judea, and to go up into Galilee. And he must needs go through Samaria.

Now the Jews had no dealings with the Samaritans who were a mixed race, and mingled the worship of Jehovah with the worship of idols. They built a temple for themselves on the top of Mount Gerizim, and between them and the Jews there was intense hatred. In the time of our Lord, however, the temple on Mount Gerizim had been long in ruins, but the hill and the city below it were regarded as sacred.

Jesus came to a city of Samaria, which is called Sychar, near to the parcel of ground that Jacob gave to his son Joseph. Joseph was buried at Shechem, and the surrounding country became the inheritance of his children.

Now there was a well of water there, known as Jacob's well. And Jesus being wearied with his long journey sat down on the low brick wall around the well, to rest, and to wait for the return of the disciples who had gone into the city to buy food.

It was about the sixth hour—near sunset—and the time when the women came out to draw water from the public wells. And there came a woman of Samaria to Jacob's well. Jesus said unto her, "Give me to drink." The Samaritan woman said unto him, "How is it that thou, being a Jew, asketh drink of me, a Samaritan woman? for the Jews have no dealings with the Samaritans."

Jesus said to her, "If thou knewest the gift of God, and who it is that saith to thee, give me to drink, thou wouldst have asked of him, and he would have given thee living water." She said unto him, "Sir, thou hast nothing to draw with, and the well is deep: from whence then hast thou that living water? Art thou greater than our Father Jacob, who gave us the well, and drank thereof himself, his sons, and his cattle?"

Jesus said to her, "Every one that drinketh of this water shall thirst again; but whosoever drinketh of the water that I shall give him, shall never thirst; but the water that I shall give him shall be a fountain of water, springing up into everlasting life."

The woman said unto him, "Sir, give me this water that I thirst not, neither come all the way here to draw." Jesus said to her, "Go, call thy husband, and come hither." The woman answered and said, "I have no husband." Jesus saith, "Thou hast well said, I have no husband: for thou hast had five husbands; and he whom thou now hast is not thy husband: in this thou hast said truly."

The woman said to him, "Sir, I perceive that thou art a prophet. Our fathers worshiped in this mountain, and ye say that Jerusalem is the place where men must worship." Jesus saith unto her, "Believe me, woman, an hour cometh when neither in this mountain nor at Jerusalem shall ye worship the Father. Ye worship that which ye know not; we worship that which we know; for the salvation is of the Jews." The Saviour, foretold by the prophets, and long waited for by the Jews, had come to deliver

THE WOMAN OF SAMARIA.

the whole world from their sins, and to teach them a better form of worship.

"An hour cometh," said Jesus, "and now is, when the true worshipers shall worship the Father in spirit and truth; for the Father seeketh such to worship him. God is a spirit, and they that worship him must worship in spirit and truth." They must give the real worship of sincere hearts. He cares not for outward forms and ceremonies. No other worship will He receive than that which is given in the right spirit. For He reads all hearts and knows which are false and which are true.

The woman said unto him, "I know that the Messiah cometh, which is called Christ: when He is come, He will tell us all things." Jesus saith unto her, "I that speak to thee am He."

At this moment the disciples appeared, and wondered at finding Jesus talking with a woman, and he a Jew, and a Rabbi! Such a thing was not tolerated by the Israelites, yet so great was their reverence for Jesus that the disciples dared not ask any questions.

Meanwhile, the woman forgetting her errand, and leaving her water-pot by the well, hurried into the city. And she said to those she met on the way, "Come, see a man who told me all the things that ever I did. Can this be the Christ?" Many gathered around to hear the tidings that she brought, some believing, and some doubting; and to prove the truth of her words they went out of the city and came to the place where Jesus was.

In the meantime, the disciples had urged Jesus to eat of the food they had brought. But he said unto them, "I have meat to eat that ye know not of."

Therefore said the disciples one to another, "Hath any one brought him food?" They were too dull to perceive that he spoke of soul-food, the strength given to him through communion with God. Jesus, who knew their thoughts, said unto them, "My meat is to do the will of him that sent me, and to finish his work." It was to be his joy, the sole object of his life, to do his Father's will, to desire to do it, as men hunger and thirst after food.

It was now the middle of December, and the harvest in that country began about the middle of April. The disciples had talked of it among themselves, and Jesus said, "Do ye not say, there are yet four months and then cometh the harvest? Lo, I say unto you, lift up your eyes, and look on the fields, for they are already white for harvesting. He that reapeth receiveth reward, and gathereth fruit to life eternal: that he that soweth and he that reapeth may rejoice together. For herein is that saying true, One soweth and another reapeth. I sent you to reap that whereon ye bestowed no labor; others have toiled, and ye reap the reward of their toil."

Jesus speaks of the gathering in of souls, which he compares to a harvest. These disciples had done no work in Samaria. Jesus himself was the sower. The good word had been dropped in the heart of a believing woman—a poor sinner—and she spread the news, and the men of Sychar were the fruits of her labors. The disciples shared in the joy of the harvest, and all those servants who come after Jesus find the field prepared for them.

Many of the Samaritans believed because of the word of the woman, which testified, "He told me all things that ever I did." To testify is to bear witness: to solemnly declare to others a fact they know nothing about. When, therefore, the Samaritans came unto Jesus they begged him to stay with them; and he abode there two days. And many more believed because of the teachings of Jesus himself, and they said to the woman, "Now do we believe, not because of thy speaking, but because we have heard him ourselves, and we know that this is indeed the Saviour of the world."

At the end of two days Jesus left Samaria and went into Galilee. For Jesus himself testified that a prophet hath no honor in his own country. But he had won honor in Judea. Therefore, when he came into Galilee the Galileans received him, having seen all things whatsoever he did at Jerusalem, for they also went to the feast. And he came again into Cana of Galilee, where he performed his first miracle, and made the water wine.

And there was a certain king's officer whose son was sick at Capernaum. When he heard that Jesus had come out of Judea into Galilee, he went unto him, and begged that he would come down and heal his son: for he was at the point of death. The man had heard of the miracles Jesus had done, and so had faith in him. Jesus therefore said unto him, "Except ye see signs and wonders ye will not believe." The king's officer saith unto him, "Lord, come down ere my child die!" Jesus saith unto him, "Go thy way; thy son liveth." And the man believed the word that Jesus spake to him, and went his way.

Cana is up in the hill country, and at least twenty-five miles from Capernaum, which is situated on the Sea of Galilee. And as the king's officer was going down, his servants met him and told him that his son lived. He inquired of them therefore the hour when he began to show signs of returning health; and they said unto him, "Yesterday at the seventh hour the fever left him." So the father perceived that it was the same hour in which Jesus had said to him, "Thy son liveth;" and his faith was increased, and he and his whole family became followers of Jesus. This Jesus again did, as a second sign, having come out of Judea into Galilee.

Jesus came once more to Nazareth, the home of his

childhood. On Friday, at sunset, the minister of the Synagogue went up on the roof of his house, and blew a loud blast from the trumpet, as a signal that all work

THE HIGH PRIEST.

was to be laid aside. Once, twice, thrice was this repeated and then the Sabbath day had begun, and the Sabbath lamp was lighted.

Jesus arose early on the Sabbath morn, and went into the Synagogue, where as child, youth, and man he had so often worshiped. Then he had kept himself in the background, and been seated according to his rank. But within a few months strange events had taken place, and the fame of Jesus had spread even to Nazareth.

It was customary for each community to build its own synagogue, but if too poor to do this, they might meet for worship in a private dwelling, a sort of "synagogue in a house." At the time of Ezra, synagogues were established in all the towns for the benefit of those who could not take part oftener than three times a year, and perhaps not so often as that, in the worship of the Temple at Jerusalem, and a special form of service was instituted. The people met there for prayer and for religious instruction.

A knowledge of ancient synagogues has been obtained through recent explorations in Palestine, and all had their entrances at the south end. It is supposed that the worshipers made a circuit to the north, where is the woman's gallery, or entered their seats by the middle of the eastern aisle. The synagogue is built of the stone of the country. Over the doors are various designs representing a seven-branched candlestick, an open flower between two lambs, or vine leaves with bunches of grapes.

At the south end, facing the north is a movable ark containing the sacred rolls of the Law and the Prophets. It is called the Holy Chest. Steps lead up to it, and in front of it hangs a curtain. Right before the ark, and facing the people, are the chief seats in the Synagogue, for the rulers and honorable members. In the middle of the Synagogue is the Lectern, or desk, from which the law is read. Those who are to read the law stand, while he who is to preach or deliver an address will sit. Beside them stands the interpreter, to explain, or to repeat aloud, what is said.

The rules are not so strict as they are in regard to the Temple, where worshipers must not enter carrying a staff, nor with shoes, nor even with dust on the

COLOSSAL LAMP.

feet, nor with scrip or purse; but the Synagogue must not be made a thoroughfare. The Jewish boys and girls were taught that they must not behave lightly in that sacred place. They must not joke, laugh, eat, talk, dress, or seek shelter there from sun or rain. Only Rabbis and their disciples might look upon it as their own dwelling, and eat, drink, and perhaps even sleep there; and under certain circumstances the poor and strangers might be fed there.

When Jesus entered the Synagogue at Nazareth, the chief ruler requested him to conduct the devotions. He would begin the service with two prayers, the first one thanking God for his many blessings, and the second asking that their eyes and their hearts may be opened to keep God's law. After this followed the Jewish Creed, which Moses taught the children of

THE ARK.

Israel, and which began, "Hear, O Israel, The Lord our God is one Lord: and thou shalt love the Lord thy God with all thine heart, and with all thy soul, and with all thy might." This was recited by all the worshipers, and was followed by another prayer, or offering of praise to the Almighty.

Then the leader took his place before the ark and repeated certain offerings of praise, or benedictions, some of which were said with bent body, and one in particular required that all should bend down. After this the priests, if there were any in the Synagogue, spoke the blessing with raised hands. This was called the raising up of hands. After the benediction there was another short prayer, at the close of which Amen was spoken by the congregation.

Then a priest, a Levite, and five Israelites read the

A LEVITE.

Law, after which the attendant handed to Jesus the Book of Isaiah which contained the passage for the day. Jesus took the scroll and unrolled it until he came to the sixty-fifth chapter, and the place where it was written, "The Spirit of the Lord is upon me, because he annointed me to preach the gospel to the poor, to heal the broken hearted, to proclaim deliverance to the captives, and recovery of sight to the blind. To set at liberty them that are bruised, and to proclaim the acceptable year of the Lord. And he closed the roll, gave it back to the attendant, and sat down. And the eyes of all in the Synagogue were fastened upon him.

And he began to say unto them, "To-day hath this scripture been fulfilled in your ears." And they

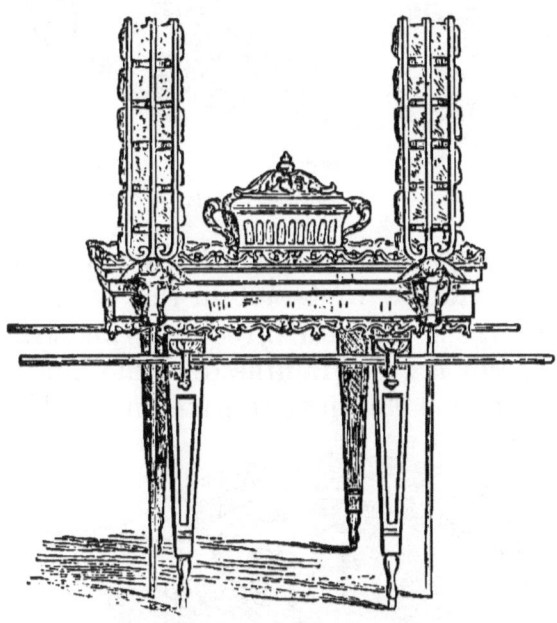

THE TABLE OF SHREW BREAD.

liked his manner and marveled at the words of grace which proceeded out of his mouth. And they said among themselves, "Is not this Joseph's son?" And he said to them, "Ye will surely say unto me this proverb, Physician, heal thyself: whatsoever we have heard done at Capernaum, do also here in thine own country."

Jesus knew that the people of Nazareth were jealous of the fame he had brought to Capernaum, and the hope that he might do even greater miracles in his early home, was their only reason for caring to see him.

Jesus said to them: "No prophet is acceptable in

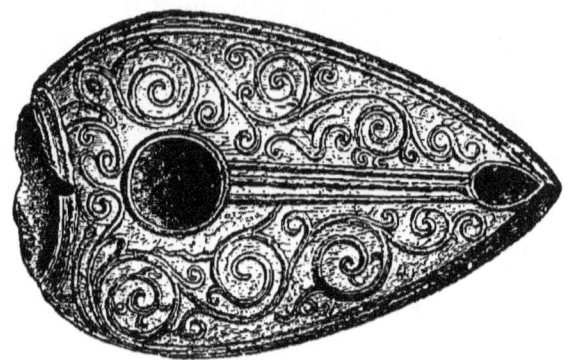

EASTERN LAMP.

his own country. Of a truth I say unto you, there were many widows in Israel in the days of Elijah, when there was no rain for three years and six months, and there came a great famine over the land. But to none of them was Elijah sent, save only to Zarephath,

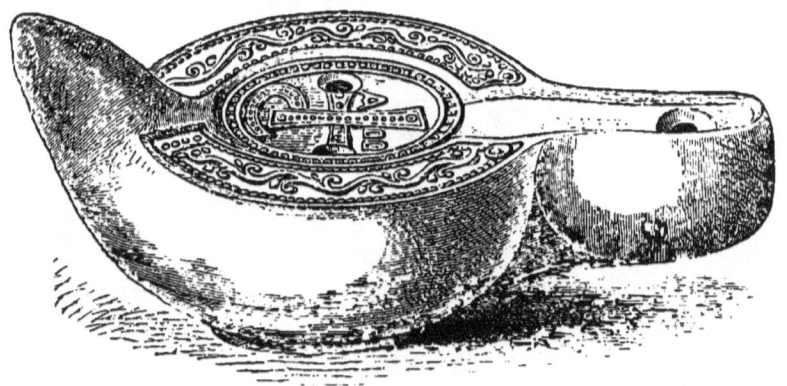

EASTERN LAMP.

a city of Sidon, where a woman dwelt that was a widow. And there were many lepers in Israel in the time of Elisha the Prophet; and none of them were cleansed, save Naaman, the Syrian."

This reference to blessings bestowed upon the Gentiles, made the whole congregation very angry. And they rose up from their seats in great wrath, and forced him out of the Synagogue, and led him to the brow of the hill on which the city was built intending to

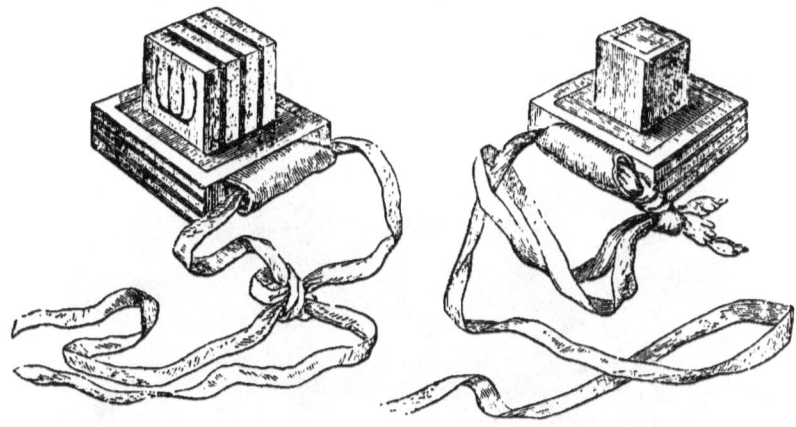

PHYLACTERIES.

throw him down headlong. But he escaped from them in some miraculous way, and went on to Capernaum, and taught there on the Sabbath day. And they were astonished at his teachings; for he spoke with great power, and as one having authority.

CHAPTER VI.

JESUS IN GALILEE—HE PREACHES FROM A BOAT—THE CALLING OF MATTHEW—CHOOSING THE TWELVE—THE SERMON ON THE MOUNT.

CAST out of his own city, Jesus went on to Capernaum, where he knew that kind friends would welcome him. It was the home of his earliest disciples, Simon and Andrew, and James and John, who, when Jesus went from Cana to Nazareth, had returned to

Capernaum, and to their work there. And here also Jesus decided to make his home while he remained in Galilee.

On the Sabbath he went into the Synagogue to teach, as was his custom. He spoke not in the dull way that the Scribes and priests were accustomed to expound the Scriptures, but in burning words that fixed the attention of the congregation. They list-

SOUTH END OF THE SEA OF GALILEE.

ened in spellbound astonishment, for never before had they heard such glowing words from the lips of any speaker.

Suddenly a strange cry broke through the stillness. A man in whom was an evil spirit—an unclean demon —entered the Synogogue, and cried out with a loud voice, "Let us alone! Ah! what have we to do with thee : thou Jesus of Nazareth? Art thou come to destroy us? I know thee who thou art; the Holy One

ON THE SEA OF GALILEE.

of God!" And Jesus rebuked him, saying, "Hold thy peace, and come out from him!" At these calm words, the demoniac fell to the ground, and screamed and writhed in a convulsion. Then the man arose cured, and in his right mind. And those who saw the miracle were amazed at the power displayed. And the fame of it went through all the country round about.

Jesus, rising from his seat in the Synagogue, went to the house of Simon. Simon was a married man, and his wife's mother was very ill, with a fever that raged violently, and the family begged Jesus to help her. He came at once, and stood over her; and at his command the fever left her, and she rose up, and busied herself about her household duties.

As soon as the sun began to set, that marked the close of the Sabbath day, throngs of people pressed to the door of Simon's humble home, bringing with them the sick, and the diseased that Jesus might cure them. He had sympathy for their sufferings, and laid his hands on all of them, and healed them. Isaiah said, "Surely he hath borne our griefs and carried our sorrows;" and Matthew interprets it, "He took our infirmities and bore our diseases." He made the afflictions of the people his own, and his soul was filled with pity.

As the day began to dawn, Jesus stole away from the crowd, and unobserved by them went off to a quiet place to pray. But he was not long alone, for the multitude sought eagerly for him, and Peter and his friends searched until they found him. And they clung to him, and begged him to stay with them, and they said, "All are seeking thee." And the crowd soon followed on, and added their entreaties.

But there were other cities besides Capernaum in need of the good tidings, and Jesus said to his disciples, "Let us go elsewhere, into the next towns, that I may preach there also; for to this end came I forth."

But the crowd would not leave him. They hung upon his words, and begged him to speak to them yet once more. Jesus, yielding to their desire, bent his

JESUS AND PETER.

steps towards the shore of the Lake of Gennesaret, or as it was usually called the Sea of Galilee. There were two boats there, and the fishermen were washing their nets. As there was no room for Jesus to stand owing to the pressure of the crowd, he entered into one of the boats which was Simon Peter's, and asked

JESUS CURING THE SICK.

him to put out a little from the land. And he sat down and taught the multitudes out of the boat.

After he had left off speaking he said to Simon: "Put out into deep water, and let down your nets for a draught." Simon answered and said: "Master, we toiled all night and took nothing, but at thy word I will let down the nets." And having done this they caught a multitude of fishes, and the net began to break. And they beckoned to their partners in the other boat to come and help them. And they came and filled both the boats so that they began to sink. When Simon Peter saw it he knelt down before Jesus saying: "Depart from me; for I am a sinful man." For amazement seized on him, and on all that were with him, at the draught of fishes which they had taken.

Jesus said unto Simon : "Fear not ; from henceforth thou shalt be a fisher of men." He was to cast the gospel net into the world's great sea, and to gather in souls in great numbers. And the disciples, when they had brought their boats to land, left all and followed Jesus.

At or near Capernaum was the place where the taxes were collected for that district. The Jews hated to pay these taxes, and hated the officers who collected them. These officers were called "publicans," and were always classed with the lowest of the people. The one at Capernaum was named Matthew, and was despised more than any others because he was a Jew. But Jesus wished to show that his disciples were chosen from among the poor and despised. Those whom men looked down upon Jesus would raise up to be his Apostles. And he said to Matthew: "Follow me." Matthew had doubtless heard of Jesus, and believed in him, and at the divine command he arose, left all, and followed his Lord and Master.

After one of these days of ceaseless toil, Jesus went up into the mountain to pray, and continued all night in prayer to God. In this way only could he gain strength for the labors of the day. He had seen that the people were at a flock without a shepherd, and that some way must be planned to keep them from going astray. They needed more teachers. So the next day, before the crowd had collected, he called his disciples unto him, and chose from among them twelve, whom he named Apostles. These were Simon Peter, and Andrew his brother, and James and John, and Philip and Bartholomew, and Matthew and Thomas, and James the son of Alpheus, and Simon, called the Zealot, and Judas the son of James, and Judas Iscariot, who became a traitor. Three of these—Peter, James and John—were very near to Christ during all of his ministry. Some are not mentioned again in the Holy Scriptures, but we must presume that they did their work in a quiet way, and were faithful in saving souls, and building up the spiritual kingdom of God.

While the choice was being made, a multitude of people were gathering from all Judea and Jerusalem, and the sea coast of Tyre and Sidon, to hear Jesus and to be healed of their diseases. And as he came down with his disciples, to a level place, the crowd pressed around him and sought to touch him, for they felt that power went out from him to help and to heal them. When all were seated on the green grass Jesus preached that memorable discourse known as the SERMON ON THE MOUNT. He spoke directly to the disciples, but intended that each one of the multitude should take the lesson to heart. Jesus said: "Blessed are the poor in spirit: for their's is the kingdom of heaven." The poor in spirit are the humble and lowly minded, who have room in their hearts for the riches of the Gospel.

"Blessed are they that mourn: for they shall be comforted." God will comfort those who mourn over their own sins, and the power of Satan in the world.

THE SHEPHERD AND THE LAMBS.

"Blessed are the meek: for they shall inherit the earth." The meek are the mild and gentle, who are more ambitious for Christ than they are for themselves. They care not for earthly honors, and shall be blessed in all their labors.

"Blessed are they which do hunger and thirst after righteousness: for they shall be filled." Those who long for God's approval as they long for meat and drink, will have it in great abundance.

"Blessed are the merciful: for they shall obtain mercy." Be good and kind yourself if you expect kindness from God and your fellow-men.

"Blessed are the pure in heart for they shall see God." Only those who have repented of their sins and led pure and holy lives, can expect to win heaven, and to be where God is.

"Blessed are the peacemakers: for they shall be called the sons of God." This is to be the reward of those who labor for the salvation of souls, and help to extend the kingdom of peace.

"Blessed are they that are persecuted for righteousness' sake: for theirs is the kingdom of heaven." Those who work for Jesus must expect crosses and persecution, and even martyrdom, but for these sufferings there is blessed reward in heaven.

"Blessed are ye when men shall revile you and persecute you, and say all manner of evil against you falsely, for my sake. Rejoice and be exceeding glad: for so persecuted they the prophets who were before you."

The Jews were looking for a Messiah who would establish a kingdom and a throne on earth, which would be the envy and admiration of all other nations. Jesus taught in these Beatitudes that the blessings to be derived from his kingdom were wholly spiritual, and that none but those who loved and served God would have any part in it.

He said to the disciples: "Ye are the salt of the earth: but if the salt have lost its savor wherewith shall it be salted? it is thenceforth good for nothing but to be cast out and trodden under foot of men." As salt seasons food, and preserves it, and keeps it from becoming stale and tasteless, so the disciples were by their lives and their teachings to keep the gospel truths fresh in the minds of the people. Good Christians are frequently and truthfully called "the salt of the earth." They were to act directly upon the souls of men who would feel better for being with them.

But this was not all. Jesus said: "Ye are the light of the world. A city set on a hill cannot be hid. Neither do men light a candle and put it under the bushel, but on a candlestick; and it giveth light unto all that are in the house. Even so let your light shine before men, that they may see your good works, and glorify your Father who is in heaven." Christ had come to bring light to those who were in darkness. It was customary in the East to build cities on high ground. The Church of Christ was to be like a city set upon a hill. Those who loved Jesus were not to do their work just in a certain circle and keep it hid from sight, but their influence was to be bright and far reaching. Their lives were to be like lights in a dark world. "Each of us must shine. You in your small corner, I in mine."

Jesus said they were not to think that he came to destroy the law. He came to prove that the law and the prophets were fulfilled in him. By his coming all that had been foretold would be brought to pass; and while heaven and earth last, he said, not one jot or one tittle shall pass from the law of God till all things were done.

A *jot* is the smallest letter in the Hebrew alphabet, and a *tittle* is the little turn at the end of the letter,

THE SERMON ON THE MOUNT.

"Whosoever, therefore, shall break one of the least of these commandments, and shall teach men so, shall be called the least in the kingdom of heaven: but whosoever shall do and teach them, shall be called great in the kingdom of heaven. For I say unto you, except your righteousness exceeds the righteousness of the Scribes and Pharisees, ye shall in nowise enter the kingdom of heaven. "Ye have heard that it was said to them of olden time: Thou shalt not kill; and whosoever kill shall be in danger of the judgment." Jesus told them that although the earthly courts only punished those who had actually committed crime, there was a higher court that proved it a crime to have angry or murderous thoughts in the heart. He said that no prayer or offering to God would be acceptable unless those angry feelings were first gotten rid of. We must ask forgiveness of those we had injured, before we asked God to forgive us our sins as we forgive those who trespass against us. We are led into sin through pride, envy, hate, or other passions. But we must not yield to them. We must not let our eyes, our feet, our hands, or our tongue offend God. We are not to swear, nor to use God's name in vain; but our speech is to be pure, and above reproach.

It was the law in olden times that a man was to revenge himself for injuries received. It was an eye for an eye, and a tooth for a tooth. But Christ taught differently. His disciples were not to strike back, but must bear twice as much as other people, and give up rather than go to law. "Whosoever shall force thee to go a mile—that is, to do extra service—go with him twain: do more even than is commanded. Give to him that asketh thee, and from him that would borrow of thee turn not thou away." Beggars were as plenty in those days as they are now, and Jesus would have his disciples kind to the deserving poor, and willing to help them.

"Ye have heard that it was said: Thou shalt love thy neighbor and hate thine enemy. But I say unto you, love your enemies, bless them that curse you, do good to them that hate you, and pray for them that persecute you, that ye may be sons of your Father who is in heaven: for he maketh his sun to rise on the evil and the good, and sendeth rain on the just and the unjust. For if ye love them which love you, what reward have ye? what merit is there in it? do not even the publicans the same? And if ye salute your brethren only, what do ye more than others? Do not even the heathen the same? Be ye therefore perfect, even as your heavenly Father is perfect."

CHAPTER VII.

THE SERMON ON THE MOUNT (CONTINUED)—THE HOUSE BUILT UPON A ROCK.

ALL Christ's teachings were against the preaching and practices of the Scribes and Pharisees. The latter took great pride in showing how religious they were. They prayed on the street corners, and if they gave away anything in charity, or did a good deed, it was always done publicly so as to be seen of men. They were hypocrites, and no true-hearted worshipers. Jesus said: "Take heed that ye do not your alms before men, to be seen of them; otherwise ye have no reward of your Father who is in heaven."

"When, therefore, thou doest alms, do not sound a trumpet before thee as the hypocrites do, in the synagogues and in the streets, that they may have the glory of men. Verily, I say unto you, they have their reward."

The blowing of a trumpet is used here as a figure of speech. It was customary for a trumpet to be blown before important personages to call attention to them. And those who call attention to their own great deeds and tell to this one and that one how much good they have done in the world, may win the praise of men, but God is not pleased with them nor their work.

"When ye pray, ye shall not be as the hypocrites are, for they love to stand and pray in the synagogues and in the broad ways that they may be seen of men. Verily I say unto you they have their reward. But thou when thou prayest, enter into thy closet, and when thou hast shut thy door, pray to thy Father who is in secret; and thy Father who seeth in secret shall reward thee openly."

On the housetop of an Eastern dwelling was a little room used for private prayer, and Jesus taught that secret prayer was a necessity. We are not to put off praying, however, until there is a chance to shut ourselves in, for even in a crowd we can be alone with God. A pious sailor hid his face in his cap whenever he prayed: that was his closet.

"But in praying use not vain repetitions as the heathen do: for they think they shall be heard for their much speaking. Be not ye therefore like unto them: for your Father knoweth what things ye have need of, before ye ask him."

But we are to ask, nevertheless. It does not matter about the words, but we must approach God in the right spirit.

"Moreover, when ye fast, be not like the hypocrites, of a sour countenance: for they disfigure their faces, that men may see that they are fasting. But thou, when thou fastest, annoint thine head, and wash thy face; that thou appear not unto men to fast, but unto thy Father who is in secret; and thy Father who seeth in secret shall recompense thee."

"Lay not up for yourselves treasures on earth where moth and rust doth consume, and where thieves break through and steal. But lay up for yourselves treasures in heaven, where neither moth nor rust doth consume; and where thieves do not break through nor steal. For where your treasure is, there will your heart be also."

We are not to fix our hearts on worldly things, that perish in the using; but we must improve our minds and hearts, and be interested in holy things, and more anxious to please God than man.

"The light (or lamp) of the body is the eye: if, therefore, thine eye be single, fixed upon God, and seeing him alone, thy whole body shall be full of light." Conscience will make thy duty plain to thee. But if thine eye be evil, if thou dost not look to God for help and strength, thy whole body shall be full of darkness. Conscience will not act, and we keep on sinning. "If, therefore, the light that is in thee be darkness, how great is that darkness." It is the worst kind of blindness when conscience is darkened, and we are left to the devices of Satan.

"No man can serve two masters: for either he will hate the one, and love the other: or else he will hold to one, and despise the other. Ye cannot serve God and mammon." Mammon means any idol that takes from us the worship due to God. We must choose whom we will serve.

"Therefore, I say unto you, be not anxious for your life, what ye shall eat, or what ye shall drink: nor yet for your body, what ye shall put on. Is not the life more than meat, and the body than raiment?" They were to trust in God. He who gave the life, would provide food to sustain it; and he who made the body would protect it.

"Behold the fowls of the air: they sow not, neither do they reap, nor gather into barns; yet your heavenly Father feedeth them. Are not ye much better than they? Which of you, by being anxious, can add one cubit to his stature?" Not to the height of the body, but to the length of life. We gain nothing by vexing ourselves with worldly cares.

"And why are ye anxious for raiment? Consider the lilies of the field, how they grow; they toil not, neither do they spin. Yet I say unto you, that even Solomon in all his glory was not arrayed like one of these. Wherefore, if God doth so clothe the grass of the field, which to-day is, and to-morrow is cast into the oven, shall he not much more clothe you, O ye of little faith?" See how God cares for the birds and the flowers. He will care for you, and supply all your needs, if you give your heart to him, and make him your chief desire.

"Be not, therefore, anxious, saying, What shall we eat? or, What shall we drink? or, Wherewithal shall we be clothed? For after all these things do the Gentiles, or heathen seek: for your heavenly Father knoweth that ye have need of all these things. But seek ye first the kingdom of God, and his righteousness; and all these things shall be added unto you. Be not, therefore, anxious for the morrow: for the morrow will take care of itself. Sufficient unto the day is the evil thereof." Each day brings its own cares and anxieties; we are not to borrow trouble. God rained down manna upon the children of Israel, when they were in the wilderness and in need of food. But they were to gather only what they needed for one day. There was not a bit to be put aside in anticipation of a greater need to-morrow. The "daily bread" we ask for in our prayers is strength from day to day, which God gives according to our needs."

The Jews were apt to be very severe in their judgment of others. Jesus said: "Judge not that ye be not judged. For with what judgment ye judge, ye shall be judged; and with what measure ye mete it shall be measured out to you." It is so in the history of the world. Those who are harsh and severe are paid back in the long-run.

"And why beholdest thou the mote that is in thy brother's eye, but considerest not the beam that is in thine own eye? Or how wilt thou say to thy brother, let me pull out the mote from thine eye; and behold a beam is in thine own eye? Thou hypocrite! Cast out first the beam from thine own eye; and then shalt thou see clearly to cast out the mote from thy brother's eye." We must get rid of our own faults before we can see clearly enough to help our brother get rid of his faults.

"Give not that which is holy unto the dogs, neither cast ye your pearls before swine, lest they trample them under their feet and turn and rend you." A certain part of the sacrifices of the Temple was reserved for the priests. This was considered sacred, and not to be given to the common people. Even so must the precious truths of the gospel, pearls of great price, be withheld from those who would reject them with contempt and trample them underfoot.

Ask, and it shall be given you; seek, and ye shall find; knock, and it shall be opened unto you. For every one that asketh receiveth; and he that seeketh findeth; and to him that knocketh it shall be opened.

They were to ask in prayer for what they had need of; peace with God. They were to seek for it as something they had lost. They were to knock, as they would at a door that was closed against them. Prayer means all this, and God always answers prayer in his own right way.

"What man is there of you of whom if his son ask bread will he give him a stone? Or if he ask a fish will he give him a serpent? If ye then, being evil, know how to give good gifts unto your children, how much more shall your Father in heaven give good things to them that ask him?" All God's gifts are good. He makes no mistakes. And when we pray, we must trust in him, for he knows our needs better than we know them ourselves.

"All things, therefore, whatsoever ye would that men should do to you, even so do ye also to them, for this is the law and the prophets." We must treat people as we would like to be treated ourselves. Do to others as you would be done by is the Golden Rule. But Christ's teaching goes further than that, and tells us to treat people as they would like to be treated themselves. Kindnesses and attentions that you would not care for, may be a great comfort and blessing to some one else. Jesus says, "Do all the good you can, to everybody you can."

The road to eternal life is represented as narrow ; that is, shut in, with no room for any worldly baggage. We must leave off everything that hinders our progress, and keep our eyes fixed on the light that guides us. The Pharisees, in the East, would naturally go through the wide gate, and make a big parade where they could be seen of men.

Jesus said: "Enter ye through the strait or narrow gate; for wide is the gate, and broad is the way that leadeth to destruction, and many there be that go in thereat. Because narrow is the gate, and straitened the way that leadeth unto life, and few there be that find it."

We know ourselves how hard it is to do right, and how easy it is to do wrong. Crowds go the way of sin, and lead low lives, and give not a thought to pleasing God ; while comparatively few attend the churches, and strive to lead holy lives and to show that their greatest desire is to love God and to keep his commandments.

"Beware of false prophets, who come to you in sheep's clothing, but inwardly are ravening wolves. By their fruits ye shall know them. Do men gather grapes of thorns, or figs of thistles? Even so every good tree bringeth forth good fruit; but the corrupt tree bringeth forth evil fruit. A good tree cannot bring forth evil fruit, neither can a corrupt tree bring forth good fruit. Every tree that bringeth not forth good fruit is hewn down and cast into the fire. Wherefore, by their fruits ye shall know them."

These false prophets were false teachers who would pretend to be disciples of Christ, and would do more harm than good. Men, like trees, are known by their fruits. From good teachers we are to look for good fruit, as the result of their teaching. Do they lead good lives? then they will teach others to lead good lives.

"Not every one that saith unto me, Lord, Lord, shall enter into the kingdom of heaven; but he that doeth the will of my Father in heaven. Many will say to me in that day, Lord, Lord, have we not prophesied in thy name? and in thy name done many wonderful works? And then will I profess unto them, I never knew you: depart from me ye that work iniquity." In that day must mean the great day of judgment. And many professing Christians—outwardly saints and inwardly sinners—will cry to Jesus for help, and plead with him to remember the good works they did in his name. They might deceive others, but him they could not deceive. He knows our hearts.

"Every one, therefore, that heareth these sayings of mine, and doeth them, shall be likened to a wise man that built his house upon a rock. And the rain descended, and the floods came, and the winds blew, and beat upon that house; and it fell not, for it was founded upon a rock. And every one that heareth these sayings of mine, and doeth them not, shall be likened unto a foolish man, that built his house upon the sand. And the rain descended, and the floods came, and the winds blew and beat upon that house, and it fell, and great was the fall of it."

THE HOUSE BUILT UPON THE ROCK.

Jesus is the rock. If we build on him, we are safe for time and eternity. Storms of sorrow, floods of grief, trials of all sorts, but rivet us closer to him, and we are not swept away. But he who builds on any other foundation but Jesus, will have nothing to cling to. When he most needs help, help will fail him. A good builder looks well to the foundation. If you are anxious to build up a good character, you must first dig down and clear away all the rubbish. Let the four walls of Temperance, Patience, Godliness and Charity be made broad, and well cemented together, with Jesus Christ the chief corner-stone; in whom all the building, fitly framed together, groweth unto a holy temple.

When Jesus had finished the Sermon on the Mount, the multitudes were astonished at his teachings. For he taught as one having authority, and not as the Scribes. Never man spake like this man.

CHAPTER VIII.

HEALING THE LEPER— THE CENTURION'S SERVANT. THE WIDOW OF NAIN— MARY MAGDALENE.

As Jesus came down from the mountain, a great multitude followed him. And as he was entering one of the small villages in that region there came a leper, and worshiped him, saying: "Lord, if thou wilt, thou canst make us clean." No one else had this power. When the dreaded disease, leprosy, came upon a man he was shut away from his family and friends, and driven out of the town or village in which he resided. He was unclean, and could not attend the services in the synagogue, and any Jew that touched him would be diseased also. Jesus was full of compassion for this wretched outcast, and when he had heard his cry of faith, "Lord, if thou wilt, thou canst make clean," he stretched out his hand and touched him, saying: "I will. Be thou clean." And immediately his leprosy was cleansed. And Jesus saith unto him, "See thou tell no man; but go thy way, show thyself to the priest, and offer the gift that Moses commanded,* for a testimony unto them." No leper, or diseased person could return to his home and friends without first seeing the priest, and getting, as it were, his discharge from the hospital. And he was to bring an offering to the altar—a gift of praise and thanks to God.

Sin is compared to the disease of leprosy, which first shows a small white spot, and then spreads all over the body. It unfits us for living with the pure and good. It is not safe for them to touch us. There is no medicine that can cure a sin-sick soul. Jesus alone can take away our sins, and make us white as snow; and this he will do if we go to him in prayer, asking to be saved from Satan's power.

The fame of Jesus spread abroad, and multitudes came together to hear, and to be healed of their infirmities. So great was the crowd that Jesus withdrew for awhile into a desert place, where he could rest and pray to God for strength. Now there was in Capernaum a centurion—an officer in charge of a hundred men—and a servant of his, of whom he was very fond, was sick unto death. The centurion, hearing that Jesus was in Capernaum, sent elders of the Jews to beg him to save the sick man's life.

The elders urged Jesus to make haste, and said that the centurion was well worthy of assistance, for he was friendly to the Jews, and had even built them a syna-

---

* Leviticus, XIV.

gogue. Jesus said at once: "I will go and heal him." And when he was not far from the house the centurion sent out some of his friends to Jesus with this message: "Lord, I am not worthy that thou shouldst

CHRIST AND THE CENTURION.

come under my roof, neither thought I myself worthy to come unto thee, but only speak the word and my servant shall be healed. For I also am a man in authority, having soldiers under me, and I say to this one, 'Go,' and he goeth, and to another, 'Come,' and he cometh, and to my servant, 'Do this,' and he doeth it." This was as much as to say: "If I can make such use of my power, you certainly can give any order and have it obeyed at once."

Jesus was surprised at hearing these words from such a man, and he turned and said to the multitude that followed him, "I say unto you, that not even in Israel have I found such great faith." And they that

EASTERN BIER.

were sent out, found on returning to the house that the sick servant was entirely well.

There was little chance for Jesus to rest now that the fame of his miracles had gone abroad, and a short time after healing the centurion's servant he left Capernaum, and set out for Nain, a small village about twenty-five miles distant. His disciples went with him, and they were followed by a great multitude. As they drew near the gate of the city they met a funeral procession, the body of a dead man being carried out for burial. He was the only son of his mother,

THE WIDOW'S SON BROUGHT TO LIFE.

and she was a widow, and many of his relatives and friends were with her.

When Jesus saw her grief he felt sorry for her, and said unto her: "Weep not." And he drew near and touched the bier, and the bearers stood still. And Jesus said: "Young man, I say unto thee, arise." And he that was dead sat up, and began to speak. And he gave him to his mother, alive and well. And great fear took hold on all; and they glorified God, saying, "A great prophet has arisen among us, and God hath visited his people. And this saying concerning him went forth throughout Judea, and all the region round about."

It was about this time that John the Baptist, whom Herod had shut up in prison, heard of the wonderful miracles that Jesus had done. And calling unto him two of his disciples, he sent them to Jesus. And when the men came unto him, they said: "John the Baptist hath sent us unto thee, saying, art thou he that should come? or do we look for another?" And while they stood there waiting for his answer Jesus cured many persons of their diseases, and hurts, and those who had lost their reason were made quite well, and of sound mind. And to many that were blind he gave sight.

Then Jesus answered John's disciples, and said to them, "Go your way, and tell John what things ye have seen and heard; how that the blind see, the lame walk, the lepers are cleansed, the deaf hear, and the poor have the gospel preached to them. And blessed is he who shall not be offended in me."

As they departed, Jesus began to speak to the multitudes concerning John. He said: "What went ye out into the wilderness to see? A reed shaken with the wind? But what went ye out to see? A man clothed in soft raiment? Behold, they that wear soft raiment are in kings' houses. But what went ye out to see? A prophet? Yea, I say unto you, and more than a prophet. For this is he of whom it is written, Behold, I send my messenger before thy face, who shall prepare thy way before thee. Verily I say unto you, among them that are born of woman there hath not risen a greater than John the Baptist, notwithstanding that he that is least in the kingdom of heaven is greater than he. And from the days of John the Baptist until now the kingdom of heaven suffereth violence, and the violent take it by force. For all the prophets and the law—that is the whole Old Testament—prophesied until John came. And if ye are willing to receive it, this is Elijah, who was to come. He that hath ears to hear, let him hear.

"But whereunto shall I liken this generation? It is like unto children sitting in the market places, who call to their fellows, saying, we have piped unto you, and you have not danced; we have wailed, and you have not mourned. For John came neither eating nor drinking, and they say, he is a madman. The Son of man came eating and drinking, and they say, behold a gluttonous man, and a wine-bibber, a friend of publicans and sinners. But wisdom is justified by her children." Those who have chosen wisely will show it by their works.

Jesus spoke to the people in this way to shame them. Many had gone out of curiosity to see John, and were neither impressed by his personal appearance, nor by the words he spoke. They looked for a king with wealth at his command, who would set up his throne in their midst, and raise the Jews to high rank. Jesus knew this, and he said that there was never a man born who was greater than John; and yet the most humble follower of Christ—he who was born of the Spirit, and born into the kingdom of heaven —that is, brought into close relations to Christ— is in a much higher position than John the Baptist. There is no higher title than Christian.

"The kingdom of heaven suffereth violence," means that heaven can only be gained by those who are in earnest. It is like a fort, to be assaulted with prayer, and taken by storm. We are to force our way in. The Jews expected that Elijah would rise from the dead, hence they would not believe that John was that prophet.

This generation were the people living in Judea at this time, many of whom laughed with scorn at the common folks who went out to hear John, and believed in his teachings. Jesus said it was like one set of children inviting another to play with them, first at a mock wedding and then at a mock funeral, in which the latter would not join. John and Jesus were the children calling to the other children—the whole gathering of Jews—who were constantly quarrelling and disagreeing. They were foolish and not wise children.

Jesus then began to speak against those cities wherein his mighty miracles were done because the people repented not. And he said, "Woe unto thee Chorazin! woe unto thee, Bethsaida! for if the mighty works which were done in you had been done in Tyre and Sidon, they would have repented long ago in sackcloth and ashes." It was the custom in the East for men who were in great sorrow, or who had had severe trials, to put on a garment, like a sack, with holes for their arms, and to strew ashes on the head.

Jesus said, "But I say unto you, It shall be more tolerable for Tyre and Sidon in the day of judgment than for you. And thou, Capernaum, which art exalted unto heaven, shalt be brought down to hell; for if the mighty works which have been done in thee had been done in Sodom, it would have stood to this day. But I say unto you, that it shall be more tolerable for the land of Sodom in the day of judgment than for thee."

Then Jesus said, I thank thee, O Father, Lord of heaven and earth, because thou didst hide these things

SIDON, AT THE PRESENT DAY.

from the wise and prudent, and reveal them unto babes. Even so, Father; for it was well-pleasing in thy sight. All things are delivered unto me by my Father; and no man knoweth the Son, except the Father; neither knoweth any man the Father, save the Son, and he to whom the Son will reveal him.

"Come unto me, all ye that labor and are heavy laden, and I will give you rest. Take my yoke upon you and learn of me; for I am meek and lowly in heart, and ye shall find rest to your souls. For my yoke is easy and my burden is light."

Not long after this Jesus was invited to dine at the house of one Simon, a Pharisee, and he went. Now it was the custom in the East for the man of the house to receive a distinguished guest with considerable honor. The master met him at the door with a kiss of welcome. Slaves removed his sandals, washed the dust from his feet, and brushed off his clothes, brought him water for his hands and face, and then combed his hair and beard and perfumed them with sweet-smelling oils. The choicest seat was given him at the table, and no one partook of the meal until after he was seated.

But when Jesus came to Simon's house there was no one at the door to receive him, and he took off his own sandals, and passed on into the dining hall. No special place was reserved for him, and he sat down in the first vacant place that offered. The guests reclined at meals on a couch that went round the table, and rested on their left arm that the right might be free to reach the food, and convey it to their mouths. As they lay thus on the couch their feet would be on the outside, and in full view of those who passed back and forth.

The doors of the eastern houses are kept open, and while the guests were at the table there came up the steps from the court-yard a woman who was bold enough to enter the dining-hall. All looked at her in surprise, as the Jews did not speak to women in public, and she was never invited to their feasts.

Worst of all, this woman was a wretched sinner. She had led a wicked life, and on that day had gone with the crowd to hear Jesus preach. His words gave promise of rest and peace, of forgiveness for past sins. As she heard him speak she felt in her soul that he was sent from God, and alone could give her strength to resist temptation. Throughout all his ministry his message was, Come. Come to ME. Those words drew her. She watched Jesus and followed him to Simon's house.

She thought not of herself nor of the shame of her being there. No one spoke as she passed on through the room, her eyes fixed on the One she had come to see. And she stood at his feet with bended form, and wept bitter tears of repentance, for she was indeed sorry for her sins.

The Eastern women were very fond of perfumes, and many of them wore a flask of sweet-smelling oil around the neck. The flask, which hung below the breast, was not always of glass, but sometimes of silver and gold, and often of alabaster, the contents being used to sweeten their breath and perfume the person.

This woman, who was known as Mary Magdalene— or Mary of Magdala—stood behind Jesus. And, as the tears gushed from her eyes, they fell on his feet, and lest they should annoy him she wiped them off with the long tresses of her hair. Then growing bolder as her faith increased she fell to kissing his feet, and anointed them with the oil from the alabaster flask she wore about her neck. She did not speak, neither did Jesus.

The Pharisee who had bidden Jesus to the feast saw what took place, and said to himself: "If this man

MAGDALENE ANOINTING THE FEET OF JESUS.

were a prophet he would have known what kind of a woman this was. And if he had known he would not have allowed her to come near him, or to touch him, for she is one of the worst of sinners."

Jesus read Simon's thoughts, and said to him: "Simon, I have somewhat to say to thee." And he saith, "Master, say on." And Jesus said: "There was a certain man who had two debtors, the one owed five hundred pence, and the other fifty. And when they had no money wherewith to pay their debts he forgave them both. Which of them therefore will love him the most?" Simon answered: "I suppose that he to whom he forgave the most." Jesus said: "Thou hast rightly judged." And, turning to the woman, he said to Simon: "Seest thou this woman? I entered into thine house, thou gavest me no water for my feet, but she hath bathed my feet with tears, and wiped them with her hair. Thou gavest me no kiss; but this woman since the time I came in hath not ceased to kiss my feet. My head with oil thou didst not anoint: but this woman hath anointed my feet with precious ointment. Wherefore, I say unto thee, her sins, which are many, are forgiven, for she loved much: but to whom little is forgiven, the same loveth little." The Jews would understand this for they were not apt to care much for those who did but little for them, but Jesus intended his words should prick Simon's conscience. His neglect of Jesus showed that he cared very little for him. The kiss of welcome, the washing of the feet, and the anointing were not absolutely necessary, but were tokens of respect and love.

The poor woman by her acts had shown intense gratitude and reverence. And Jesus said unto her: "Thy sins have been forgiven." She knew it. She felt it in her soul, and now all was rest and peace. And those that sat at meat with him, began to say within themselves, "Who is this that even forgiveth sins?" Jesus said to the woman, "Thy faith hath saved thee: go in peace." And she, the first one who had come to Jesus, asking for spiritual help, passed out of darkness into light. By her faith in Jesus she had entered into the kingdom of heaven. It was heaven to be at peace with God, and to know her sins were all forgiven.

CHAPTER IX.

JESUS AT THE SEASIDE—HE TEACHES IN PARABLES—THE SOWER—THE WHEAT AND THE TARES—GRAIN OF MUSTARD SEED—HIDDEN LEAVEN—HIDDEN TREASURE—THE PEARL OF PRICE—THE DRAG NET—THE STORM ON THE LAKE—THE HERD OF SWINE.

Jesus was now on the high tide of success as a popular preacher. Crowds gathered to hear him, and listened spell-bound to his words. Although he was born of the Jewish race, there was in his face, form, and manner, something that distinguished him from other men, and commanded the most respectful attention from pious worshipers. His voice held them by its firm, clear tones, and his words haunted them forever after. But the Pharisees were on the watch to tangle him in his talk, for they were exceedingly jealous of him.

Early one spring morning Jesus and his disciples went down by the sea-shore. As he sat there the crowd began to gather, and he was forced to enter one of the boats, from which he preached to them in parables. This was the favorite mode of teaching among the Jews, but their parables differed from those that Jesus used. A parable is a fable, in which a lesson is taught by a series of word-paintings, and Jesus chose the most familiar scenes to illustrate his meaning.

His first parable was that of the Sower. "The Sower went forth to sow his seed; and as he sowed, some fell by the wayside, and it was trodden down; and the birds devoured it. Some fell upon the rock; and

THE SOWER.

as soon as it grew up it withered away because it had no moisture. And some fell in the midst of thorns, and the thorns grew up with it and choked it. Others fell on good ground, and grew up and brought forth fruit a hundred fold. And when he had said these things, he cried: "He that hath ears to hear, let him hear."

The lesson in this parable was: Take heed how ye hear the gospel message; and although the meaning seems quite clear to us, because of the light thrown upon it in the New Testament, it was not so easy for those who heard it to understand, and take it home to themselves.

The disciples asked Jesus what this parable meant. And he said: "The seed is the Word of God. Those by the wayside are they that have heard the word, but taken none of it to heart. They are careless and indifferent, and Satan puts temptations in their way, lest they should believe in Christ and be saved. Those on the rock are they who when they have heard the word receive it with joy, and for awhile believe in Jesus and obey his teachings. But the seed can take no root, and when trials and persecutions come these fickle followers go back to the world, and give no more attention to spiritual things. Some of the seed fell in the midst of thorns, and these are they that have heard, and go forth earnest and eager, as young converts. But they are selfish, and care more to please themselves than to please God. The thorns are the cares of the world, the love of dress, society, or business, which choke the good seed and keep it from coming to perfection. Have you not seen young people who gave promise of becoming good Christians, workers in the Church and Sunday-School? For awhile they were faithful and earnest, but ere long they were drawn away, and there was no room in their hearts for the growth of spiritual things.

The seed that fell on the good ground are such as, having heard the word with honest and good hearts, hold it fast, and bring forth fruit with patience. These are they, who, in the midst of storms and trials, stand firm in the lot in which God has placed them, and bring forth fruit to his glory.

Another parable Jesus set before them, saying,

The kingdom of heaven is like to a man who sowed good seed in his field. But while the men slept, his enemy came and sowed tares among the wheat, and went away. But when the blade sprung up and brought forth fruit, then appeared the tares also. And the servants of the householder came and said unto him: "Sir, didst thou not sow good seed in thy field? How

THE ENEMY SOWING TARES.

then, did these tares get in?" He said to them: "An enemy hath done this?" The servants said unto him: "Wilt thou then that we go and gather them up?" But he said: "Nay, lest haply while ye gather up the tares ye root up also the wheat with them. Let both grow together until the harvest: and in the time of the harvest I will say to the reapers, Gather up first the tares, and bind them in bundles to burn them: but gather the wheat into my barn."

Another parable he put forth, saying: The kingdom of heaven is like to a grain of mustard seed, which a man took and sowed in his field: which indeed is the least of all seeds: but when it is grown it is greater than the herbs, and becometh a tree, so that the birds come and lodge in the branches thereof.

The meaning of this was that those who heard the word of God aright, though they had but little faith, it would grow and spread out, and become the means of bringing others to Christ.

And still another parable spoke Jesus unto them, saying: The Kingdom of Heaven is like unto leaven, which a woman took, and hid in three measures of meal, till it was all leavened.

Leaven is another name for yeast. Yeast is put into flour to make it rise, and only a small quantity is needed. Bread is unwholesome without yeast, and life is dull and heavy without Jesus in it. He lightens us. There is always evil along with good, but the more of Jesus we have in our hearts and lives the better can we work against all evil influences.

Then Jesus sent the multitude away and went into the house, and his disciples came to him, asking him to explain the parable of the tares of the field. Tares look so much like the real wheat that it is difficult to tell them apart. For this reason they cause a great deal of trouble if allowed to grow up in the same field. As an old proverb says: "Ill weeds grow apace."

Jesus said to his disciples: "He that soweth the good seed is the Son of Man. The field is the world. The good seed are the sons of God—those who grow up good Christians—and the tares are the sons of evil —those who lead wicked lives. The enemy that sowed them is the devil." In the world these two classes of men grow up side by side, and by many cannot be told apart.

"The harvest is the end of the world, and the reapers are the angels. As, therefore, the tares are gathered up and burned in the fire, so shall it be at the

LEAVEN.

end of the world. The Son of Man shall send forth his angels, and they shall gather out of his kingdom all things that offend—all stumbling-blocks that have hindered others from doing good works, and all workers of iniquity. And shall cast them into a furnace of fire; and there shall be weeping and gnashing of teeth. Then shall the righteous shine forth as the sun in the kingdom of their Father. He that hath ears to hear, let him hear."

Mysterious as these sayings were, the disciples could guess at their meaning. Children were taught to be obedient to their parents; and sons of God were those who obeyed God's word, and did good works in the

SEEKING GREAT PEARLS.

world. Those who did nothing to please God, but led selfish, sinful lives, would realize at the Last Day how wicked they had been, and shame and sorrow would burn within them like a furnace of fire that no tears could quench. There is no excuse for those who have the Gospel preached to them.

Jesus spoke yet other parables to the disciples in

the house, and said to them: "The Kingdom of Heaven is like a treasure hidden in a field, which a man found, and kept hid, and in his joy he went and sold all that he had and bought that field."

To find Christ is to find a precious treasure, worth all the wealth of this world.

"Again," said Jesus, "the kingdom of heaven is like to a man that is a merchant seeking pearls. And when he finds one pearl of great price he goes and sells all that he has and buys it." Jesus is the "pearl of great price." No matter what else we have, we are poor without him. We are to be as eager to obtain this pearl as is the merchant who deals in gems, and wants the best thing in the market. It will cost something to have Jesus in the soul. He will not share a divided heart. Are we determined to have him at any cost? Then we will sell all we have—get rid of everything that is worthless in comparison—and buy the one great pearl which so enriches the owner.

"Again," said Jesus, "the kingdom of heaven is like unto a net, that was cast into the sea, and gathered up every kind of fish. And when it was full, they drew it to the shore, and sitting down, gathered the good into vessels, and the bad they cast away. So shall it be at the end of the world; the angels shall come forth, and sever the wicked from among the just. And shall cast them into the furnace of fire: and there shall be weeping and gnashing of teeth. Have ye understood all these things?" They say unto him: "Yes, Lord."

All sorts of people are caught in the Gospel net and drawn into the various churches, many of whom are not true Christians. But we are not to judge them. We are to leave that to God, who will separate the bad from the good at the Last Day.

And he said unto them: Therefore every scribe who

hath been made a disciple for the kingdom of heaven, is like to a man that is a householder, who bringeth forth out of his treasure things new and old. Ministers and teachers are to use their knowledge of the Bible to instruct others, and to make clear the truths of the Old Testament as well as of the New. Christ

PARABLE OF THE NET.

taught his disciples, as he teaches us, that we are not to seek him just for our own selfish benefit, but are to illuminate and enrich our own lives and brighten the lives of those around us.

From day to day Jesus continued to teach the crowds, whom it was not easy to dismiss, even at nightfall. But one evening Jesus said to his disciples: "Let us go over to the other side." And they took him as he was into the boat, and made not the least preparation for the journey. And there were also with him other small boats.

Ere he left the shore, a certain scribe came and said

STILLING THE TEMPEST.

unto him: "Master, I will follow thee whithersoever thou goest." And Jesus said to him: "The foxes have holes, and the birds of the air have nests, but the Son of Man hath not where to lay his head." Jesus meant that if he went with him, he would have to accept poverty, and privation, for Jesus knew that the

Scribe was on the lookout for earthly honors and promotion.

And one of his disciples said to him: "Lord, suffer me first to go away and bury my father." But Jesus said: "Follow me; and leave the dead to bury their own dead." This was to teach that the first and most important work in life is to follow Christ. True disciples will obey at once, and make no excuses.

While the boats were on their way over the sea, or Lake of Galilee, there came up a sudden storm, which swept over them with great fury. The water came in, and the men were in great terror. In the stern of the of the boat, on a low bench where the steersman sat to rest, was pillowed the head of Jesus. The disciples were vexed to find him asleep, for they had supposed that with Jesus in the boat it would surely be plain sailing. And they wakened him, and said: "Master, Master, dost thou not care to save our lives?" And Jesus arose, and rebuked the wind and the waves; and said unto the sea: "Peace, be still." And the wind ceased, and there was a great calm. And Jesus said to the disciples: "Why are ye so fearful? Where is your faith?" And they marveled exceedingly, and said one to another: "Who then is this man, that even the wind and the sea obey him?"

Christians must not expect to escape trouble. There will be storms of sorrow, and great trials, but with Jesus in the boat with us we cannot sink. We are to charge him with neglect, but to pray to him for strength and courage. Life is a stormy sea, and our cry at all times should be: "Lord, save, or we perish!"

The Sea of Galilee was six miles wide, and the eastern shore was quite thinly inhabited. They landed at Gadara, in what was called the land of the Gadarenes.

And as Jesus left the boat there met him a madman,

who came out from among the tombs, and was so exceedingly fierce that no one dared pass that way.

In eastern countries those who were so unfortunate as to lose their reason were not shut up, as they are with us, but were allowed to roam at will. There were no hospitals for these poor afflicted ones, so they took refuge in caves and among the tombs, where they

JESUS AND THE DEMONIAC.

made night and day hideous with their yells and cries. Men had sought to bind this man with ropes or chains, but he burst the bonds asunder, and no one had strength to tame him. Night and day he was in the mountains, and among the tombs, crying out and cutting himself with stones. And when he saw Jesus from afar off, he ran and fell down at his feet, crying out with a loud voice: "What have I to do with thee, Jesus, thou Son of the Most High God? I beseech in God's name, torment me not." For the man had writhed in agony, when Jesus said: "Come forth, thou unclean spirit." And Jesus asked the demon: "What is thy name?" And he answered, saying, "My name is Legion; for we are many." And he begged that he might not be sent out of the country.

Now there was near, on the mountain a great herd of swine feeding. And the demons besought him, saying: "Send us into the swine, that we may enter into them." And Jesus said, "Go." And they immediately left the man and entered into the swine, and the herd—which numbered about two thousand —ran violently down a steep place, and were drowned in the sea. And they that fed them, fled in great fright and astonishment, and told it in the city and throughout all the country round about. And a great mass of people went out to see what had been done. And they come to Jesus, and behold he that was possessed with the devil; ay, who had a legion of them, was sitting, clothed, and in his right mind! And those who had seen the miracle told what had been done to the madman and the swine. And they begged Jesus to depart out of their borders. And when Jesus was in the boat, the poor demoniac prayed that he might be with him. Jesus suffered it not, but said unto him: "Go to thy house and unto thy friends, and tell them what great things the Lord hath done for thee, and how he had mercy upon thee." And he went and began to make known in Decapolis the great things that Jesus had done for him, and all those who heard him marveled greatly.

It is not known whether this miracle was performed at Gadara or Gergesa. It matters little. The people were heathens, and thought more of saving their property, than of saving souls. The loss of the swine, from the sale of which they made much money, was more to them than the healing of a madman, and the fear of further damage made them long to get rid of this worker of miracles.

So Jesus turned his back on them, and entering the boat was soon on his way over to Capernaum.

CHAPTER X.

HEALING OF THE PARALYTIC—MATTHEW'S FEAST—THE RAISING OF JAIRUS'S DAUGHTER—TWO BLIND MEN—THE DUMB DEMONIAC—JESUS SENDS OUT THE TWELVE APOSTLES.

THERE were many on the shores of Capernaum watching for Jesus's return. They knew his boat, and as soon as they caught sight of the sail the word went forth that the Great Teacher was on his way back to them. When Jesus landed he went directly to Peter's house, where he made his home when in Capernaum. There the people gathered so there was not room for them, and the court-yard was crowded even out to the street.

The houses in the East were built low, and with a flat roof which was reached by a flight of steps inside and outside of the house. In the crowd were four men who had brought with them a sick friend that Jesus might cure him of his dreadful disease. He had been stricken with paralysis, and could move neither hand nor foot. Being helpless himself, these friends took him up, bed and all, and brought him to Jesus, and their disappointment was great when they found themselves shut out by the crowd. What should they do? Return without having accomplished their errand? This was not to be thought of for a moment. Quickly they devised a plan—for necessity sharpens one's wits—and proceeded to carry it out.

The roof itself was paved with brick or stone, or hard cement, and around it was a railing at least three feet high. It would have been difficult for them to break through this, but they must get to Jesus in some way.

Jesus stood under a covered gallery that ran around the court-yard and opened into the various apartments, so that the members of the family could sit in their own rooms, and hear all that was going on outside. The friends of the paralytic took their burden up the outer staircase, broke through the tiles on the roof, and let down the bed with the sick man upon it in front of the place where Christ was sitting.

We may imagine the surprise of the crowd at this strange interruption, the fear and anxiety portrayed in the faces of the four men on the roof, the awe-struck appeal in the eyes of the poor paralytic. It was a strange scene. A deep silence fell on all around, broken at last by the voice of Jesus, who, seeing the faith of these men, said to the paralytic: "Be of good cheer. Thy sins are forgiven thee."

Then the Scribes and Pharisees began to talk among themselves, saying: "Who is this that speaketh blasphemies? God alone can forgive sins." But Jesus, perceiving their thoughts, said unto them: "What reason ye in your hearts? For whether is it easier to say, thy sins are forgiven thee? or, Arise and walk? But that ye may know that the Son of Man hath power upon earth to forgive sins," he said unto the palsied, "I say unto thee, Arise, and take up thy couch and go unto thine house." And immediately the man, who had been a perfectly helpless man, rose up before them, and taking up the bed on which he had lain for so long a time, set out for his home, praising God as he went. And all who saw it were amazed, and they

HEALING OF THE PARALYTIC.

glorified God, and were filled with fear, saying: "We have seen strange things to-day. We never saw anything like this before."

From the house, Jesus went down to the sea-shore, and a great multitude followed him. After he had

THE PARALYTIC CURED.

taught them for awhile, he went to the house of Matthew, who had made a great feast and invited Jesus and his disciples to attend it. As Matthew was himself a publican, a large company of the same class of men were seated at the table. Yet with no show of scorn, Jesus and his disciples sat with them at the feast.

This made the Scribes and Pharisees very angry, and they found much fault with the disciples, saying: "Why do ye eat and drink with the publicans and sinners?" Jesus heard of their murmurs, and said, to them: "They that are in health have no need of a physician; but they that are sick. I am not come to call the righteous, but sinners to repentance."

They said unto him: "The disciples of John fast often, and make prayers, and likewise also do the disciples of the Pharisees. But thy disciples eat and drink with publicans and sinners."

Jesus said to them: "Can ye make the sons of the bride-chamber fast while the bridegroom is with them? But there will come a time when the bridegroom shall be taken away from them; and then shall they fast in those days."

Jesus referred to himself as the bridegroom. He was with his disciples, and it was a time for rejoicing. When he left them, then there would be a good reason for their fasting.

He spake also a parable unto them, saying: "No man putteth a patch of new cloth upon an old garment, for that which filleth it up taketh from the garment, and a worse rent is made. Neither do men put new wine in old bottles, else the bottles burst, and the wine runs out, and the skins are ruined. But they put new wine into fresh bottles, and both are preserved together."

In olden times, bottles were not made of glass, but of leather. New wine ferments, or works, and the vast amount of gas would stretch the old bottles and cause them to burst. But by putting new wine into new bottles, both would stretch together. Jesus meant to teach by this parable that the new religion would break through all the old Jewish rites and ceremo-

CURED BY TOUCHING HIS GARMENT.

nies. Those notions of caste, of feeling that one man was better than another, must be done away with. Jesus came to the poor, and the lowly-minded, and they were made new men through him.

The feast was scarcely over, and Jesus was still speaking, when there came to him one of the rulers of the synagogue, a man named Jairus. And he fell down at the feet of Jesus in great grief, for his only daughter, twelve years of age, was dying. And he besought Jesus, saying: "My little daughter is at the point of death; I pray thee that thou wilt come and lay thy hands on her, that she may be healed, and brought back to life."

Jesus went with the ruler, and a great multitude followed him, and crowded against him. In the throng was a woman who had had a dreadful disease for twelve long years. She had been under the care of many physicians, had spent all the money she had, and was no better, and if anything much worse. When she heard of the wonderful things that Jesus had done, she thought to herself, perhaps he can cure me! He may succeed where every one else has failed! Her faith was great, and she said: "I will not trouble him, or ask him to put himself out of the way to attend to my wants, but so great is his power that if I can only touch his robe it will do me good. Who am I that he should speak to me?" Feeling thus, she pushed her way through the crowd, and panting and breathless came near to Jesus, who moved in great haste towards the ruler's house. The wind blew his outer robe away from him, and the poor woman, watching her chance, touched the hem of his garment as it came within reach of her hand. And straightway the trouble she had had for twelve years was cured; and she felt that she was entirely well.

Jesus, being conscious that the power from him had gone forth, turned about and facing the crowd, said:

"Who touched my garments?" His disciples said to him: "Thou seest the multitude crowding and pushing against thee, and yet thou sayest, 'Who touched me?'" Jesus said: "Somebody touched me;" and looked around to see who it was. The woman, feeling that she could not hide herself, came fearing and trembling, and fell down at his feet. And she told him before all the people why she had touched him, and how she was healed immediately. Jesus said unto her: "Daughter, thy faith hath made thee whole; go in peace."

While he yet spoke there came a servant from the ruler's house, saying to him, "Thy daughter is dead; trouble not the master." But Jesus, hearing it, said: "Fear not; only believe." And when he came to the house, he allowed no one to enter with him save Peter, James, and John.

It was the custom in the East, for hired mourners to gather at the house where one lay dead, and to weep and wail in token of their sympathy. Already were they lamenting the death of Jairus's daughter, when Jesus came into the house. And seeing the tumult, and seeing the people weeping and wailing, he said: "Why make ye this noise, and weep so greatly? The child is not dead, but sleepeth." And they laughed him to scorn. But when he had put them all out of the house, he taketh the father and mother of the child, and with Peter, James, and John entered the room where the young girl was. Taking her by the hand, Jesus said unto her: "Rise, my child." And straightway she arose, and walked, and was in her usual health. And those who saw her were amazed, and filled with awe. And Jesus charged them strictly to tell no one of this miracle, lest it should excite the people. And he commanded the parents to give the child something to eat. They were not to expect the child to be kept alive on spiritual food. The body

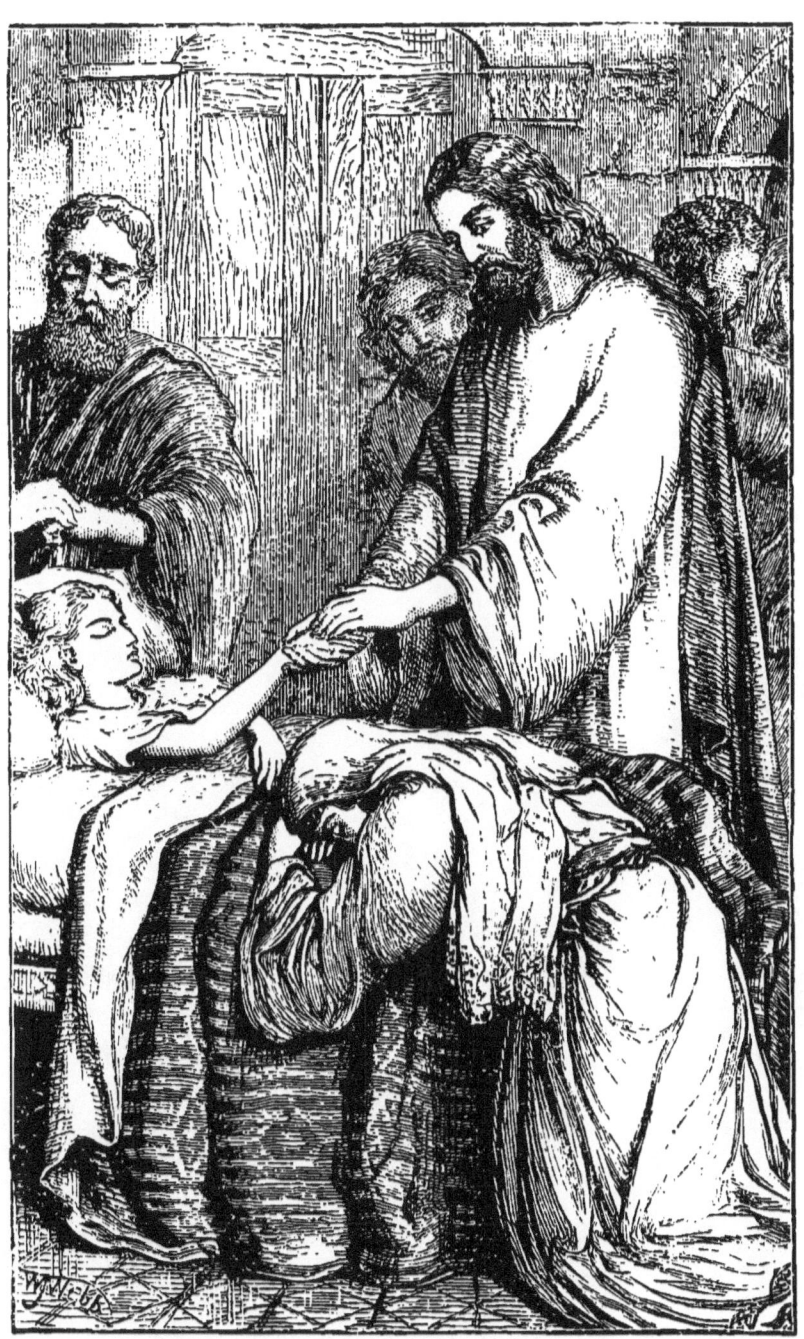

JAIRUS' DAUGHTER.

needs nourishing, and the child was to eat her accustomed food in order to be kept in good health. Those who are anxious to save their souls are not to neglect their bodies, and go without food.

Those who saw the girl dead must afterwards have seen her alive, and thus the name and fame of Jesus spread through all that part of the land.

Crowded as the day had been with exciting events, there was still more to follow. As Jesus left the house of the ruler the multitude kept close behind him, and with the throng came two blind men, crying: "Have mercy on us, thou Son of David!" These blind beggars usually sat by the roadside near the large towns, and asked aid of all the passers by. Their hearing was very sharp, and a great deal of the talk had come to their ears, and in the hope of being cured they had followed after the great Wonder-worker, who healed the sick, and gave the blind their sight.

Jesus let them cry on until he came to a certain house, and then he turned and said to them: "Believe ye that I am able to do this?" They answered: "Yes, Lord." Then touched he their eyes, saying: "According to your faith be it done unto you." And their eyes were opened; and Jesus charged them strictly, saying: "See that no man know it." But their joy was so great that they could not keep silence, and they went forth and spread abroad his fame in all that country. By this means they brought down on Jesus the hatred of his enemies.

They had no more than gone when there was brought unto Jesus a dumb man possessed with a devil. A dumb demoniac! And when the devil was cast out, the dumb man spake. And the multitudes marveled, saying: "Never was such a thing seen in Israel." But the Pharisees said: "He casteth out devils because he is himself the prince of devils." And Jesus went about all the cities and villages, teaching in their synagogues, and preaching the gospel of the kingdom, and healing every disease, and every sickness.

When Jesus looked upon the crowd that followed him, he was moved with great pity, because they were distressed and scattered about as sheep without a shepherd. And he said to his disciples: "The harvest is plenteous but the laborers are few. Pray ye, therefore, the Lord of the harvest that he send forth laborers into the harvest."

The people were willing to hear, but could not, unless there were more teachers. So he called unto him the twelve disciples, and gave them power over unclean spirits, to cast them out, and to heal every disease and every sickness.

The names of the twelve apostles were: Simon, who was called Peter, and Andrew, his brother; James, the son of Zebedee, and John, his brother; Philip, and Bartholomew; Thomas, and Matthew, the publican; James, the son of Alpheus, and Lebbens, whose surname was Thaddeus; Simon, the Canaanite, or Zealot, and Judas Iscariot, who turned traitor.

These twelve Jesus sent forth, charging them not to go among the Gentiles, or to enter a city of the Samaritans, but to go rather to the lost sheep of the house of Israel. If they went to to the heathen, or half-heathen first, the way would have been closed to the hearts of the Jews, who were to form the foundation for the Christian church.

Jesus said to them: "As ye go, preach, saying, 'The kingdom of heaven is at hand.' Heal the sick, cleanse the lepers, raise the dead, cast out devils. Freely ye have received, freely give." They were not to labor for gain, but what Jesus had taught them they were to teach unto others.

He told them to take no gold, nor silver, nor brass, in their purses, nor any wallet for baggage. Neither were they to take two coats, nor a change of shoes, nor an extra staff, for the workman is worthy of his meat. With no luggage they would be free from care, and must be content with such food as was given them.

Jesus said: "Into whatsoever city or town ye enter inquire who in it is worthy, and there stay until ye are ready to leave the place. As ye enter a house salute it." The Eastern salutation meant: "Peace be unto ye." "And if the house be worthy let your peace come upon it. But if be not worthy—if the head of the house is not a good man—let your peace return to you." They were to have no fellowship with those who lived in the house. "And whosoever shall not receive you as their guests, nor hear your words, when ye depart out of that house or that city, shake off the dust from your feet. Verily I say unto you, it shall be more tolerable for the land of Sodom and Gomorrah in the day of judgment, than for that city." All these towns and cities that refused to hear the Word of God preached in them, by Jesus himself, or by his disciples, were in a short time a heap of ruins.

Jesus said to the apostles: "Behold, I send you forth as sheep in the midst of wolves: be ye therefore wise as serpents, and simple as doves." Like serpents, they were not to court danger, and were to avoid it as much as possible, without being cowardly. Their enemies were fierce and cruel, and Jesus said: "Beware of men"—that is the wolves—"for they will deliver you up to the judges, and will scourge you in their synagogues. And ye shall be brought before governors and kings for my sake, for a testimony to them and the Gentiles. But when they deliver you up, be not anxious as to how or what ye shall speak, for it shall be made known to you in that hour what ye shall speak. For it is not ye that speak, but the spirit of your Father which speaketh in you. And brother shall deliver up brother to death, and the father the child, and children shall rise up against their parents, and cause them to be put to death. And ye shall be hated of all men for my name's sake; but he that endureth to the end the same shall be saved.

"But when they persecute you in one city, flee to another, for verily I say unto you ye shall not have gone through the cities of Israel till the Son of Man be come. The disciple is not above his master, nor the servant above his lord. It is enough for the disciple that he be as his master, and the servant as his lord. If they have called the master of the house Beelzebub"—the prince of devils—"how much more shall they speak evil of those of his household?" The disciples must not expect better treatment than Christ received. If wicked men could be harsh and cruel to Jesus, the master and Lord of all, they would certainly be as severe to his servants and to all who bore his name. And they were to learn from him how to bear up under their trials.

Jesus said: "Fear them not, therefore, for there is nothing covered that shall not be revealed; and hid that shall not be known. What I tell you in the darkness that speak ye in the light; and what ye hear in the ear, that make known upon the housetops." They were to be bold in preaching; and the truths that Jesus had taught them privately, they were to make known publicly, and with a loud voice.

"Be not afraid of those who kill the body, but are not able to kill the soul; but rather fear him who is able to cast both body and soul into hell." Strive to please God rather than men, and have more fear of his displeasure than of anything that man can do unto you. "Are not two sparrows sold for a penny?" These birds are so small that they are always sold in pairs. "Yet, small as they are, not one of them falls to the ground without the knowledge of your Heavenly Father The very hairs of your head are all numbered." God takes special care of you. "Be not afraid, therefore, ye are of more value than many sparrows. Every one, therefore, who shall confess me before men, him will I also confess before my Father who is in heaven. But whosoever shall deny me before men, him will I also deny before my Father who is in heaven." We confess Christ by our daily walk and conversation, and by our acts and deeds; and we deny him by our un-Christian lives.

Jesus said: "Think not that I came to send peace on earth. I came not to send peace, but a sword. For I came to set a man at variance against his father, and a daughter against her mother, and a daughter-in-law against her mother-in-law. And a man's foes shall be they of his own household. He that loveth father and mother more than me is not worthy of me; and he that loveth son and daughter more than me is not worthy of me. And he that taketh not his cross, and followeth after me, is not worthy of me."

It is not always easy to follow Christ. There may be stumbling-blocks in the way. Father or mother may be opposed to it, and sisters and brothers may treat the idea with scorn, and make it very hard for the young convert to "stand up for Jesus."

"He that loveth father or mother more than me is not worthy of me; and he that loveth son or daughter more than me is not worthy of me." Religion often causes breaking up of family ties. If any trouble arises, we are not for the sake of peace to give up Jesus. We are to love our own, but to love them less than we do Jesus. "He that taketh not his cross, and followeth after me, is not worthy of me."

Here was a foreshadowing, a hint, of the manner of his own death. As I bear my cross, do you bear yours, and prove that you are worthy to be my disciple. "He that findeth his life shall lose it: and he that loseth his life for my sake shall find it."

Christ must be first in our thoughts, and before all

the pleasures and comforts of this life. Greater gain will be ours through serving him, and we will be happy in this life and in the life to come.

"He that receiveth you, receiveth me: and he that receiveth me receiveth him that sent me. He that receiveth a prophet in the name of a prophet shall receive a prophet's reward; and he that receiveth a righteous man in the name of a righteous man shall receive a righteous man's reward."

Wherever there was love and regard for Christ there would his disciples be received with favor. The message they brought would be a blessing to all hearts.

"And whosoever shall give unto one of these little ones a cup of cold water only, in the name of a disciple, verily I say unto you he shall in no wise lose his reward." The smallest kindness done to one of these disciples, for the master's sake, will be remembered and rewarded. We are better for every act of kindness we perform. We are not to feel self-satisfied, there is no gain in that; but if we can help along the cause of Christ by helping those who are bearing the gospel message, we are doing a good work, and our hearts will be comforted and strengthened.

CHAPTER XI.

THE POOL OF BETHESDA—HEALING OF THE HELPLESS CRIPPLE—THE DISCOURSE THAT FOLLOWED—JESUS RETURNS TO GALILEE—TWELVE APOSTLES SENT OUT—THE MURDER OF JOHN THE BAPTIST.

AFTER Jesus had sent out the twelve apostles, he continued his labors as before, and visited the cities through Galilee, where the people were awaiting for him, and anxious to hear him. It was now the autumn of the year, and the fertile fields were clothed in their richest beauty.

There was at this time a feast in Jerusalem. The name of the feast is not exactly known, but is sup-

THE POOL OF BETHESDA.

posed to be the Feast of Purim, which commemorated the deliverance of the Jews, through the influence of Queen Esther. It was not held in the Temple, but in private houses, and though it had become rather a gay festival, many devout Jews attended it with thankful recollections of God's dealing with Haman and Mordecai.

Jesus went up to Jerusalem. In the city, and close to the Sheep Gate, was a pool, inclosed with five porches, which bore the name of Bethesda, or House of Mercy. In the five porches surrounding this pool lay a great multitude of sick people—the blind, the lame, and those whose bodies or limbs were wasted— waiting to be healed. It was the popular idea that an angel came down and stirred the water, causing it to bubble up, and only he who first stepped into the pool would be cured. We may imagine the scene when the water began bubbling up, or was "troubled," as the people said. Many springs have this way of gushing from time to time, and angels have nothing to do with the movement. But what the people could not understand they laid to the angels, and it was a fact that at certain periods the pool was more thoroughly charged with gas, and wonderful cures were performed. At such times the crowding and pushing must have been great, and the wails and cries of the disappointed ones must have filled the air.

Among this sickly crowd was one who had been half paralyzed for thirty-eight years. Buoyed up with hope, and then cast down with disappointment, he had visited this health resort year after year, and still was no better.

Jesus had probably been among the wealthy Jews, and wearied of them. They were self-satisfied and trifling, and so he turned from them on the Sabbath, and went down among the sick and suffering. And he saw the half-paralyzed man lying there, and observing that he had been a long time in that state, he said: "Wilt thou be made whole? Do you want to be well?"

The sick man answered him: "Sir, I have no friend to hurry me into the pool when the water is troubled;

but while I am on the way another steps down before me." He thought he must do something himself to effect a cure, but though his will was strong, he had not the physical strength. He thought only of his bodily ailments: but the question of Jesus referred to his soul's health. "Do you want to be a Christian? Do you want to be cleansed from your sins?"

Jesus said to the sick man: "Rise, take up thy bed, and walk." He did not hesitate, but rose at once, as Jesus had commanded. And immediately he was made well; and rolling up the mattress which laid upon the ground, had formed his bed, he walked off with it upon his shoulders.

It was the Sabbath day on which this miracle was performed, and the law of Moses forbade that any work should be done on that day. As he went out on the street, he was met by a number of Jews—Priests, Levites, and Pharisees—who said unto him that was cured: "It is the Sabbath day, and it is not lawful for thee to take up thy bed."

But he answered them: "He that made me whole, the same said unto me, 'Take up thy bed and walk.'" These men clung to the law of Moses, and would not permit any different teaching. So they asked him: "Who is the man, that said unto thee 'Take up thy bed and walk?'" But he that was healed knew not who he was. The man had never seen him before, and Jesus had slipped out of the crowd and was soon out of sight.

Some time afterwards when Jesus was in the Temple-Courts he saw this same man whom he had healed at Bethesda, and he said unto him: "Behold, thou hast been made whole; sin no more, that some worse thing come not unto thee." The man went away, and told the Jews that it was Jesus who made him whole. And for this cause did the Jews persecute Jesus, because he did these things on the Sabbath day. And they stood face to face with him and charged him with being a great sinner.

Jesus answered them: "My Father worketh until now; I also work." God works right on, and takes no rest. Jesus came on earth to do his will; and if he gave rest from sin on the Sabbath day, it made the day more glorious. He could break no law.

For this cause, therefore, the Jews sought the more to kill him, because he not only broke the Sabbath, but also called God his own Father, making himself equal with God.

Then answered Jesus, and said unto them: "Verily, verily, I say unto you, the Son can do nothing of himself but only that which he seeth the Father do; for what things soever he doeth, these things the Son also in like manner doeth. For the Father loveth the Son, and showeth him all things that he himself doeth. And he will show him greater works than these, that ye may marvel." They would be amazed and awe-stricken.

"For as the Father raiseth up the dead and maketh them live, so the Son also putteth new life into those whom he will. For the Father judgeth no one, but hath given all judgment unto the Son. That all may know the Son even as they know the Father. He that knoweth not the Son, honoreth not the Father which sent him.

"Verily, verily, I say unto you, he that heareth my word, and believeth him that sent me, hath eternal life, and cometh not into judgment, but hath passed out of death into life."

Those who believe in Jesus, are free from the old Mosaic law. It becomes a dead letter to them, and they walk in a new life, for a new spirit works within them.

"Verily, verily, I say unto you, an hour cometh, and now is, when the dead shall hear the voice of the Son of God; and they that have heard shall live. For even as the Father hath life in himself, so gave he to the Son also to have life in himself. And he gave him authority to execute judgment, because he is a Son of Man." He is the Giver of Life to those who hear his voice and he is also the judge of men.

"Marvel not at this, for an hour cometh in which all that are in their graves shall hear his voice; and they that have done good shall go forth unto a resurrection of life; and they that have done evil unto a resurrection of judgment. I can of mine own self do nothing. As I hear, I judge, and my judgment is just, because I seek not mine own will, but the will of him that sent me."

In the courts of law a man cannot plead his own cause. He must have witnesses to testify in his behalf; that is, to speak for him, and tell of his previous good character. Jesus said: "If I bear witness concerning myself, my witness is not true. Another beareth witness concerning me, and I know that the witness he witnesseth concerning me is true. Ye have sent unto John, and he hath borne witness unto the truth. But the witness that I have is greater than man; howbeit these things I say that ye may be saved. He was a burning and a shining light, and ye were willing for a season to rejoice in his light." John's work had been to point to Jesus. He was the lamp God had lighted to guide men in the right path. But they thought more of John himself than they did of his message, and their souls were not saved.

Jesus said: "But the witness that I have is greater than that of John; for the works the Father hath given me to do, the very works that I do, bear witness concerning me, that the Father hath sent me. And the Father who sent me, he hath borne witness concerning me. Ye have neither heard his voice at any time, nor seen his form. And ye have not his word abiding in you, because him whom he sent ye believe not." Every word and deed of Jesus showed that he was doing God's work, and that God had sent him. But the hearts of the Jews had not been touched, nor their eyes opened, else they would have recognized God's voice when Jesus spoke, and would have seen the Father manifested in the Son.

"Ye search the Scriptures," said Jesus, "because ye think that in them ye have eternal life: and it is they that bear witness concerning me. And ye will not come to me that ye may have life." The Jews searched, that is, studied the sacred writings, for it was their belief that if the words of the law were imprinted on their hearts they were safe for this life and for the life to come. But it is not so. Eternal life can only come through Jesus; and if they had studied the word of God aright they would have been looking for Jesus and given him a royal welcome. Not that he was self-seeking. He cared not for the praise and glory of men. "But I know you," he said, "that ye have not the love of God in your hearts. I am come in my Father's name, and ye receive me not. If another shall come in his own name, him ye receive. How can ye believe who seek the glory of men rather than the glory of God? Do not think that I will accuse you to the Father. There is one that accuseth you, even Moses in whom ye trust. For if ye believed Moses, ye would believe me; for he wrote concerning me. But if ye believe not his writings, how will ye believe my words?"

Never before had Jesus spoken so plainly, and his words were likely to call upon himself the intense hatred of the Jews. He had dared to make himself equal with God, and this in their eyes was the greatest of crimes. Jesus knew that it would not be safe for him to remain in Jerusalem, for already the Scribes and Pharisees were plotting to put him to death. Every moment his life was in danger. So while the crowd was held spellbound by the majesty of his presence, and the eloquence of his words, he slipped away without being seen, and went back into Galilee.

Meanwhile John the Baptist had been shut up in prison, by order of Herod Antipas, the son of Herod the Great. He had expected to succeed his father as King of Judea, but Herod the Great, a few months before his death, put the name of Archelaus, another son, in place of Antipas, and the latter became "Tetrarch," or Governor, over the fourth part of the Roman province. He took his ill-fortune in good part, and made a faithful Governor over Galilee and Perea. He fortified the capital, and built up Tiberias, where he had a splendid palace. He had two other palaces, one at Julias, and the other at Machærus, where he spent considerable of his time. He was not so cruel as his father, but he was a weak man and very superstitious.

He made frequent visits to the Emperor of Rome, and at such times was the guest of his brother Herod Philip, who had been disinherited by his father, and lived as a private person. In return for the hospitality received, Herod Antipas fell in love with Philip's wife, Herodias, notwithstanding he had a wife of his own, to whom he had been married for many years. But the Herods were a wicked race, and given to all sorts of vices.

Herodias herself was a wicked and ambitious woman, and preferred to reign as a Princess, even though she committed sin in order to obtain the position. Herod promised to marry her, and to get a divorce from his true wife, who was an Arabian princess. She, however, did not wait to be divorced, but, feeling herself insulted, fled with great haste to her father, who broke off at once all friendly relations with his son-in-law, and afterwards declared war against him.

John's preaching had attracted Herod's attention, and out of curiosity he had sent for him to come to the castle, and really seemed to be under a good influence. But there was one thing he did not like. John was a bold preacher, and not afraid to speak the truth even before princes. Herod had committed a great crime in marrying Herodias, who was not only his brother's wife but his own niece, and John had frequently said to him: "It is not lawful for thee to have thy brother's wife."

This made Herodias very angry, and she desired that John should be put to death; but this Herod would not do. He feared John, knowing him to be a just and holy man, and he also feared the multitude who regarded him as a prophet. But for her sake he had John seized, and bound and put in one of the deep dungeons of Fort Machærus. What a cruel fate for one who had lived all his life out of doors, and longed to be at work for Jesus. and to lead men to repentance.

It was while shut up in this dark dungeon that he heard of the fame of Jesus, and of the crowds that followed after him. And he sent messengers to inquire: "Art thou the coming One? or do we wait for another?" John was in doubt. His own trial had weakened his faith somewhat. But before the messengers returned it had been made clear to him that his life work was done. The Messiah had come.

It was in the early spring, and near the time for the Passover, when Herod made a feast on the anniversary of his coming into power, as Tetrarch. For many months Herodias had sought to rid herself of John the Baptist, for whom she had an intense hatred, and now a wicked plan formed itself in her mind. At the

SALOME BEFORE HEROD,

time of her marriage to Herod Antipas she had a little daughter named Salome, who had now grown into a tall and graceful maiden. The feast was at its height. All the lords of Herod's court, the military officers, and chief men of Galilee, were there, and the sounds of music and shouts of revelry were heard far beyond the castle walls. The guests had been served with the choicest viands and the costliest wines, and every sense had been gratified. The king could offer nothing further.

This then was Herodias's hour. She sent her beautiful young daughter to dance before Herod and his guests. The girl was as bold and brazen as her mother, and her dancing pleased the half-intoxicated men who sat at the king's table. Her coming was an agreeable surprise, and Herod swore with a loud voice so that all could hear that he would give the girl whatever she asked of him.

Salome stole out to ask her mother what it should be; what reward should she claim from the king? Her mother said: "Ask for the head of John the Baptist." The girl did not shrink with horror from such a request, but came back at once to Herod, and said: "Bring me here on a platter the head of John the Baptist."

There was silence for a few moments in the castle hall. All were roused from their half-drunken stupor by the strange request. What would Herod do? For months he had tried his best to prevent this thing, and in his heart he dreaded to rouse the enmity of the people. But he was weak and superstitious, and because he had sworn to the girl, and before the assembly, that he would give her what she asked for, he felt bound to redeem his pledge. So he sent and had John beheaded in the prison, allowing him no time to prepare for death, and his head was brought in on a large dish, and given to the maiden. And she took the ghastly burden in her hands, and carried it to her mother.

When John's friends, his faithful disciples, heard of it they came and reverently bore away the headless corpse and gave it proper burial, and went and told Jesus, who decided at once to leave Capernaum.

About the same time the apostles of Jesus return-

HERODIAS WITH THE HEAD OF JOHN THE BAPTIST.

ed from their mission, and told him all that they had done and taught. They had preached repentance, had healed the sick, and cast out devils, and might have done much more had their faith been stronger.

Meanwhile Herod, the Tetrarch, had heard of Jesus, and of the wonderful miracles that he performed. And he was perplexed, because that some had said that John had risen from the dead, and others that

Elijah, or some one of the old prophets had appeared. Herod said: "John I beheaded; but who is this of whom I hear such things?" And he was anxious to see Jesus. Not that his soul might be cleansed, and be saved from the power of Satan, but to satisfy himself that John had not risen from the dead to torment him.

Herod lived a wicked life, and died a violent death, and in a few years his beautiful palaces were a heap of ruins.

CHAPTER XII.

FIVE THOUSAND FED—JESUS WALKS ON THE SEA—THE DISCOURSE AT CAPERNAUM ABOUT EATING WITH UNWASHED HANDS.

Jesus, hearing of Herod's alarm, resolved at once to leave Capernaum, fearing there might be a rising among John's disciples to avenge his cruel murder. The twelve apostles had returned from their mission, and, although very weary, were kept so busy with crowds coming and going that they had no chance to rest, and scarcely time to eat.

So Jesus said to them: "Come ye, by yourselves, into a desert place, and rest awhile apart from the crowd." And they went in a boat to a quiet place on the eastern shore of the lake, near Bethsaida. As soon as the people saw them departing, they ran together there on foot, by the land way, and some of them reached the place in time to welcome those in the boat.

Jesus went up among the hills to rest and pray, and there he sat awhile and taught his disciples. When he came forth from his retirement, and saw the great crowds that had gathered, he was moved with compassion for them, for they seemed as sheep without a shepherd. It was an opportunity not to be lost. There was no time for him to rest. His work must go on.

The Passover was near at hand, and thoughts of that and the scenes that would follow, must have filled his mind. And as he moved among the multitude, when the day was far spent, he turned to Philip and said: "Where are we to get bread that these may eat?" This was to test Philip, for Jesus himself knew what he was about to do.

Philip answered him: "Two hundred pennyworth of bread is not sufficient for them, if each one had ever so little." The question went around among the disciples. They said: "This is a desert place; and the day is far spent. Send them away, that they may go into the country round about, and into the villages, and buy themselves somewhat to eat." But they were not to buy. The disciples must give them. "Shall we go and buy food for them?" they asked. No. That was not what Jesus meant. They must give of their own store. How many loaves had they? Let them go and see.

Andrew, Simon Peter's brother, found a fisher lad who had five barley loaves and two fishes. "But what are they," said Andrew, "among so many?"

Jesus said: "Make the people sit down." And they were seated on the grass in companies of a hundred, and of fifties. And Jesus took the five loaves and two fishes, and looking up to heaven blessed and brake them, and gave them to his disciples to set before the people. And they did all eat and were filled.

Then Jesus said to his disciples: "Gather together the pieces that nothing be lost." And they took up twelve baskets full of that which remained of the loaves and fishes. And they that did eat were about five thousand men, women, and children.

This wonderful miracle made a great impression upon the people, and they said: "This is truly the

FEEDING THE MULTITUDE.

Prophet, the coming One for whom the world has waited." As far back as the days of Moses it had been said to the children of Israel: "The Lord thy God will raise up unto thee a prophet from the midst of thee, of thy brethren, like unto me; unto him ye shall hearken." Others had foretold of the coming of One who should do wonderful things; and the people felt sure that he was now with them in the person of Jesus.

Jesus perceived that it was their intention to carry him off by force to Jerusalem and make him their king. This would surely bring on a conflict with the Roman Government, and hasten his own death. The disciples shared in the excitement; so Jesus commanded the twelve to leave him, and go down to Capernaum, and wait for him there. After which he dismissed the multitudes and went up into the mount to pray where none but God could see him.

Night came on, and there he was all alone with his Heavenly Father. The labors of the day had been great, and he needed to be strengthened and refreshed with prayer. Hardly had the disciples taken to their boat than the sky became overcast, and the wind blew a gale. All night they labored in the midst of a tempestuous sea, and at daybreak were only half way across the lake, a distance of three miles. Jesus had looked out after them, and seen how hard they rowed against wind and tide. They had used their own strength as far as it would go, and now they had need of him.

It was in the dusk of the morning, when the sun was expected soon to rise, that the disciples looked up and saw a form walking by them on the sea. It came near the boat, and they, supposing it was a ghost, cried out in great fear. But a well-known voice spoke to them, saying: "Be of good cheer. It is I; be not afraid!" Peter, greatly excited, exclaimed: "Lord, if it be thou, bid me come to thee upon the waters." Jesus said, "Come." And going down from the boat, Peter walked on the waters to go to Jesus.

As long as his eyes were fixed on Jesus all went

JESUS WALKING ON THE SEA.

well, but as soon as he noticed the great waves and saw how rough the wind was, he began to sink, and cried out: "Lord, save me!" Straightway Jesus stretched forth his hand and took hold of him, and said: "O thou of little faith, wherefore didst thou doubt?" And when they came into the boat the wind ceased, and the sea was calm. And all those that were in the boat worshiped Jesus, saying: "Of a truth thou art the Son of God."

We are to learn from this that Jesus is always ready to help us. He may seem to leave us, but it is only that we may use our own efforts, and pray the more earnestly. "Weeping may endure for a night, but joy cometh in the morning." When tossed about with great waves of trouble, and feeling ready to sink, one cry for help will bring him to our side, and his outstretched hand will save us from the doubts or sins that drag us down. In all the storms of life, if we but listen, we can hear the voice of Jesus saying: "Be of good cheer. Fear not. I am with thee."

When they had crossed over to the land, they came to Gennesaret, and as soon as the people heard of it they carried their sick ones around on beds to the place where he was, and, through all the towns and villages where he was to pass, they laid the sick in the market places that they might touch, if it were, the border of his garment. And as many as touched him were healed of their diseases.

The next day when the multitudes saw that there was no other boat save the one the disciples had gone off in, and that Jesus went not with them, they, supposing he was somewhere among the hills, set out, forthwith to look for him. While they were still in wonder and doubt, other boats came from Tiberias, and the boatmen told the people that neither Jesus nor his disciples had gone there. So as many as could get into the small boats, came to Capernaum, seeking for

Jesus. And, when they found him, they said unto him: "Rabbi, whence comest thou hither?"

Jesus answered them and said: "Verily, verily, I say unto you, ye seek me not because ye saw the miracles, but because ye did eat of the loaves and were satisfied. Work not for the food which perisheth, but for that food which abideth unto eternal life, which the Son of Man shall give unto you; for on him the Father's seal is set."

Christ is meat and drink to the believer. He gives himself to us, but we must first work hard to put everything out of the way that hinders his approach. We must make a place worthy of the gift. But these people of the East were fond of magic, and many of those who had seen the signs and wonders Jesus had done, were anxious to learn the secret of those mysteries, so that they might increase their wealth, and exhibit their powers. They said therefore to Jesus: "What must we do that we may work the works of God?" Jesus answered: "This is the work of God, that ye believe in him whom he sent." They said: "What then doest thou as a sign that we may see and believe thee? What dost thou work? Our fathers did eat manna in the wilderness, as it is written: 'He gave them bread out of heaven to eat.'" Jesus said unto them: "Verily, verily, I say unto you, Moses gave you not the bread from heaven, but my Father giveth you the bread out of heaven—the true bread. For the bread of God is that which cometh down out of heaven, and giveth life unto the world." They said unto him: "Lord, evermore give us this bread."

Jesus said unto them: "I am the bread of life; he that cometh to me shall never hunger; and he that believeth in me shall never thirst. But I would have you know that ye have indeed seen me, and believe not. All that which the Father giveth me shall come

CHRIST THE CONSOLATOR.

to me; and him that cometh to me I will in no wise cast out. For I came out of heaven not to do mine own will, but the will of him that sent me. And this is the will of him that sent me, that of all which he hath given me I should lose nothing, but should raise it up at the last day. For this is the will of my Father, that every one who beholdeth the Son and believeth in him should have eternal life; and that I should raise him up at the last day."

What the Jews needed was faith in the Lord Jesus. They had seen all the signs and wonders he did, and yet did not believe in him, or obey God's Word. Jesus calls himself the BREAD OF LIFE. We depend on bread to satisfy our hunger. When the children of Israel were in the wilderness without food, God rained down manna from heaven, which they ate in place of bread. This manna was but a sign, or symbol of the bread that God would send down out of heaven to save the souls of men. Not only to give them peace and comfort in this life, but to prepare them for an endless life in heaven.

Some of the Jews understood Jesus, and saw that his words had a spiritual meaning. But there were others, open enemies of Jesus, who were offended at his speech. They murmured among themselves, and said: "Is not this Jesus the son of Joseph, whose father and mother we know? How then can he say that he came down out of heaven?"

Jesus answered them and said: "Murmur not among yourselves. No one can come to me except the Father which sent me shall have drawn him: and I will raise him up at the last day. It is written in the prophets, 'They shall all be taught of God.' Every one that hath heard from the Father, and hath learned, cometh unto me. Not that any one hath seen the Father, save he which is from God, he hath seen the Father. Verily, verily, he that believeth hath everlasting life. I am the bread of life. Your fathers did eat manna in the wilderness and died. This is the bread which cometh out of heaven, that any one may eat thereof, and not die. I am the living bread which came down out of heaven. If any one eat of this bread he shall live forever. The bread that I will give is my flesh, for the life of the world."

The Jews took hold of these words, and said among themselves: "How can this man give us his flesh to eat?" Jesus therefore said unto them: "Verily, verily, I say unto you, except ye eat the flesh of the Son of Man and drink of his blood, ye have no life in yourselves. Every one that eateth my flesh and drinketh my blood hath eternal life; and I will raise him up at the last day. For my flesh is food indeed, and my blood is drink indeed."

They must feed on him in their hearts by faith; make Jesus a part of themselves, just as what they ate and drank became a part of themselves.

"He that eateth my flesh and drinketh my blood, dwelleth in me, and I in him. As the living Father sent me, and I live because of the Father; so he that eateth me, he also shall live because of me. This is the bread which came out of heaven; not as your fathers did eat and died. He that eateth this bread shall live forever."

These things he said as he was teaching in a synagogue at Capernaum. And many of the disciples when they heard this, said: "This is an hard saying; who can hear him?" They did not hear aright, and therefore did not understand. But Jesus knowing in himself that his disciples murmured concerning this he said unto them: "Does this offend you? Does this cause you to stumble? What then if ye shall see the Son of Man ascending where he was before?" Then the sense they had put upon his words would have no meaning. For how could they eat the flesh of one who was not with them?

Jesus said: "It is the spirit that maketh life; the flesh profiteth nothing. The words that I spake unto you, they are spirit, and they are life. But there are some of you that believe not."

For Jesus knew from the beginning who they were who believed not, and who it was that would betray him. And he said: "For this cause have I said unto you that no one can come unto me, except the spirit have been given unto him by the Father." Their hearts had not been prepared to receive the words of Jesus.

Upon this, many of those who had set out to follow Jesus and to be his disciples went back to their homes and their trades, and walked no longer with him.

Jesus therefore said unto the twelve apostles: "Would ye also go away? Is it your wish to leave me?" Simon Peter answered him: "Lord to whom shall we go, if we leave thee? Thou hast the words of eternal life. And we believe and know that thou art the Holy One of God."

Jesus answered them: "Did not I choose you twelve? and one of you is a devil?" Now he spoke of Judas, the son of Simon Iscariot; for he was about to betray him, being one of the twelve. Yet none of the disciples knew of it, save only Judas himself.

Then came to Jesus certain Scribes and Pharisees who had come up from Jerusalem on purpose to watch him, and to find an excuse for putting him out of the way. They had heard much of the wonderful miracle of the feeding of the five thousand, and were quite offended that Jesus should permit his disciples to eat without washing their hands.

The custom of washing the hands before meals had come down to them from the time of Moses, and the

Jews were very particular in regard to it. To touch food with unclean hands was thought to be a great sin, and one not likely to go unpunished. Stories were told of loss of property, sickness, and terrible calamities, that were brought about by eating food without first washing the hands.

Therefore the Scribes and Pharisees came to Jesus, saying: "Why do your disciples break the law of Moses, for they wash not their hands when they eat bread?" Jesus said: "Why do ye break the commandments of God, for the sake of your old custom? For God said: Honor thy father and thy mother; and he that speaketh evil of father or mother shall surely die."

But the Jews had made a law that if any one dedicated all his property to God he would be free from the care of his parents.

Jesus therefore said unto them: "Ye hypocrites! Well did Isaiah prophesy of you, saying: 'This people draweth nigh unto me with their mouth, and honoreth me with their lips, but their heart is far from me. In vain do they worship me, with their false teachings.'"

When he had called the people unto him, he said: "Hear and understand. Not that which entereth into the mouth defileth the man, but that which cometh out of the man."

The disciples said to him: "Knowest thou that the Pharisees took offence when they heard this saying?" Jesus said: "Let them alone: they are blind guides; and if the blind lead the blind, both shall fall into the pit."

When they had left the multitude and entered into the house, Peter came to Jesus and asked him to explain to the twelve the meaning of the parable. Jesus said, "Even yet are ye also without understanding?" Had they been more spiritually minded they would surely have known what was meant. Everything that goes into the mouth in the shape of food, affects the body, and not the heart. But out of the heart come evil thoughts, murders, thefts, all sorts of crimes, frauds, and blasphemies.

These are the things that make a man unclean in the sight of God, and a clean heart is more necessary than clean hands.

CHAPTER XIII.

IN THE CORNFIELD—THE LORD'S PRAYER—THE BLIND AND DUMB DEMONIAC—THE PHARISEES ASK FOR A SIGN—JESUS DINES WITH SCRIBES AND PHARISEES—UNWASHED HANDS—ANGER OF HIS ENEMIES—THE PARABLE OF THE RICH FOOL—BE YE ALSO READY.

THE Jews were very strict in keeping the Sabbath, and would have no work done inside or outside of the house on that day. They had already found much cause for complaint because Jesus had healed the sick on the Sabbath, and done many things that showed that his teachings were different from those of Moses.

One Sabbath day Jesus and disciples were walking through a field of grain. Corn such as we know about did not grow in the East, but there were large fields of wheat and barley. The disciples, being hungry, plucked some of the ears of grain and began to eat them. But when the Pharisees saw it, they said unto Jesus: "Behold, thy disciples do what is not lawful to do on the Sabbath." They claimed that rubbing the ears of wheat together was the same as reaping, and therefore work. Jesus said unto them: "Have ye not read what David did when he was hungry, and they that were with him? How he entered into the house of God, and did eat the shew-bread, which was not lawful for him to eat, neither for those who were with him, but was only for the priests? Or have ye not read in the law, how the priests in the temple

IN THE CORNFIELDS.

profane the Sabbath and are blameless? But I say unto you, that in this place is one greater than the temple. But if ye had known what this meaneth, I will have mercy, and not sacrifice, ye would not have condemned the blameless. For the Son of Man is Lord even of the Sabbath.

All that leads to him is Sabbath-keeping. All that leads away from him is Sabbath-breaking. If the

THE WITHERED HAND.

Jews had read the Word of God aright, they would have known that God would rather have men good and kind to each other, than to have them bring the choicest of their flocks or herds to be burned on the altar as an offering to him. Kind acts done on the Sabbath make the day more holy. It is said, "The Sabbath was made for man, and not man for the Sabbath." This does not mean that we are free to do as we please on that day; but we are to do all the good we can, and whatever is needful or helpful will be part of our service to Christ. If we sit and read the Bible from morn till night, and neglect doing needful duties, and acts of kindness, we are not keeping the Sabbath in the right way.

On another Sabbath, Jesus went into a synagogue and taught there. And among the crowd was a man with a withered hand. The Scribes and Pharisees watched Jesus, to see if in any way they might accuse him of breaking God's laws. Jesus who knew their thoughts, said unto them: "What man is there among you, who, if he have one sheep, and it falls into the pit on the Sabbath day, will not lay hold of it and lift it out? How much then is a man better than a sheep. So then it is lawful to do good on Sabbath days." Then he said to the man with the withered hand: "Stand up where all can see you." And the man arose, and stood up in full view of all those in the synagogue. Then saith he to the man: "Stretch forth thine hand." And he stretched it forth, and it was healed, and as perfect as the other.

Then the Pharisees were in a great rage, and met together to form a plot to destroy him. But Jesus knowing it, withdrew from that place, and many followed him and were healed of their diseases.

It is said that Christ's enemies were "filled with madness." So great was their hatred of him that they acted like men who had lost their reason. And he who came only to do good, was roughly treated, and scorned by the spies from Jerusalem, who dogged his footsteps at every turn.

Early one morning Jesus stood praying in a lonely

place among the hills, for in the East the people stand and do not kneel in prayer. And one of the disciples came to him and said: "Lord teach us to pray, even as John also taught his disciples." And he said unto them: "When ye pray, say: Our Father, who art in Heaven, hallowed be thy name, thy kingdom come, thy will be done on earth as it is in heaven; give us this day our daily bread, and forgive us our trespasses as we forgive those who trespass against us, and lead us not into temptation, but deliver us from evil; for thine is the kingdom, and the power, and the glory, forever and ever. Amen."

This seems a simple prayer, and yet how much does it contain! We first give praise to our Heavenly Father, and ask that the Kingdom of Christ be established on earth, and God's commandments obeyed here as they are in heaven. Not my will, O Lord, but thine be done, should be the prayer of every Christian. For if we truly believe in Jesus, we will feel that whatever he does is for our good, although it may not seem so at the time. Faith does not see beyond the veil, but waits with patience and submission to the will of God.

GIVE US THIS DAY OUR DAILY BREAD.

When we pray thus, we ask for strength and grace to last us through the day. We do not ask for to-morrow's portion. It is as though we said, "Lord, help us through the trials and sorrows of the day, and may we find comfort in thee."

FORGIVE US OUR TRESPASSES.

Means forgive us our sins as we forgive those who sin against us. Think of it!

Are we ready to forgive the sins and offences of those with whom we associate? Is it not more easy to find fault, and to magnify the sins and shortcomings of others? Christ teaches that we must forgive all those who have injured us, before we ask God to forgive us the sins we have committed against him.

LEAD US NOT INTO TEMPTATION.

Satan sets traps for our feet. The world is full of them, and only through God's grace can we escape them. With our hand in his hand we are safe. If caught in the snare, he will deliver us. For he alone can put the right spirit into man, and by his power lift him above the things of earth. And God must have all the praise.

The word AMEN, signifies "So let it be"—and was joined in by the whole congregation at the end of each prayer. After giving this form of prayer to his disciples, Jesus said unto them, "Which of you shall have a friend, and shall go to him at midnight, and say to him, 'Friend, lend me three loaves. For a friend of mine has come to me from a journey, and I have nothing to set before him.' And he from within shall answer and say, 'Trouble me not. The door is now shut, and my children are with me in bed. I cannot rise and give thee.'

"I say unto you, though he will not rise and give him, because he is his friend, yet because of his importunity—his persistent knocking—he will arise and give him as much bread as he needs. And I say unto you, ask and it shall be given you ; seek, and ye shall find ; knock, and it shall be opened unto you. For every one that asketh receiveth ; and he that seeketh findeth; and to him that knocketh it shall be opened. If a son shall ask bread of anyone of you who is a father, will he give him a stone? or if he ask for a fish will he give him a serpent? If ye then, being evil, know how to give good gifts unto your children, how much more shall your Heavenly Father give the Holy Spirit to them that ask him?"

We are to ask God for what we need, as a child asks its earthly father for the food it craves. If once asking does not bring an answer, we must ask again. We knock once at the door of a friend's house. The door does not open. We knock again. The door is still shut. We grow more anxious, and with throbbing heart and eager fingers knock once more. Then, just as we have about given up hope, the door opens, and the joy is greater because of the delay.

God answers every prayer. If you do not get the thing you ask for, it is because it is not best for you to have it. God knows our needs better than we know them ourselves. "In some way or other the Lord will provide."

Afterwards there was brought unto Jesus a demoniac, who was blind and dumb, and he healed him so that he spoke, and his sight came back to him. And all the people were amazed, and some cried out: "Is not this the son of David?" But when the Pharisees heard it they said: "This man casts out devils through Beelzebub the prince of devils."

Jesus, knowing their thoughts, said unto them: "Every kingdom which acts against itself will destroy itself; and every city or house divided against itself shall not stand. If Satan cast out Satan, he is divided against himself. How then shall his kingdom stand? If I, by Beelzebub, cast out devils, by whom do your sons cast them out? therefore they shall be your judges."

The Pharisees claimed that Jesus was in league with Satan, but Jesus proved that their reasoning did not hold good. Satan never rebukes sin, and how could Jesus make use of him to drive out sin? He is sin himself.

The kingdom of Christ cannot be built up by wicked men. Jesus said: "If I cast out devils by the Spirit of God, then the kingdom of God is come unto you.

How can one enter a into strong man's house, and spoil his goods, except he first bind the strong man, and then he will spoil his house. He that is not with me it against me; and he that gathereth not with me scattereth abroad."

Jesus proved that his power was divine. If he was not stronger than Satan he could not gain the victory over him. Satan's house is man's heart. His goods are the evil thoughts and deeds with which we fill our lives until Satan is driven out, and a new Master takes possession.

"Therefore, I say unto ye," saith our Lord to his enemies, "every sin and blasphemy shall be forgiven; but the blasphemy against the Spirit shall not be forgiven. And whosoever speaketh a word against the Son of Man it shall be forgiven him; but whosoever speaketh against the Holy Spirit, it shall not be forgiven him, neither in this world, nor in the world to come. Either make the tree good and the fruit good; or else make the tree evil and its fruit evil. For by the fruit the tree is known." "Ye brood of vipers! how can ye, being evil, speak good things? for out of the abundance of the heart the mouth speaketh. The good man out of the treasure of his heart bringeth forth good things; and the evil man out of the evil treasure bringeth forth evil things. And I say unto you, that every idle word that men shall speak, they shall give an account thereof in the day of judgment. For by thy words thou shalt be justified; and by thy words thou shalt be condemned." With our lips we either confess or deny Christ, and by our words and deeds show whether we are with Him, or against Him.

Then certain of the Scribes and Pharisees answered him, saying, "Master, we would see a sign from thee." They were not satisfied with the miracles they had seen, for they might have been done by magic. But a sign out of heaven would prove to them that he had dealings with the Most High. Jesus said that no sign should be given them but that of the prophet Jonah. For as Jonah was three days and three nights in the belly of the whale, so should the Son of Man be three days and three nights in the heart of the earth. "The men of Nineveh," he said, "shall stand up in the judgment with this generation, and shall condemn it; because they repented at the preaching of Jonah, and behold one greater than Jonah is here. The Queen of the South shall stand up in the judgment with this generation, and shall condemn it; for she came from the ends of the earth to hear the wisdom of Solomon; and, behold, one far greater than Solomon is here." Yet the Jews were not drawn toward him, nor did they give heed to his words.

"When the unclean spirit has gone out of the man, he passeth through dry places, seeking rest, and findeth none. Then he saith, I will return into my house from whence I came out; and when he is come he findeth it empty, swept, and garnished. Then goeth he, and taketh with himself seven other spirits more wicked than himself, and they enter in and dwell there, and the last state of that man is worse than the first. Thus shall it be also with this wicked generation." Jesus spoke in a sort of parable to the Jews. The meaning of it was that when the evil spirits were driven out of a man, the empty spaces must be filled with pure thoughts, else wicked ones would troop in, and the man would be a greater sinner than he was before.

While Jesus was yet speaking, behold, his mother and brethren stood without in the crowd, seeking to speak to him. They had become anxious about him, knowing the enmity of the Scribes and Pharisees, and that they were plotting to take away his life.

Some one called the attention of Jesus to them, saying, "Behold, thy mother and thy brethren stand without, seeking to speak to thee." Jesus said unto him that told him, "Who is my mother? and who are my brethren?" and he stretched forth his hand towards his disciples, and said, "Behold my mother and my brethren! For whosoever shall do the will of my Father who is in heaven, he is my brother, and sister, and mother." Jesus loves us with a human as well as a divine love. His closest relations are with his disciples, those who obey God; and he teaches us that we must not be drawn away from doing God's work because of the anxiety of near and dear friends.

While Jesus had been speaking, a certain Pharisee came and asked him to dine with him. And Jesus went into the man's house and at once sat down to the midday meal. When the Pharisee saw this he marveled that Jesus had not first washed his hands before dinner. The Lord said unto him, "Now do ye Pharisees cleanse the outside of the cup and platter; but your heart is full of robbery and wickedness. Ye fools, did not he that made the outside make the inside also? Rather give for alms such things as ye have within; and behold all things are clean to you." Jesus meant that the most important thing was to have a clean heart. These men were greedy and grasping, they robbed the poor, and did all sorts of wickedness. These things soiled a man, and made him filthy in the sight of God, though his skin might be as white as soap and water could make it.

Jesus did not spare them, for the time had come for plain speaking, and he said: "Woe unto you, Pharisees, for ye tithe the mint, and the rue, and all manner of herbs, and pass over judgment and the love of God: but these ye ought to have done, and not have left the other undone." The Israelites were bidden to pay a tithe, or tenth part of the fruits of the field and of the trees, as an offering to the Lord. The Scribes and Pharisees paid these tithes, which cost them little and were of small value, but gave not their hearts to Him, which were the only offerings he desired.

"Woe unto you, Pharisees," said he, "for ye love the chief seats in the synagogue, and the salutations in the market-places. Woe unto you, hypocrites, for ye are as the tombs which appear not, and the men that walk over them know not they are there."

They would pretend to be good, and so do a great deal of harm to those who believed in them and trusted them.

At this point, one of the lawyers who were present said to Jesus, "Master, in saying thus thou dost reproach us also." Jesus answered : " Woe unto you lawyers also, for ye load men with burdens with one of your fingers ! Woe unto you, for ye build the tombs of the prophets, and your fathers killed them! So then ye bear witness that ye approve of the deeds of your fathers. Therefore also said the wisdom of God, 'I will send unto them prophets and apostles, and some of them they shall kill and persecute, that the blood of all the prophets shed from the foundation of the world may be required of this generation ; from the blood of Abel to the blood of Zachariah who was slain between the altar and the temple.'

"Woe unto you, lawyers, for ye have taken away the key of knowledge. Ye entered not in yourselves, and them that were entering ye hindered." If the lawyers had taught the law correctly they would have led the people to Christ. But this they had not done.

Jesus was alone among those who hated him. He had been invited to partake of the midday meal, not out of any kindness of heart, but that they might heap more abuse upon him. They were false friends, and Jesus knew it, as his words plainly showed. They might deceive others, but him they could not deceive. The feast was broken up, and all the guests crowded around Jesus, and plied him with questions, watching him closely that they might catch him off his guard, and find something of which to accuse him.

As Jesus passed out of the house he found a great crowd assembled, so great that they trod upon one another. And, speaking first to his disciples, he said: "Beware ye of the leaven of the Pharisees, which is hypocrisy! For there is nothing covered that shall not be revealed, nor hidden that shall not be known. Wherefore, whatsoever ye have said in the darkness shall be heard in the light; and that which ye have whispered in inner places shall be proclaimed upon the housetops. And I say unto you, my friends, be not afraid of them that kill the body, and after that have no more that they can do. But fear him who after he hath killed the body hath power to cast the soul into the fires of hell." He told them that God loved them, and that the Son of Man would confess before God those who confessed him before men.

One among the crowd, who had been thinking more of earthly things than of heavenly, said unto Jesus, "Master, speak to my brother that he divide his inheritance with me." Jesus said unto him, "Who made me a judge or a divider over you?" And speaking to all he said, "Take heed, and keep yourselves from all covetousness." Be not greedy of gain, "For a man's wealth in this life consists not in the abundance of his possessions."

And he spoke a parable to them, saying: "The ground of a rich man brought forth plentifully. And he reasoned within himself, saying, "What shall I do, because I have not where to bestow my fruits?" And he said, "This will I do: I will pull down my barns and build larger ones, and there will I bestow all my grain and my goods. And I will say to my soul, Soul, thou hast much goods laid up for many years; take thine ease; eat, drink, and be merry." But God said unto him, "Thou fool, this night thy soul shall be required of thee; and then who will own the things which thou hast last provided? So is it with him that layeth up treasure for himself, and is not rich toward God."

Jesus told his disciples not to vex themselves with worldly cares, nor to be anxious for to-morrow. He who fed the ravens, and made the flowers of the field more gorgeous than the robes of King Solomon, would surely provide for the wants of those whose lives were of more value. Why could they not trust in him?

It was useless to heap up riches in this world, for we had to die and leave them, and they would cause much strife among our heirs. But we should seek for heavenly riches, and have more care for the soul than for the body. "Sell that ye have," said Jesus, "and give alms; make yourselves purses that never grow old, and lay up treasures in heaven that never fail, where no thief comes near to rob nor moths to destroy. For where your treasure is, there will your heart be also."

How true that is! If we love spiritual things, our thoughts will dwell on the higher life; but if we love the world and its pleasures, our thoughts will dwell on these lower things, and drag us down.

We are to think less of self, and to use our wealth to give to those who are poor and needy. The heavenly treasures never grow old, but the longer we have them the brighter they grow.

The Orientals—as the people of the East are called

—wore long garments that, unless belted or girded around the waist, they could not walk in or serve at table. Therefore he said to them: "Let your loins be girded about, and your lamps burning. And be ye yourselves like unto men that wait for their lord, when he will return from the marriage feast; that when he cometh and knocketh, they may straightway open unto him. Blessed are those servants whom the Lord, when he cometh, shall find watching. Verily I say unto you, that he shall gird himself, and make them sit down to meat, and will come forth and serve them. And if he shall come in the second or third watch, and find them so, blessed are they. But know this, that if the master of the house had known what hour the thief was coming, he would have watched, and not have left his house to be broken into. Be ye also ready, for in such an hour as ye think not the Son of Man cometh."

The returning Master is Jesus, and we are always to be ready for his coming. Good and faithful servants, having nothing to hide, do not fear to have their master come in at any time. We do not know when we are to die. Many have been struck down when in the full flush of health. It matters not when we go, if we are only ready to go.

Peter said unto him, "Lord, speakest thou this parable unto us, or even to all?" The Lord said: "Who, then, is the faithful and wise steward, whom his lord shall set to rule over his household, to give them their meat in due season? Blessed is that servant whom his lord when he cometh shall find so doing. Of a truth I say unto you that I will set him to rule over all that he hath. But if that servant say in his heart, "My lord delayeth his coming;" and shall begin to beat the menservants and maidservants, and to eat, and drink, and be drunken; the lord of that servant shall come in a day when he expecteth him not, and in an hour he knoweth not, and shall cut him asunder, and appoint his portion with the unfaithful."

The servant who knew his lord's will, and made not ready, nor did according to his wishes, shall be beaten with many stripes. But he that knew not, and did things worthy of punishment, shall be beaten with few stripes. For to whom much is given much shall be required. And to whom men have committed much, of him they will ask the more.

Jesus answered Peter's question by showing how faithfulness was rewarded and unfaithfulness punished. The Lord will judge his people as he finds them. The more confidence men have in us, the more responsibility we have, the greater reason is there for our being faithful. Those who know the right and do the wrong are more sinful than those who have been brought up in ignorance.

"I am come," said Jesus, "to cast fire upon the earth, and what will I, if it be already kindled! But I have a baptism to be baptized with; and how am I straitened till it be accomplished!"

He refers here to his own death, and the depth of his sufferings. There was a weight upon him, a human shrinking from the awful doom.

"Suppose you," he says, "that I am come to bring peace on the earth? I tell you, nay; but rather a sword;" and he speaks of the strife that will arise because of him. Then he said to the multitudes also: "When ye see a south wind blowing, ye say there will be a scorching heat; and it cometh to pass. Ye hypocrites! ye know how to judge the signs on the face of the earth and the sky, but how is it that ye know not how to tell the signs of this time? Why even of yourselves judge ye not what is right? For as thou art going with thine adversary to the magistrate, on the way give diligence to be released from him, lest he drag thee to the judge, and the judge shall deliver thee to the officer, to be cast into prison. I say unto thee thou shalt by no means come out till thou hast paid the very last mite."

The adversary—or foe with whom we fight—is the holy law of God. The magistrate is God himself. On the way, ere it is too late, we must make our peace with God, and by repentance and faith secure forgiveness of our sins. For those who come before the Judge on the Last Day, without having been released from Satan's claim, will be punished forever.

CHAPTER XIV.

JESUS LEAVES CAPERNAUM — THE SYRO-PHŒNICIAN WOMAN — THE DEAF-AND-DUMB MAN — FOUR THOUSAND FED — CÆSAREA PHILIPPI — PETER'S CONFESSION.

By this time the Scribes and Pharisees had begun to show so much enmity to Jesus that it was not safe for either him or the disciples to remain among them. So Jesus withdrew from Capernaum, and went out to the borders of Tyre and Sidon. This country was inhabited by Gentiles, or heathen people, and Jesus went into a house and remained there, that it might not be known that he was in the place. But as a lamp shines out into the darkness and is seen afar, so this Light that was to light the world could not be hid. Soon it was noised about that he who had done so many signs and wonders was in their midst, and a poor Syro-Phœnician woman heard of it. She had a little daughter who was very sick and in great pain, and the mother's heart was filled with agony and longings for her relief.

She had done all she could, but the child only

JESUS AND THE SYRO-PHŒNICIAN WOMAN.

grew worse, and when she heard of the wonderful cures that Jesus had performed, she made up her mind to go to him for help. She was a Greek and a heathen, and as she came to the house where Jesus was, she cried out, "O Lord, thou Son of David, have mercy upon me! My daughter is grievously vexed with a demon." Jesus spoke not, and the disciples, knowing his desire to remain hidden, said to him, "Send her away, for she crieth after us."

Then Jesus said to the woman, "I was sent only to the lost sheep of the House of Israel." But she threw herself at his feet and cried, "Lord, help me!" And he said to her, "It is not meet to take the children's bread, and throw it to the dogs." She answered, "Even so, Lord; yet the dogs eat the crumbs that fall from the master's table." Then Jesus said unto her, "O woman, great is thy faith! Be it done unto thee even as thou wilt." And her daughter was healed from that hour.

This heathen woman understood the parable at once. Having faith, she saw more clearly than the Jews, who rejected Christ. They, the Jews, called the heathen "dogs," and did not treat them with common civility, and would not think of sitting at the same table with them. But in every Jewish household there were a number of small dogs, called *house dogs*, that kept under the table and ate up the crumbs that fell down, or the bits that were thrown them.

The woman had faith to believe that there was enough of God's grace for those at the table and under the table. The crumbs would satisfy her. She did not deserve much, for she felt that she was a guilty sinner. And when she went to her own house, she found the child lying in bed, weak, but quiet, for the demon had left her.

Jesus, leaving the coast, came through Sidon and Decapolis, a region of ten cities on the eastern shore of the Sea of Galilee. And they brought unto him one who was deaf, and had an impediment in his speech, and begged Jesus to lay his hand upon him.

Jesus took him away from the crowd, and put his fingers into the deaf ears, and he spat, and touched the tongue that was dumb. And looking up to heaven, he sighed, and said unto him, "*Ephpheta*," which is, "Be thou opened." And his ears were unstopped, and his tongue loosed, so that he heard and spoke plainly. And Jesus charged the people to tell no one, but the more he charged them. a great deal more did they publish it, and were astonished beyond measure, saying, "He hath done all things well. He maketh even the deaf to hear and the dumb to speak."

Crowds still continued to follow Jesus, many being drawn to him by curiosity, because of his wonderful miracles. Some were held by the power of his words, and so great was their charm that they listened day after day, and forgot even the need of food. Jesus, touched by their faith, called his disciples unto him, and said: "I have pity on the multitude, because they have been with me now for three days, and have had nothing to eat. And if I send them away fasting to their own homes they will faint by the way, for many have come from a long distance."

The disciples said, "Where can we find bread enough for them in such a desert place?" He asked them how many loaves they had, and they answered, "Seven, and a few little fishes." Then he commanded the multitude to sit down on the ground, and he took the seven loaves and the fishes, and having given thanks he brake them, and gave to the disciples, and they distributed them among the people. And they did all eat, and were filled. And there was left seven baskets, full of broken pieces. And there were fed at this time about four thousand men, women, and children.

After this, Jesus sent away the multitude, and immediately entered into a boat with his disciples, and went into the borders of Magdala and the regions of Dalmanutha. It is supposed that the boat landed at some point between these two places, which are on the western shore of the Sea of Galilee, and in a lonely spot, for Jesus sought rest and retirement.

Hardly had he set foot on shore, however, when the Pharisees and Sadducees, the bitterest enemies of Jesus, came forth to meet him, intent to do all they could to hinder his preaching. They were men of great influence among the people, the Pharisees, because of their religious zeal, and the Sadducees, because of their wealth and rank. They looked upon Jesus as a false prophet not worth listening to. If he was indeed the Christ he claimed to be, let him give them a sign, and let that sign be from heaven.

Jesus sighed, and, in deep sorrow of heart, said, "Why doth this generation seek for a sign? Verily I say unto you, there shall no sign be given to them." And he turned his back upon them, and entering the boat, crossed over to the other side of the lake.

Now the disciples had forgotten to buy bread, and had with them in the boat but one loaf. Jesus knowing it charged them to beware of the leaven of the Pharisees and Sadducees. "What does he mean?" they said. "Is it because we have brought no bread with us?" Jesus, grieved at their lack of understanding, said unto them, "Why reason ye because ye have no bread? Are your eyes not yet opened after seeing all these miracles? Have ye your heart yet hardened? Having eyes ye see not, and having ears hear not, and do ye not remember when I brake the five loaves for the five thousand, how many baskets full of broken pieces took ye up?" They said unto him, "Twelve." "And when the seven loaves were given to the four thousand, how many baskets full of pieces took ye up?" They said, "Seven." And he said unto them, "How is it that ye do not yet understand?"

So great was their love and reverence for Jesus that they listened awestruck to his words, and dared not ask him the questions that disturbed their hearts. But slowly the truth dawned upon the disciples that Jesus meant they were to beware of the teachings of the Pharisees and Sadducees.

When the boat landed at Bethsaida, Julias, a blind man, was brought to Jesus to be healed. And he took hold of the blind man by the hand and brought him out of the village. And, spitting on his eyes, he laid his hands upon him, and asked him if he saw anything. The blind man looked up and said, "I see men as trees walking." His friends or some of the disciples were near, and he saw them, but not clearly.

Then Jesus put his hands again upon his eyes, and made him look up; and he saw all things plainly. And Jesus sent him to his own home, saying, "Do not even enter the village."

Leaving Bethsaida, Julias, Jesus, and his disciples went on to Cæsarea Philippi. This city stood at the foot of Mount Hermon, and commanded a fine view of the surrounding country. The fields were rich with grain, and on all sides were olive groves, vines, mulberry trees, and a wealth of flowers in full bloom. At one time the Greeks lived here, and worshiped *Pan*, the god of woods and fields, and they gave to the place the name of *Paneas*. At the time of our Lord's visit it was in the hands of Herod Philip, who had been made governor of that region by the Emperor Augustus.

Driven out of Judea and Galilee by the hatred of the Jews, Jesus came in sadness of spirit to this part of the Gentile world. There were no crowds following him now. He was alone, save for the disciples who were never very far off. As he came from the retired spot where he had been praying, he asked his disciples, "Whom do men say that I, the Son of Man, am?" And they said, "Some say John the Baptist, some Elijah, and others Jeremiah, or one of the prophets." And he said unto them, "But whom say ye that I am?" Peter said, "Thou art the Christ, the Son of the living God." Jesus said, "Blessed art thou Simon, son of Jonas, for flesh and blood hath revealed it not unto thee, but my Father who is in heaven. And I also say unto thee that thou art Peter, and upon this rock I will build my church; and the gates of hell shall not prevail against it. And I will give unto thee the keys of heaven; and whatsoever thou shalt bind on earth shall be bound in heaven, and whatsoever thou shalt loose on earth shall be loosed in heaven." And he charged his disciples to tell no man that he was Jesus the Christ.

Never had Jesus spoken to his disciples like this. He had confessed his power in words they could not mistake. Up to this time Peter had been called Simon. *Petros* means *stone* or *rock*, and because Peter had faith to believe and boldness to confess Christ, on him or, rather, in that way should the Church of Christ be built up. He was to act as the steward of God, and whosoever he received into the Church on earth, God would receive into the kingdom of heaven. God made choice of him that by his mouth the Gentiles should first hear the words of the Gospel, and at his bidding he baptized in the name of the Lord. *

From that time forth Jesus began to speak more

---

* Acts xv., 7; Acts x., 48.

familiarly with his disciples, and to show them that he must go to Jerusalem, and suffer many things from the elders and chief priests and Scribes, and be killed, and on the third day be raised up. Peter took him aside and began to rebuke him, saying: "Be it far from thee, Lord! This thing shall never be done unto thee!" But he turned, and said to Peter: "Get thee behind me, Satan! Thou art a stumbling-block unto me; for thou mindest not the things of God, but only the things of men."

Peter, out of human sympathy, wished to save Jesus from suffering and death, now realizing that God's will must be done. He had tempted him as the devil tempted him in the early part of his ministry, and tried to turn him from the path marked out for him. But Jesus rebuked him, as he rebukes all who shrink from the trials of a Christian life.

Then said Jesus to his disciples: "If any one would come after me let him deny himself, and take up his cross and follow me. For whosoever would save his life shall lose it; and whosoever would lose his life for my sake shall find it. For what shall a man be profited, if he gain the whole world, and lose his own soul? or what shall a man give in exchange for his soul?"

The gain of the world — the love of wealth and fashion, and the love of self will lead to a greater loss—the loss of the higher life, and the joys that enrich the soul.

"For the Son of Man shall come in the glory of his Father with his angels, and then shall he render unto every man according to his deeds. Verily I say unto you there be some standing here who shall not taste of death till they see the Son of Man coming in his kingdom."

Thus did Jesus warn them against selfish pleasures, and point out the highest duty of man. He spoke also of his final coming after his resurrection of a day not being very far off and to quiet their fears said that some of those standing there should not taste death until the Son of Man had come into his kingdom. The power of Christ would be felt on earth, and his church be built in the hearts of men.

CHAPTER XV.

THE TRANSFIGURATION—HEALING THE LUNATIC BOY—WHICH SHALL BE GREATEST?—THE TRIBUTE-MONEY—THE NINETY AND NINE—JESUS REJECTED BY THE SAMARITANS—"I GO NOT UP YET TO THE FEAST."

SIX days have passed, and at the close of the Sabbath Jesus and three of his disciples—Peter, and James, and John—climb the path that leads to the heights of Hermon. While Jesus was praying a great change came over him. His face shone as the sun, and his garments were as white as snow, and of dazzling brightness. At the same time Moses and Elijah appeared talking with him, and they spoke of his death which was about to take place in Jerusalem.

But Peter and they that were with him were heavy with sleep, yet, having remained awake, they saw his glory and the two men that stood with him. And Peter said: "Lord, it is good for us to be here. Let us make here three tabernacles—one for thee, and one for Moses, and one for Elijah."

While he was yet speaking behold a bright cloud came over the top of Mount Hermon, and hid the shining ones from the gaze of the disciples. And a voice out of the cloud said, "This is my beloved

Son, in whom I am well pleased; hear ye him." When the disciples heard it they were awestruck, and fell on their faces in great terror. The very light and glory of heaven had fallen upon them, and they had heard the voice of God! The silence which followed was like that of death.

Presently, they felt a gentle touch, and the voice of Jesus said to them, "Arise, and be not afraid!" And, lifting up their eyes, they saw no one save Jesus only. In the early dawn of the next morning Jesus and his disciples came down the mountain path that led to the valley, where they had left their companions. And Jesus commanded them not to tell what they had seen until after he was risen from the dead. And they spoke of it to no one. Among themselves, however, they spoke often of the vision, and of the strangeness of Elijah's appearing. They had been taught in the Old Testament to look for his coming, but supposed he would make a longer stay. What did it mean?

They put the question to Jesus, and asked why the Scribes taught that Elijah must first come. Jesus said, "Truly, Elijah cometh first to prepare men to receive the Gospel." Elijah had come already, and they knew him not, but did with him as they pleased. In like manner would the Son of Man suffer at their hands. Then the disciples understood, for the first time, that Elijah had come again on the earth in the person of John the Baptist. He had come to lead Israel to Christ, but they would not heed his cry, "Repent, and be saved!"

While Jesus, and Peter, and James, and John were descending the mountain, a great multitude had collected on the plain below. The disciples had failed to cure a lunatic boy, and the Scribes were vexing them with all sorts of questions, and were in a great rage. As soon as the multitudes saw Jesus they were greatly amazed, and running to him saluted him. And he asked the Scribes, "Why do ye dispute with them?" But before they could answer a man rushed out from the crowd, and throwing himself at the feet of Jesus, cried out, "Master, I have brought unto thee my son who has a dumb spirit. And wheresoever it seizeth him it teareth him, and he foams at the mouth, and grindeth his teeth, and withereth away."

Jesus said to the multitude: "O faithless generation! how long shall I be with you? How long shall I bear with you?" Then turning to the father, he said, "Bring him to me." And they brought the lunatic boy; and, when he saw Jesus, the spirit within him tore him grievously, and he fell to the ground, and writhed about, foaming at the mouth.

Jesus asked the father, "How long has he had this sickness?" The father answered: "From childhood. And ofttimes it has thrown him into the fire and into the waters to destroy him. But if thou canst do anything, have compassion on us, and help us."

"*If thou canst believe*, all things are possible to him that believeth." Straightway the father of the child cried out, "Lord, I believe; help thou mine unbelief!" His faith was weak, but it led to prayer. Jesus, seeing that the multitude were drawing near, rebuked the unclean spirit, saying, "Thou deaf and dumb spirit, I command thee come out of him, and enter no more into him."

And the spirit cried out, and threw the boy into spasms, and then came out of him, leaving him so weak and exhausted that many who saw him said, "He is dead."

But Jesus took him by the hand and raised him up; and he stood on his feet completely cured.

When Jesus came into the house, the disciples

asked him privately, why they could not cast out devils as he did, and why they had failed in curing the lunatic boy. Jesus frankly told them it was because of their unbelief. "This kind," he said, "can come out by nothing but prayer." With more faith they could do more and blessed work for Christ.

Paul says, "I can do all things through Christ who strengtheneth me." All things are ours, if Christ is ours. Jesus left Cæsarea Philippi, and passed through Galilee, not by the main roads, but along the by-paths, that his presence might not be known. He wished to talk with his disciples, and to prepare their minds for his death, which was so soon to take place. They had wondered at the miracles he had done, and he said, "Let these sayings sink down into your ears, for the Son of Man shall be delivered up into the hands of men." But they understood not what he meant, for it was hid from them, and they feared to ask him about it.

And they came to Capernaum; and when Jesus entered the house he asked the disciples what they had disputed about on the way. And they were ashamed to tell him, for they had disputed with one another as to which should be the greatest in the kingdom Jesus was about to set up. The rest of the disciples were jealous of Peter, and James, and John, supposing that they would hold high rank in the future kingdom.

Jesus, sitting down, called the twelve around him, and said, "If any one would be first in the kingdom he shall be last of all." And he took a child, and set him in the midst of them; and taking him in his arms he said unto them, "Whosoever shall receive a little child in my name receiveth me; and whoso receiveth me, receiveth not me but him that sent me."

He is nearest to Christ who has the least thought of self; we must stoop low to save souls, and think that no work is mean that is done in his name.

John answered him, saying, "Master, we saw one casting out devils in thy name, and he followeth not us; and we forbade him because he followeth not us." But Jesus said: "Forbid him not, for there is no one that shall do a mighty work in my name and be able to speak evil of me. For he that is not against us is for us."

If those who are not followers of Jesus strive to do good work for him they must not be discouraged. Their faith will increase, and they may thus be brought into the fold.

Clasping the child more closely in his arms, Jesus said: "Whosoever shall give you a cup of water to drink in my name, because ye belong to Christ, verily I say unto you he shall in no wise lose his reward. And whosoever shall offend one of these little ones that believe in me, it were better for him that a mill-stone were hung about his neck, and he were cast into the sea."

Jesus takes care of his own, and the least kindness shown to them is the same as if shown to him. He warns us against the guilt of leading little children away from Christ, and of teaching them to do wrong. The whole blame will rest upon us, and we shall be terribly punished.

Jesus said: "See that ye despise not one of these little ones; for I say unto you, their angels in heaven do always behold the face of my father who is in heaven. For the Son of Man is come to save that which was lost." He despiseth no one. "How think ye, if a man have a hundred sheep, and one of them be gone astray, doth he not leave the ninety and nine and go into the mountains and seek that which has gone astray? And if so be that he find it, truly I

JESUS BLESSES THE CHILDREN.

say unto you he rejoiceth over it more than over the ninety and nine which went not astray. Even so it is not the will of your Father who is in heaven that one of these little ones should perish." Those who do not know how to care for the lambs are not fit to take care of the sheep. Jesus loves the little ones, and his arms are always open to receive them. He is like a tender shepherd, who is unwilling that any of his flock should be lost. He does not leave them to be eaten up by wolves, but goes out after them, and brings them home safely in his arms. Little ones are to feel that they have a friend in Jesus.

Jesus said unto them, "If thy hand cause thee to offend, cut it off; for it is better to enter life maimed than having thy two hands to enter into the fire that is never quenched. And if thy foot cause thee to offend, cut it off; for it is better that thou enter halt into life than having thy two feet to be cast into hell. And if thine eye cause thee to offend, pluck it out; for it is better that thou enter the kingdom of God with one eye than having thy two eyes to be cast into hell. For every one shall be salted with fire."

"Salt is good, but if the salt have lost its saltness wherewith will ye season it? Have salt in yourselves, and be at peace with one another."

Jesus teaches several lessons by these figures of speech. If our right hand leads us into sin we must deny ourselves, and be as if the hand were cut off. How much better for him that stole, or murdered, if he had had no hands at all! Our feet lead us often into sin, but we must turn away and walk with Jesus if we would escape the fire that eats into the soul. How often the eye causes us to sin. We see that our neighbors are better off than we are, we covet their wealth, their fine homes and worldly pleasures, and sell our souls in order to obtain these things that perish with the using. Better for many that they had been blind than, having two eyes, to fall into the mire of sin. Better for us to be blind—to have our eyes put out—if only in that way can we be brought to know Christ, and to be followers of Jesus. "Every one shall be salted with fire," said Jesus. Salt is a great purifier and preserver. Without it much of our food would be tasteless. Fire also purifies, and takes the dross from the pure gold and silver. So the trials and sacrifices we meet with in the Christian life are to sweeten and refine us, to make us more pure and holy. If the taste is lost from salt there is no way of putting it back again; but if we have salt in ourselves, if we season the message so that the Gospel is made attractive, many will be drawn to us, and souls will be saved. If we feel the salt losing its power, we can, by prayer, obtain a fresh supply, and only in this way can we gain strength for the work we have to do for Jesus.

While they were at Capernaum the time came for the collection of the temple tax. For in addition to the tithes—the tenth part of the fields, the flocks, and the herds—every male Jew over twenty years of age had, at a certain time of the year to pay in a half shekel for the support of the temple. A shekel is worth from fifty to seventy cents, and this money was used to purchase the sacrifices and to pay for the incense, the shew-bread, and all the other expenses of the temple services. As many of the worshipers came from a long distance they could not take with them the young cows, or the sheep that were to be laid on the altar, but had to buy them of the dealers whose shops were near the temple.

They that received the tribute-money came to Peter and said, "Doth not your master pay the half shekel?" Peter saith, "Yes," and went into the house to get it. But Jesus prevented him, saying: "What thinkest thou, Simon? Of whom do the kings of the earth receive toll — from their own sons or from strangers?"

And when Peter said, "From strangers," Jesus said unto him: "Surely, then, the sons are free. But

PETER AND THE TRIBUTE-MONEY.

lest we should cause others to offend, go thou to the sea, and cast a hook, and take up the first fish that cometh up. And when thou hast opened its mouth thou shalt find a piece of money—a shekel—that take, and give unto them for thee and me."

The money was usually paid in the month of March, but priests and eminent rabbis were free from the tax; and, as Jesus had been absent from the city, the debt had been allowed to stand.

But there was no reason why Jesus should pay this tax when he himself was the temple of the living God. Had Peter thought a moment he would not have spoken so rashly, but as he had confessed the debt Jesus arranged that he should pay it by his own efforts. Thus the law was kept, and no one's feelings were hurt.

It was now the autumn of the year, and the Feast of Tabernacles was at hand. It began on the fifteenth of October, and lasted for eight days, and was a time of great rejoicing.

Already were pilgrims on their way to Jerusalem to put up booths in which they could live during the festive week. These booths were made of the boughs of olive, palm, and other trees, and were a great protection from the rays of the midday sun, as well as a shelter at night.

For some months Jesus had walked in Galilee, for he would not walk in Judea because the Jews there —the leaders of the people—sought to kill him. But now all Galilee was astir, for the Feast of the Tabernacles was one of the great feasts of the year.

This harvest feast reminded Jesus of the ingathering of souls. And choosing seventy disciples, he sent them out, two and two, into every city and place to prepare the people for his coming. And he said to them: "The harvest is plenteous, but the laborers are few. Pray ye, therefore, the Lord of the harvest that he would send forth laborers into his harvest. Go your ways. Behold I send you forth as lambs in the midst of wolves. Carry no purse, no wallet, and no sandals, and salute no man by the way." It was the custom of the Jews to

THE SENDING OUT OF THE SEVENTY.

speak to no one when on the way to prayer. "And into whatsoever house ye shall enter first say, 'Peace be to this house.' And if a son of peace be there, your peace shall rest upon it, but if not it shall turn to you again."

They were to seek out those worthy to receive the message they brought, and in that house were to remain, sharing with them the food they gave, for the laborer is worthy of his hire. They were not to go from house to house in search of ease, or better food, but to eat such food as was set before them.

They were to heal the sick in these places, and to say to them: The kingdom of God is come nigh unto you. In case the people did not receive them into their houses they were to go through the streets and warn them that the kingdom of God is near.

And he said that the same woes would come upon these cities and towns where the people refused to receive the seventy, as would come upon those that rejected him. And great was the ruin of those cities and towns!

Jesus said to them as he says to all who go out to preach and teach in his name, "He that heareth you heareth me, and he that despiseth you despiseth me, and he that despiseth me despiseth him that sent me."

As the route from Capernaum to Jerusalem lay through Samaria, Jesus sent messengers on ahead to prepare food and shelter for him and the large party with him. But in the first village the messengers entered the people refused to receive him, giving as an excuse that, as his mission was to the Jews, the Jews must befriend him.

When his disciples, James and John, saw this they were very angry, and said, "Lord, wilt thou that we command fire to come down from heaven, and burn them up, even as Elijah did?" But Jesus said, "The

Son of Man is not come to destroy men's lives, but to save them." And they passed on to another village.

The seventy were not gone for any great length of time, and returned in a joyful state because powers had been given them to heal diseases and to cast out devils. Jesus warned them not to rejoice too much in the power they possessed—not to glory in their

SIDON.

power to save souls—but to make it their chief joy that their own names were written in the Book of Life.

Then began he, as on a former occasion, to upbraid the cities wherein most of his mighty works were done: "Woe unto thee, Chorazin! woe unto thee, Bethsaida! for if the mighty works which were done in you had been done in Tyre and Sidon, they would have repented long ago in sackcloth and ashes. But I say unto you, it shall be more tolerable for Tyre and Sidon in the day of judgment than for you. And thou, Capernaum, which art exalted unto heaven, shalt be brought down to hell—that is, the place of the dead. For if the mighty works which have been done in thee had been done in Sodom it would have stood till this day. But I say unto you that it shall be more tolerable for the land of Sodom in the day of judgment than for thee."

Then Jesus turns from these sorrowful thoughts, and looking upward gives praise to God, saying: "I thank thee, O Father, Lord of heaven and earth, because thou hast hid these things from the wise and prudent, and revealed them unto babes. Even so, Father, for so it seemed good in thy sight. All things were delivered to me of my Father: and no man knoweth the Son but the Father, neither knoweth any man the Father, save the Son, and he to whom the Son willeth to reveal him."

The wise and prudent were the proud Jews, the well-informed Scribes and Pharisees. The children were those who had believing hearts. Simple and trustful as babes they understood the Gospel. They might be ignorant of many things, but they knew about the love of Jesus, and believed in him.

And with his heart filled with love to these little ones whom he would fain clasp in his arms, he spoke those words of gracious invitation which have brought peace and rest and balm to many a bleeding heart:

"Come unto me all ye that labor and are heavy laden, and I will give you rest. Take my yoke upon you, and learn of me, for I am meek and lowly in heart, and ye shall find rest unto your souls. For my yoke is easy, and my burden is light."

Jesus and his party left Samaria, and went towards

one of the Jewish villages. Here they were met by a certain man, a Scribe, who said: "I will follow thee whithersoever thou goest." And Jesus said unto him: "The foxes have holes, and the birds of the air have nests, but the Son of Man hath not where to lay his head." And Jesus said to another, "Follow me. Be my disciple." But the man said: "Suffer me first to go and bury my father." Jesus said unto him: "Let the dead bury their own dead, but go thou and preach the kingdom of God." Better to leave the dead unburied than disobey the call of Jesus. Another said: "Lord, I will follow thee, but first suffer me to bid farewell to those that are at my house." Jesus said unto him: "No man, having put his hand to the plough, and looking back, is fit for the kingdom of God."

The plough used in the East was easily overturned and, therefore, required close attention. When a man put his hand to the plough, intending to turn up the soil, and fit it for seed sowing, he must keep his hand there and not be looking behind him, or his work would be wasted. So those who have made up their minds to give up the world and follow Jesus, must fix their gaze on him, and give their whole hearts to the work.

It was the intention of Jesus to go quietly up to Jerusalem at the time of the great Thanksgiving feast, but his brethren urged him to do otherwise. They said unto him: "Depart hence, and go into Judea, that thy disciples also may behold the works that thou doest. For no one doeth anything in secret, who seeks to be known openly."

The brethren of Jesus did not believe in him, or his claims to be the Messiah. Therefore they said to him: "If thou doest these miracles, make it known to everybody." Jesus said unto them: "My time is not yet come, but your time is always ready."

It was safe for them to go at any time and mingle with the wicked Jews. "The world cannot hate you," said Jesus to his brethren, "but me it hateth, because I bear witness concerning it, that its works are wicked. Go ye up to the feast. I go not up to the feast, because my time is not yet fulfilled." And when he had said these things unto them, he abode still in Galilee. And when his brothers had been gone for a day or two, then Jesus went up also to Jerusalem, but in secret, and by a road not frequented by the public.

The Jews, therefore, sought him at the feast, and said, "Where is he?" And there was much whispering among the multitudes because of him; some saying, "He is a good man;" while others said, "No, he is not; for he leads the common people astray." But both sides, through fear of the Jews, dared not speak out their thoughts aloud. They only half believed, and therefore were not bold.

CHAPTER XVI.

THE FEAST OF TABERNACLES—THE SPEECH NEAR THE TREASURY — THE JEWS PICK UP STONES TO THROW AT HIM.

By the 14th of October—or *Tishri*—the streets of Jerusalem were thronged with pilgrims, and the city presented a gay appearance. Booths made of fresh green boughs were in the streets and court-yards, and even on the housetops, a leafy reminder of the days when the children of Israel were led through the wilderness, and had no other sort of houses to live in.

The next day the feast began, and at the first dawn of morn, the priests blew their silver trumpets twenty-one times to awaken the sleepers. This was done each day; and all day long the smoke of the bullocks that burned on the altar of sacrifice rose high on the air.

The crowds as they met in Solomon's Porch, or elsewhere, talked in low tones about Jesus, and wondered where he was, and why he did not appear.

All at once Jesus came into the temple, unnoticed and unheralded, and was found teaching in one of the halls that open out of the temple-courts. No one knew by what road he came, nor why his disciples were not with him; and we are not told how and where he lodged during the feast.

The Jews listened to him in astonishment, wondering how a man who had not been taught in their schools could become such a skilled and powerful teacher.

Jesus, knowing their thoughts, answered them as if they had spoken aloud: "My teaching is not mine, but his that sent me. Those who have the will to do his will in my teaching will hear the voice of God. If a man speaks from himself, he seeks his own glory; but he who seeketh the glory of him who sent him, cannot be a false messenger, but his words are true. Did not Moses give you the law, and yet none of you keepeth the law? Why seek ye to kill me?"

Jesus had done nothing, and yet these men who professed to keep the whole law of Moses, were seeking to kill him.

The people who knew not the designs of the Jews, answered Jesus: "Thou hast a demon! Thou talkest like a madman! Who is there that seeketh to kill thee?"

Jesus said unto them: "I have done one miracle, and ye all marveled and are angry with me because I healed a man on the Sabbath day."

He referred to the miracle at the Pool of Bethesda, which had roused all the hatred of the Scribes and

Pharisees. And, though Jesus had done many other miracles in Jerusalem, all the good he had done was forgotten, and only this thing remembered—that he had broken one of God's commandments.

Jesus showed them how they kept to the *letter* and not the *spirit* of the law, and asked them to be as kind and just in judging him, as they were in judging themselves. Some of those who lived in Jerusalem said: "Is not this he whom they seek to kill? And, lo, he speaketh out boldly, and they say nothing unto him! Can it be that the rulers know that this is the Christ? It cannot be! For we know who this man is, and from whence he came; but when the Christ comes, no one will know."

Then Jesus raised his voice so that all could hear him, and said: "Ye both know me, and ye know from whence I came; and I have not come of myself, but he that sent me is true whom ye know not. I know him, because I am from him, and he sent me."

These were sharp words, for the men of Jerusalem claimed to know God, and to be well-read in the Scriptures. To be found fault with in this way roused all their hatred, and they sought therefore to seize Jesus, and to put a stop to his teachings. But he escaped from them, and no one laid hands on him, for his hour had not yet come.

Others in the crowd were drawn to Jesus. Their faith was stirred, and they believed in him, and they said among themselves: "When the Christ comes will he do more signs than these which this man hath done?"

Although the multitudes had spoken in secret in regard to Jesus, the Scribes and Pharisees had heard of it, and fearing many might be won over to him, the chief priests sent out officers with orders to seize him. But Jesus felt no fear. He said: "Yet a little while I am with you, and then I go unto him that sent me. Ye shall seek me, and shall not find me; and where I am, ye cannot come."

The Jews therefore said among themselves, "Where will he go that we cannot find him? Will he go among the Greeks and teach them? What does he mean when he says, 'Ye shall seek me and shall not find me, and where I am ye cannot come?'"

Every morning while the Jews were assembling in the temple-courts, one of the priests went down to the Pool of Siloam, and brought up water from thence in a golden urn. Amid the sounding of trumpets and the singing of hymns of praise and thanksgiving, the priest poured the water on the altar, as a type of the pouring out of the Holy Spirit. In the evening the rejoicing was kept up in the courts of the women with singing and music, and the blaze of the great lamp lit up the temple, and could be seen all over the city.

The people chanted the *Hallel* from the Psalms of David,* which was a hymn of thanksgiving, beginning with, "Praise ye the Lord!" and ending with, "O give thanks unto the Lord, for he is good; for his mercy endureth forever." As they sang this they waved the palm branches they carried in their hands, and at the end of each section the priest blew a threefold blast, while the people bowed down to worship.

To this was added a praise song from Isaiah: "Behold God is my salvation; I will trust, and not be afraid; for the Lord Jehovah is my strength and my song; he also is become my salvation."

"Therefore with joy shall ye draw water out of the wells of salvation. And in that day shall ye say, 'Praise the Lord, call upon his name, declare his

---

* Psalms cxiii, cxviii: Isaiah xii,

WAVING THE BRANCHES AT THE FEAST OF TABERNACLES.

doings among the people. Cry out and shout, thou inhabitant of Zion: for great is the Holy One of Israel in the midst of thee.'"

Thus they sang each day with ringing voices, but with dull hearts, for they did not understand the meaning of the words. They did not know that the Messiah was even then with them.

It was now the last and great day of the feast. For seven days had the water been poured upon the altar, in memory of the miraculous supply of water in the wilderness. And now the services were at an end. The priests marched seven times around the altar and passed out of the temple. The people pulled the willow branches from the altar, and beat the palm branches to pieces. By afternoon all the booths were torn down, and the pilgrims made ready for the homeward march.

After the pouring on of the water, and after the people had given thanks and prayed that God would send them salvation and prosperity, there was a pause—a solemn hush. Then Jesus stood up, and cried out with a loud voice, so that his words could be heard throughout the temple: "If any one thirst, let him come unto me and drink. He that believeth in me, as the Scripture said, out of his heart shall flow rivers of living water." And this spake he concerning the spirit which they that believed in him were to receive; for the spirit was not yet given, because Jesus was not yet glorified.

Some of the multitude therefore when they heard these words, said: "Of a truth, this is the Prophet." Others said: "This is the Christ." Some said: "What, doth the Christ come out of Galilee? Hath not the Scripture said, that the Christ cometh out of the seed of David, and from Bethlehem, the village where David was?" There arose therefore a division among the multitude because of him. And some of them would have seized him, but no man dared to lay hands on him.

The officers who had been sent out by the chief priests and Pharisees listened awestruck to the words of Jesus, and lingered near him for a day or two without power to arrest him.

Seventy of the chief priests and Pharisees formed a court of law, called the Sanhedrin, and when the officers came back without their man, the chief priests and Pharisees said unto them: "Why have ye not brought him?"

To this question the officers could only answer, "Never did any man speak like this man." Whether it was the charm of his voice or his presence that held them spellbound they could not tell. But they were powerless to do him harm.

Then said the Pharisees with a sneer, "Have ye also been led astray? Hath any one of the rulers or the Pharisees believed in him? Ye can see for yourselves that none of the learned ones are drawn toward him, but only the ignorant and foolish people that know not the law. And their unbelief brings with it a curse."

But among the rulers of the Jews was one Nicodemus, he who came to Jesus by night and was secretly his friend. He had partly overcome his fears, and said to the other members of the Sanhedrin, "Doth our law judge a man, except it have first heard from himself and learned what he hath done?" They answered and said unto him: "Art thou also of Galilee? Search and see that out of Galilee ariseth no prophet." And Nicodemus was left alone, to mourn that he had not done more for Jesus.

On the eighth day no work was done, the festive rites were at an end, but the temple was still thronged with worshipers. In the evening Jesus sat in the Court of the Women, near to the Treasury, where the thirteen chests were with trumpet-shaped mouths, into which the Jews threw their gifts. In this court were four immense candelabra, over fifty feet in height, beautifully gilded, at the top of which lamps were lit that illumined the whole city. Around these lamps, which were the pride of Jerusalem, the people gathered and joined in the songs and dances of the Harvest-feast.

As the water symbolized the rock that was opened for them in the wilderness, so was the light a symbol of the Pillar of Fire—both of them referring to Christ and his coming.

Again, therefore, Jesus spoke unto them, saying, "I am the light of the world; he that followeth me shall not walk in darkness, but shall have the light of life." The Pharisees, therefore, said unto him, "Thou bearest record of thyself, and thy record is not true." Jesus said unto them, "Even though I bear record of myself my record is true, because I know whence I came and whither I go; but ye know not whence I come or whither I go. Ye judge after the flesh by outward appearance. I judge no one. But even if I judge, my judgment is true, because I am not alone, but I and the Father that sent me.

"In your own law also it is written that the testimony of two men is true. I am he that beareth witness of myself, and the Father that sent me beareth witness concerning me. Then they said unto him, "Where is thy Father?" Jesus answered, "Ye know neither me nor my Father. If ye knew me, ye would know my Father also." While Jesus thus spoke the people stood awestruck, and though he was in the very stronghold of his enemies, not one of them laid hands on him for his hour had not yet come.

Knowing how they felt toward him, Jesus said to them, in the saddest of tones, "I go my way, ye shall seek me, and in your sins ye shall die.

Whither I go ye cannot come." They thought he spoke of his dying, and said, "Will he kill himself? because he saith whither I go ye cannot come."

This was the only separation they thought of, though Jesus spoke to them so plainly.

Jesus said unto them, "Ye are from beneath. I am from above. Ye are of this world, I am not of this world. I said therefore unto you that ye shall die in your sins. For if ye shall not believe that I am, ye shall die in your sins."

They said therefore unto him, "Who art thou?" Jesus said unto them, "Even the same that I told you from the beginning. Why am I even speaking to you at all?

"I have many things to speak and to judge concerning you. Nevertheless he that sent me is true; and the words which I have heard from him, these do I speak unto the world." His hearers understood not that he spoke of God, their Heavenly Father.

Jesus therefore said, "When ye have lifted on high the Son of Man, then shall ye know that I am, and that of myself I do nothing; but even as the Father taught me speak I these things. And he that sent me is with me; he hath not left me alone, because I do always the things that are pleasing to him." God will be with those who do his will. As he spoke these words many of his hearers believed on him. They were drawn toward him, and felt that his mission must be divine.

Jesus, knowing their hearts, spoke to those who believed in him, saying, "If ye abide in my word, if ye continue to have faith in me, then are ye indeed my disciples. And ye shall know the truth, and the truth shall make you free."

He meant that they would be drawn to Jesus, see him in the right light, and be freed from the power of Satan. The Jews put a different meaning to his words, and therefore said, "We are Abraham's seed and were never in bondage to any one. How sayest thou then, ye shall become free?"

Jesus answered them, "Verily, verily, I say unto you, every one who doeth sin is the slave of sin. And the slave has no claim to a place in the house, but the son dwells there forever. If the son therefore shall make you free, ye shall be free indeed."

The Jews thought that being heirs of Abraham, they were sons of God. Jesus wished them to understand that Abraham could not give them an entrance into heaven, and so long as they were the slaves of sin they would have no place in God's house. Christ was the only one who could open the door to them, and through him they might become sons of God.

Jesus said, "I know that ye are Abraham's seed; but ye seek to kill me, because my word has not found its way to your hearts. I speak the things which I have seen with the Father, ye do that which ye have heard from your father."

They said unto him, "Abraham is our father." Jesus saith unto them, "If ye are Abraham's children do the works of Abraham. But now ye seek to kill me, a man that hath spoken to you the truth which I heard from God. This did not Abraham. Ye do the works of your father."

Jesus showed that if they were true sons of Abraham, they would have some of his spirit and faith, and they would know him and love him, and not seek to kill him. But they failed to understand Jesus when he spoke of the Father, so plainer words must be used. When he said, "ye do the works of your father," they thought he charged them with being heathens, and worshipers of idols. They said therefore, "We have one Father, even God."

Jesus said unto them, "If God were your Father ye would love me, for I come forth from God. I have not come of myself, but he sent me. Why do ye not know my speech? Because ye cannot hear my word." What Jesus taught was hateful to them. They could not bear to hear it. The reason was as Jesus said:

"Ye are of your father, the devil, and the works of your father it is your will to do. He was a man-killer from the beginning, and stood not in the truth because there is no truth in him. Whenever he speaks a lie he speaks it because he loves falsehood, for he (Satan) is a liar, and the father of all those who tell lies. But because I tell you the truth ye believe me not."

This proved that they were not children of God, but children of the devil.

"Which of you can charge me with sin? If I say truth, why do ye not believe me? He that is of God, heareth the words of God; for this cause ye hear not, because ye are not of God."

Were they children of God they would take the teachings of Jesus to their hearts, but his words seemed only to rouse their hatred. And the Jews answered, and said unto him, "Say we not well that thou art a Samaritan, and hast a demon?" No one but a madman, they thought could utter such words as these.

Jesus answered, "I have not a demon; but I honor my Father, and ye do dishonor me."

The Jews hated the Samaritans, and their taunt was the same as if they had said, "Thou art a child of the devil, and hast a demon." Jesus denied this, for his whole desire was to glorify his Heavenly Father. "I seek not my glory," he said; there is one that seeketh and judgeth. Verily, verily, I say unto you, if a man hath kept my word he shall not see death."

Then said the Jews to him, "Now we know that

thou hast a demon. Abraham is dead, and the prophets, and thou sayest, 'If a man have kept my word he shall never taste of death.' Art thou greater than our father, Abraham, who died? And the prophets who died. Whom makest thou thyself?"

Ah, these wily Jews thought that they had found him out. By his own words they had caught him at last, and proved that their charges were true!

Jesus answered, "If I glorify myself, my glory is nothing; it is my Father that glorifieth me, of whom ye say he is your God. Yet ye have not known him; but I know him; and if I should say I know him not, I shall be like unto you, a liar. But I know him, and keep his word. Your father, Abraham, rejoiced to see my day; and he saw it, and was glad."

Abraham longed to see this day, and through faith in the promise of God he saw it in the far distance and was filled with joy and gladness. But the Jews, who despised Jesus, and rejected him as their Saviour, did not the works of Abraham. Nor could they understand what Jesus meant when he said, "Your father, Abraham, rejoiced to see my day."

Therefore they said to him, "Thou art not yet fifty years old, and has thou seen Abraham?" Jesus said, "Before Abraham was born, I AM." The thought of Jesus as a Saviour of men was in God's heart long before Abraham was born.

His words threw the Jews into a great rage. This man of low rank and birth claimed to be superior to Abraham, the father of the faithful! It was rank blasphemy! And rushing from the Porch out into the Court of the Gentiles, they picked up stones to throw at him. But Jesus hid himself for the moment, behind one of the columns, or in one of the many small rooms, and then making his way through the crowd passed out of the temple.

His hour had not yet come, and no one could harm him.

CHAPTER XVII.

THE MAN BORN BLIND—THE PARABLE OF THE SHEEP-FOLD—JESUS SAYS, I AM THE DOOR—HE LEAVES GALILEE.

As Jesus passed out of the temple, he saw a man who had been blind from his birth. And the disciples asked him, saying. "Rabbi, who did sin, this man or his parents, that he should be born blind?" It was the common belief that special sins in the parents would cause special diseases in their children.

Jesus answered, "Neither did this man sin, nor his parents; but he was born blind that the works of God might be made manifest in him. I must work the works of him that sent me, while it is day. The night cometh, when no one can work. Whensoever I am in the world, I am the light of the world."

When he had thus spoken, he spat on the ground, and made clay of the spittle, and with this clay anointed the eyes of the blind man. And he said unto him, "Go, wash in the Pool of Siloam." The meaning of the word Siloam, is "sent," or "sent forth." Jesus did not need to make use of the waters. But he wished to draw out the man's faith, to make him feel that he owed his cure to One sent of God to open the eyes of the blind. And the man went away, and washed, and came back cured of his blindness.

The neighbors, therefore, and those who had seen him previously and knew that he had been blind all his life, said, "Is not this the blind beggar we used

THE "POOL OF HEZEKIAH," JERUSALEM.

to see sitting by the roadside?" Some said, "It is he." Others said, "No, but he is like him." But the man himself said, *"I am he."*

They said therefore to him, "How then were thine eyes opened?" He answered, "The man that is called Jesus made clay, and anointed mine eyes, and said unto me, "Go to Siloam, and wash." I went away therefore, and washed, and I received my sight." And they said unto him, "Where is he?" He answered, "I know not."

Then they brought the man to the Pharisees, that they might make a charge against Jesus. For it was on the Sabbath day that Jesus made the clay and opened his eyes, and thereby broke the Jewish law, which forbade any work being done on that day.

Again therefore the Pharisees asked him how he had received his sight. And he said unto them, "He put clay on my eyes, and I washed, and do see." Therefore said some of the Pharisees, "This man is not from God, because he keepeth not the Sabbath day." Others said, "How can a man that is a sinner do such miracles?" And there was a division among them, some being for, and others against Jesus.

They say therefore unto the blind man again, "What sayest thou of him that opened thine eyes?" And he said, "He is a prophet." But the Jews did not believe that the man had been born blind and received his sight until they had called upon his parents to inquire concerning the truth of the matter. And they asked them, saying, "Is this your son, who ye say was born blind? How then doth he now see?" His parents answered and said, "We know that this is our son, and that he was born blind. But by what means he now seeth, we know not; or who opened his eyes, we know not; ask him, he is of age; he shall speak for himself."

These things said his parents because they feared

the Jews, for the Jews had already declared that whoever confessed that Jesus was the Christ should be put out of the synagogue.

To a Jew this was a terrible punishment. He would be shunned like a leper, and would sit on the ground, and bear himself like one in deep grief. He would not shave, but would let his beard and hair grow wild and shaggy. He would not bathe nor anoint himself, and if he died in the meantime stones would be thrown at him, and curses, and no one would be permitted to mourn for him. Henceforth he was as one dead, for he could not study with the others, for no one was to have speech with him, or even show him the road. He might buy such food as he needed to keep himself alive, but it was forbidden that any one should eat or drink with him. Therefore, in their dread of being put under ban, the parents of the blind man said, "He is of age; ask him."

The Jews, wishing to force from the man a confession that Jesus was an impostor, called him up before them a second time, and said unto him, "Give God the glory. We know that this man is a sinner." He answered, "Whether he be a sinner, I know not; one thing I do know and that is, that whereas I was blind, now I see."

They said therefore to him again, "What did he do to thee? how opened he thine eyes?" He answered them, "I have told you already and ye did not hear; wherefore would ye hear it again? would ye also become his disciples?" And they cursed him, and said, "Thou art his disciple; but we are Moses's disciples. We know that God hath spoken unto Moses; but as for this man, we know not whence he is."

The man answered and said unto them, "Why, herein lies the marvelous thing, that ye know not from whence he is, and yet he opened my eyes. We know that God heareth not sinners; but if any man be a worshiper of God, and do his will, him he heareth. Since the world began was it not heard that any one opened the eyes of a man who was born blind. If this man were not from God, he could do nothing."

These Jews thought they were doing the will of God by holding on to the law of Moses. The blind beggar, having his eyes opened, saw more clearly, had more faith, and undertook to lead the Jews out of darkness into light. We are blind until Jesus touches our eyes, and being saved ourselves our first impulse is to try and save others. But these rulers of the Jews, these wise Rabbis, were furious at being spoken to in this way, and by such a man. They Christ's disciples indeed? Far from it! The charge stung them to the quick!

They answered and said unto him with scorn, "Thou wast altogether born in sins, and dost thou teach us?" And they put him out and left him to his fate, thinking it were better if he had remained a blind beggar at the roadside.

But there was one watching over him who had been born blind, and when Jesus heard that the Jews had cast him out he found him, and said, "Dost thou believe in the Son of God?"

He answered and said, "Who is he, Lord, that I may believe in him?" Jesus said unto him, "Thou hast both seen him, and it is he that talketh with thee." And he said, "I believe, Lord;" and he worshiped him.

In his heart he had seen Jesus. He was no longer in the dark, and trusting to blind guides, but Jesus, the Light of the world, had shone in upon him.

And Jesus said, "For a judgment came I into this world, that they which see not may see, and that they which see may become blind." Now some of the Jews had followed Jesus, not being led away by the teachings of the Pharisees, and these, when they heard his words, said unto Jesus, "Are we blind also?" Jesus said, "If ye were blind, ye would not have sin; but now ye say, 'We see;' and are guilty of sin."

Their sin was in not coming to Jesus. The light was at their door, and yet they sat in darkness. It was their own fault.

Jesus felt a great pity for these people, who were as a flock without a shepherd; and he spoke to them in a sort of parable. The sheep-fold was a large open space inclosed by a fence or by walls of no great height. There was but one door to the fold, and this was kept by a porter, who would let in only those who had a right to enter. In the morning the shepherds come to lead forth their flocks, and each shepherd knows his own flock, and calls them by name, and leads them out. Then the Eastern shepherd puts himself at the head of his flock, and goes before them to lead them in the right way. For they follow his voice.

Should any one try to get into the fold, by climbing the fence, or some other way, the one on guard would know at once that he was a thief or a robber, and had no right there. He wishes to get near the flock, and to lead them in the wrong direction. So there were good and false teachers in the world, and that they might know how to tell them, Jesus said unto those before him, "He that entereth not by the door into the sheep-fold but climbeth up from some other quarter the same is a thief and a robber. But he that entereth in by the door is a shepherd of the sheep. To him the porter openeth, and the sheep hear his voice, and he calleth his own sheep by name, and leadeth them out. When he hath put out all his own sheep, he goeth before them, and the sheep follow him, for they know his voice. A stranger will they not follow, but will flee from him, for they know not the voice of strangers." This parable said Jesus unto them, but they understood not the meaning of his words.

Jesus, therefore, said unto them again, "Verily, verily, I say unto you, I am the door of the sheep. All that came before me are thieves and robbers, but the sheep did not hear them. I am the door; by me if any man enter in he shall be saved, and shall go in and out and find pasture. The thief cometh not but that he may steal and kill and destroy. I came that they may have life and abundance of good things."

Jesus said, "I am the door." He was to lead his flock out of the Jewish fold, into the rich pastures of the kingdom of God. Some had falsely claimed the place that belonged to him, but those who trusted in God were kept from these deceivers. These false shepherds had sought their own good, and not that of the flock, and would not care for their lives or their safety.

Jesus said, in contrast to this: "I am the good shepherd. The good shepherd layeth down his life for the sheep. But he that is an hireling and not a shepherd, whose own the sheep are not, beholdeth the wolf coming, and leaveth the sheep, and fleeth, because he is only hired, and careth more to save his own life than to save the sheep. And the wolf catches them, and they are scattered. I am the good shepherd, and I know my sheep, and am known of mine even as the Father knoweth me and I know the Father. And I lay down my life for the sheep. And other sheep I have, which are not of this fold; them also I must lead, and they shall hear my voice. And they shall become one flock, one shepherd. Therefore doth the Father love me because I lay down my life that I may take it again. No man taketh it from me, but I lay it down of myself. I have power to lay it down, and I have power to take it again. This commandment I received of my Father."

There were others, Gentiles, outside the Jewish fold. They were his, and they knew his voice, and followed him. He must die to save the life of his sheep, and would then rise again, to gather them all into one flock and to be their shepherd. This was his mission on earth. This was the work God had sent him to do.

There arose a great strife among the Jews because of these words. Many of them said, "He hath a devil and is mad, why hear ye him?" Others said: "These are not the words of one that is possessed by a devil. Can a devil open the eyes of the blind?"

Thus ended the visit of Jesus to the Feast of the Tabernacles. In spite of all that he had said and done, the greater part of the Jews looked upon him with hatred. He had more enemies than friends in Jerusalem; and, feeling that his life was in danger, he withdrew from the city, and went into Galilee to visit his old home at Capernaum, which he was soon to leave forever.

In the meantime the seventy whom Jesus had sent out had returned with great joy, for power had been given them to heal the sick, and also to cast out devils. Jesus told them not to rejoice too much over the power they had, but to be chiefly glad that their names were written in the Book of Life.

There were some present at that time who told him of the Galileans whose blood Pilate had mingled with their sacrifices. The Galileans were known to be hot-blooded, and at some feast in the temple they got into a quarrel with Pilate's soldiers and several of them were killed. The Jews thought that it was terrible to die under such circumstances, and a proof of God's displeasure. Jesus answered and said: "Suppose ye that these Galileans were sinners above all the Galileans, because they have suffered these things? I tell you nay; but, except ye repent, ye shall perish in like manner. Or those eighteen upon whom the tower in Siloam fell, and slew them, think ye that they were sinners above all the men that dwell in Jerusalem? I tell you, nay: but except ye repent ye shall all likewise perish."

And he spake this parable: "A certain man had a fig-tree planted in his vineyard, and he came seeking fruit thereon, and found none. Then said he to the vine-dresser, 'Behold, these three years I come seeking fruit on the fig-tree, and find none. Cut it down: why cumbereth it the ground?' And he, answering, saith unto him, 'Lord, let it alone this year also till I shall dig about it, and manure the roots; and if it bear fruit after that, well; and, if not, then thou shalt cut it down.'"

The owner of the vineyard is God. The vine-dresser is our Lord. The fig-tree is the Jewish nation, and the vineyard is the world. The fig-tree, if in good condition, bears fruit at the end of three years; but Jesus had been preaching to the Jews for three years with no results from his labors. Still he pleads for them, and holds out the hope that, by care and attention to the roots, on which its life depends, it would yet bear fruit to God's glory.

The feast of the Dedication of the Temple took place in Jerusalem two months after the Feast of Tabernacles. Brief as was the time that Jesus could stay at his home, the Pharisees could not let him remain in peace. Pretending to be alarmed for the safety of Jesus, they came to him saying, "Get thee out, and depart from this place, for Herod wishes to kill thee." And he said unto them, "Go and say to that fox, 'Behold, I cast out devils and heal men to-day and to-morrow, and the third day come to the end.'"

THE UNFRUITFUL TREE.

The meaning of this is, I shall stay in your territory for three days, healing the sick of their diseases, and doing my work, and at the end of the third day will continue my journey.

He was not afraid of Herod's threats, and said to the Pharisees, "Nevertheless, I must go on my journey to-day and to-morrow, and the day following, for it cannot be that a prophet perish out of Jerusalem." In that city many a holy man had been put to death, and Jesus, knowing what was to take place there, cried out, with a sad voice : "O Jerusalem, Jerusalem! that killeth the prophets, and stoneth them that are sent unto thee, how often would I have gathered thy children together, even as a hen gathereth her brood under her wings, and ye would not! Behold, your house is left unto you desolate, forsaken ; and I say unto you, ye shall not see me until ye shall say, 'Blessed is he that cometh in the name of the Lord!'"

And when he had finished these sayings, Jesus departed from Galilee, and came into the borders of Judea beyond the Jordan. And great multitudes followed him, and he healed them there.

CHAPTER XVIII.

IN PEREA—WHO IS MY NEIGHBOR?—PARABLE OF THE GOOD SAMARITAN—THE MAN WITH THE DROPSY—THE GREAT SUPPER—THE LOST SHEEP—THE LOST PIECE OF MONEY—THE LOST SON.

JESUS passed through Perea, and as he taught in one of the synagogues there, a certain lawyer stood up to question him and to see if he could tell him anything new or strange. And he asked him, saying, "Master, what shall I do to inherit eternal life?" Jesus said unto him : "What is written in the law? How readest thou?" The lawyer said, "Thou shalt love the Lord thy God with all thy heart, and with all thy soul, and with all thy strength, and with all thy mind, and thy neighbor as thyself." Jesus said unto him: "Thou hast answered right. This do and thou shalt live."

But he, wishing to justify himself and to prove that he led a righteous life, said unto Jesus, "And who is my neighbor?" Jesus said, in reply: A certain man was going down from Jerusalem to Jericho, and he fell among robbers, who stripped him, and beat him, and went away leaving him half dead.

By chance a certain priest was going down that way, and when he saw the poor helpless man he passed by on the other side. By chance also a Levite, one who taught the law and served in the temple, came to the place and looked at the man, and passed by on the other side.

Haply a Samaritan journeyed that way and came to the place where he was. And when he saw him he was moved with compassion. He did not ask who the man was, or how he received his wounds. His only thought was that he needed help. So he went to him, and mixing together some oil and wine which were used as remedies in the East, he bound up the wounds. Then he lifted him on his own beast, and walking by his side, brought him to one of the inns or khans where travelers were lodged free of expense. But they were charged for any food that might be furnished man or beast, and for any care taken of the latter. In this case the Samaritan took care of the wounded man himself, and stayed with him all that night.

The next morning, when he was obliged to continue his journey, he gave to the host two Roman coins, each one of which was worth about eight cents of our money. A penny a day—eight cents—was a laborer's wages, and the Samaritan told the landlord to take care of the man, and if he was obliged to spend any more money he would pay him back when he came that way again.

"Which of these three, thinkest thou, was a neighbor unto him that fell among thieves?"

The lawyer said, "He that had pity on him."

And Jesus said, "Go, and do thou likewise."

Thus did Jesus teach a lesson of love to all mankind. We make ourselves neighbors by being kind to those who are in need of help. We are not to turn aside from those who are not related to us, or who are perhaps in a lower walk of life. But with willing hands, ready feet, and pitying hearts, we are to do good to all we can. In this way we show our love to Christ. It is not enough to know the law. We must do it from our hearts.

It was twenty-one miles from Jerusalem to Jericho, over a desert road that was infested by robbers. A man stripped, and beaten, and left for dead, was in a sad plight, depending for his life on those who might chance to pass that way. Jesus brought out the cruelty and pride of the Jews, by making the priest and the Levite pass by on the other side. How had they read the word of God? The Jews looked down on the Samaritans, but here was one of that hated race doing noble work, and serving God with a truer spirit than did the self-righteous Scribes and Pharisees. Shall the heathen put us to shame?

It came to pass that "Jesus went to the house of one of the rulers of the Pharisees to eat bread on the Sabbath day. The Jews gave feasts on the Sabbath, the food being cooked the day before. A number of guests were present at this feast, most of them being Pharisees, who did all they could to entangle Our Lord in his talk. And there came in a man with the dropsy.

Jesus, knowing the thoughts of the Pharisees, said unto them, "Is it lawful to heal on the Sabbath, or not?" But they held their peace. And he took hold of the man and healed him, and then sent him away. And he said unto the Pharisees, "Which of you, if an ass or an ox fall into a pit, will not straightway pull him out on a Sabbath day?"

And they could make no answer to these things, but only hated him the more. And he spoke a parable to the guests, when he saw how they chose the chief places at the table, saying, "When thou art invited to a marriage-feast, sit not down in the chief place lest haply a more distinguished man than thou be among the guests. And the host shall come and say to thee, 'Give place to this man,' and thou shalt go with shame to take the lowest seat at the table. But, when thou art bidden, go and sit down in the lowest place, that when he who invited thee comes into the room, he may say unto thee, 'Friend, go up higher.' Then shalt thou have honor in the presence of every one that sits at meat with thee. For every one that exalted himself shall be humbled, and he that humbleth himself shall be exalted.

Jesus had spoken to the guests, who were self-seeking and full of pride, thinking themselves better than other men. Jesus then turned to the host, who in the same spirit had invited to his feast only the rich and those of his own class.

Jesus said to him: "When thou makest a dinner or a supper, call not thy friends, nor thy brethren, nor thy kinsmen, nor thy rich neighbors, lest haply they also bid thee again, and a recompense be made thee. But when thou makest a feast, call in the poor, the maimed, the lame, and the blind. And thou shalt be blessed, because they have not wherewith to recompense thee. For thou shalt be recompensed in the resurrection of the just.

When one of those who sat at the table heard these words, he said, "Blessed is he that shall eat bread in

CASTING OUT THE GUEST WHO HAD NO WEDDING GARMENT.

the kingdom of God!" feeling certain that he would be among the number.

But Jesus said unto him: "A certain man made a great supper, to which many were invited. And, at supper time, he sent out his servant to say to those who were bidden, 'Come, for everything is now ready.' And they all, with one consent, began to make excuse. The first said unto him, 'I have bought a piece of land, and must needs go out and see it; I pray thee have me excused.' And another said, 'I have bought five yoke of oxen, and am going out to try them; I pray thee have me excused.' And another said, 'I have married a wife, and therefore I cannot come.' And the servant came and told his lord these things. Then the master of the house, being angry, said to his servant, 'Go out quickly into the streets and lanes of the city, and bring in hither the poor, the maimed, the halt, and the blind.' And presently the servant came back, and said, 'What thou didst command me to do is done, and yet there is room.' And the lord said to the servant, 'Go out into the highways and hedges, and beg them to come in, that my house may be filled. For I say unto you, that none of those that were bidden shall taste of my supper.'"

The meaning of the parable is this: God had prepared a great feast to which the Jews, his chosen people were, invited. Isaiah* had written, "In this mountain shall the Lord of hosts make unto all people a feast of fat things." And further on he had said, "Lo, this is our God; we have waited for him, and he will save us. This is the Lord." Yet they did not seem to remember. For when the master sent out his servant to tell those who were invited that everything was ready they made all sorts of

---

*Isaiah xxv, 6.

excuses. They did not care for the feast, and would not give up any of their worldly plans in order to be present.

Then the master sent out the servant, and bade him go into the broad streets and quiet lanes, and to bring in those who in their poverty and wretchedness would shrink from coming to so rich a feast. Even when this was done, there was room, and to spare. For the lord's house was large and he had spread a great feast.

Then he sent his servant out again, telling him to go among the highways and hedges, and to bring in the outcast and the strangers, and those who were worn and weary with life's journey. These would make excuses, of course, and say they did not know the master of the house, and had no clothes to appear in.

The messenger was to tell them of God's great love, to make them feel that Jesus was their friend, and to bring them with him to the Master, that the house above might be filled.

Jesus had but few friends now, and many foes, and wherever he went he was followed by the Scribes and Pharisees who watched him closely. As he went through Perea, however, on his way to Jericho, many publicans and sinners drew near unto him to hear him. The Scribes and Pharisees murmured at this, saying, "This man receiveth sinners, and eateth with them."

These purse-proud men felt that they had done Jesus a great honor by inviting him to their feasts and making him their guest, and they did not like him to lower himself in this way.

Jesus spoke unto them this parable, saying, "What man of you, if he had a hundred sheep, and lost one of them, would not leave the ninety and nine in the wilderness, and search for the lost one till he find it? and when he hath found it he layeth it on his shoulders, rejoicing. And when he cometh home he calleth together his friends and his neighbors, saying unto them, 'Rejoice with me; for I have found my sheep which was lost.' I say unto you, that even

THE LOST SHEEP.

so there shall be joy in heaven over one sinner that repenteth more than over the ninety and nine just persons who have no need of repentance."

If a man have a hundred sheep, and lose one of them, he might say, "That is not much of a loss.

Let him go." But Jesus—the Good Shepherd—knowing how easy it is for the sheep to wander, follows after the lost one, seeking for it everywhere. When he finds it, he takes it up in his arms, and with tender care places it upon his shoulders. In this way he bears us and all our burdens, and being brought near to him by our wounds and sorrows, we find what a loving Saviour he is, and keep close within sound of his voice forever after.

When a child is lost, how we wait and watch for the one word that will give the good news. And when the cry of "saved!" is heard on the air, there is rejoicing in every home, and all hearts are glad. How much greater the joy of angels over the saving of a lost soul. Love and pity will work wonders.

Again Jesus speaks a parable, saying, "What woman having ten pieces of silver, if she lose one piece doth not light a candle and sweep the house, and search diligently until she find it? And when she hath found it, she calleth together her friends and neighbors, saying, 'Rejoice with me; for I have found the piece which I had lost.' Even so, I say unto you, there is joy in the presence of the angels of God over one sinner that repenteth."

The lost piece of money represents a lost soul which a woman goes forth to rescue. The candle or lamp, she takes is the Holy Spirit, which throws a light on the word of God, and enables her to see her duty clearly. All is still, and she searches diligently, praying earnestly, that out of the filth and dust of the world she may find this piece of money, which now that it is lost seems worth more than all her possessions. What joy is hers when she can bring it into the house of God, and know that it is safe! A joy in which all the angels share!

In both these parables, Jesus showed what men would do when they lost their worldly goods. If the loss of a sheep or a coin, could so disturb the peace of mind, how much greater ought to be the distress when a human soul was lost!

And he said, "A certain man had two sons; and the younger of them said to his father, 'Father, give me the portion of goods that falleth to me.' And he divided unto them his living, giving to each the amount of property the law allowed him. And not many days after the younger son gathered all his money together, and took his departure into a far country, and there he wasted his substance in riotous living. And when he had spent all there arose a mighty famine in that land, and he began to be in want. And he went and joined himself to one of the citizens of that country, and he sent him into his fields to feed swine. And he would fain have filled himself with the husks that the swine did eat. They were fed, but no man gave food to him. So great was his hunger that he was almost driven mad. But when he came to himself, he said, 'How many hired servants of my father's have bread enough and to spare, and I perish here with hunger! I will arise and go to my father, and will say unto him, "Father, I have sinned against heaven, and in thy sight, and I am no more worthy to be called thy son; make me as one of thy hired servants."' And he arose, and came to his father.

"While he was yet a great way off, his father saw him, and was moved with compassion, and ran, and fell on his neck, and kissed him. And the son said unto him, 'Father, I have sinned against heaven, and in thy sight, and am no more worthy to be called thy son.' But the father said to his servants, 'Bring hither the best robe and put it on him; and put a ring on his hand, and shoes on his feet. And bring hither the fatted calf, and kill it; and let us eat and be merry; for this my son was dead, and is alive again; he was lost, and is found.' And they began to be merry.

"Now his elder son was in the field; and as he came and drew near to the house, he heard music and dancing. And he called to him one of the servants, and asked what these things meant. And he said

THE PRODIGAL'S RETURN.

unto him, 'Thy brother is come; and thy father hath killed the fatted calf, because he hath received him safe and sound.' And he was angry, and would not go in; therefore his father came out and entreated him. But he answering said to his father, 'Lo, these many years have I served thee, nor transgressed I at any time thy commandments ; and yet thou never gavest me so much as a kid, that I might make merry with my friends. But when this thy son came, who had wasted his substance in riotous living, thou didst kill for him the fatted calf.' And he said unto him, 'Son, thou art ever with me, and all that is mine is thine. It was meet that we should make merry and be glad ; for this thy brother was dead, and is alive again ; was lost, and is found.' "

The prodigal son is he who wastes the talents God has given him. This one wished to be free from all restraint, and to make his own way in the world, so he went off into a far country. He spent his money with a lavish hand, and made friends with the very lowest. After awhile conscience smote him, and he sought relief in work. To a Jew, there could be nothing more degrading than to feed swine ; the flesh of which he was forbidden to eat. This man might have fed on the pods of the carob tree, which he gave to the swine, but would not satisfy his hunger. It was a craving for something better.

Then he thought of the goodness of God, and his own guilt in thus wandering away among sinners. He was ashamed of his conduct, but felt in his heart that his father would forgive him. Penitent, and humble he turned his face toward home. His father who had been on the lookout for him, saw him coming and ran out to meet him. God's loving arms are about us, and the penitent one is forgiven ere he has confessed his sins by word of mouth. The lost is found, and there is joy in heaven.

The elder son was a picture of the Pharisees, who had served God in a slavish sort of way. They were jealous of the publicans and sinners, and would not share in the same feasts with them. These men, like the elder son, looked for reward for their services, while the truly repentant sinner is willing to give up all worldly honors, and to take the place of a servant, if God will only take pity on him and forgive him; and he is welcomed as a child of God, and there is joy in heaven.

CHAPTER XIX.

PARABLE OF THE UNJUST STEWARD—DIVES AND LAZARUS—THE COMING OF THE KINGDOM—IS IT LAWFUL?—SUFFER THE LITTLE ONES TO COME UNTO ME—THE UNMERCIFUL SERVANT.

JESUS spoke other parables, and this one of the unjust steward was directed more particularly to the disciples, and to those who believed in Jesus, and was to warn them against the sin of self-righteousness. He said, "There was a certain rich man who had a steward, who took care of all his possessions, and the same was accused of having wasted his property. And he called him, and said unto him, 'What is this that I hear of thee? Give an account of thy stewardship; for thou canst no longer be a steward.' And the steward said within himself, 'What shall I do, if my lord taketh away the stewardship from me? I cannot dig; to beg I am ashamed. I am resolved what to do, that when I am put out of the stewardship, they may receive me into their houses.'

"So he called every one of his lord's debtors unto him, and he said unto the first, 'How much owest thou unto my lord?' And he said, 'A hundred measures of oil.' And he said unto him, 'Take thy bill, and sit down and write fifty.' Then said he to another, 'And how much owest thou?' And he said, 'A hundred measures of wheat.' And he saith unto him, 'Take thy bill, and write fourscore.' And the lord commended the unjust steward because he had done wisely; for the children of this world are wiser than the children of the light.

"And I say unto you, make to yourselves friends of the Mammon of unrighteousness, that when ye shall fail, they may receive you into everlasting hab-

THE UNJUST STEWARD.

itations. He that is faithful in that which is least is faithful also in much; and he that is unjust, or unrighteous, in the least, is unrighteous also in much. If therefore ye have not been faithful in the unrighteous Mammon, who will commit to your trust the true riches? And if ye have not been faithful in that which is another's, who will give you that which is your own? No servant can serve two masters: for either ye will hate the one, and love the other; or else ye will cleave to one and despise the other. Ye cannot serve God and Mammon."

Mammon means worldly wealth. The riches we possess do not belong to us, but we hold them in trust, and must give an account of the manner in which they are spent. The owner of a large estate has to have a steward in whom he can place confidence. The steward collects his rents, sells goods, signs all the bills, and handles all the money. This one in the parable being proved dishonest, still further cheats his employer by cutting down the bills of those who had bought goods and had not paid for them. His master found out the trick, but praised the steward for his shrewdness.

Christians must be faithful to their trust, and make a wise use of their wealth and all their powers, not that they may gain earthly friends who live in fine houses, but that they may make friends with the saints above, and secure an entrance in the heavenly home.

The Pharisees, who were great lovers of money, heard all these things; and they mocked at Jesus, with words and gestures. And he said unto them, "Ye are they that justify yourselves before men; but God knoweth your hearts. For that which is highly esteemed in the sight of men, is abomination in the sight of God.

"The law and the prophets were until John the Baptist came, who brought the good tidings of the kingdom of God, and every man forceth his way into it. But it is easier for heaven and earth to pass, than for one mite of the law to fail."

The Pharisees pretended to be very strict in keeping the law, but though men might think them pure and good, God knew that they broke the law every day of their lives. They were harsh in their judgments of publicans and sinners, while their own conduct was that of the worst. Their selfishness and hypocrisy were known to Jesus and he taught them, in the parable of Dives and Lazarus, the danger they were in if they loved the riches of this world too well. He said to them :

"Now there was a certain rich man, who was clothed in purple and fine linen, and fared sumptuously every day. And a certain beggar named Lazarus was laid at his gate, full of sores. He longed to be filled with the crumbs that fell from the rich man's table, food that could well have been spared and cost nothing, but he was left to himself, and to add to his misery, even the dogs came and licked his sores.

And it came to pass that the begger died, and was borne away by the angels into Abraham's bosom ; and the rich man also died, and was buried. And in hell he lifted up his eyes, being in torment, and seeth Abraham afar off, and Lazarus in his bosom; he cried and said, 'Father Abraham have mercy on me, and send Lazarus, that he may dip the tip of his finger in water, and cool my tongue ; for I am in anguish in this flame.' But Abraham said, 'Son, remember that thou in thy lifetime receivedst thy good things, and Lazarus in like manner evil things: but now he is comforted, and thou art tormented.' And besides all this, between us and you there is a great gulf fixed; so that they who wish to pass from hence to you may not be able ; nor can any cross to us from thence.

"Then he said, 'I pray thee therefore, Father Abraham, that thou wouldest send him to my father's house—for I have five brethren—that he may testify unto them, lest they also come to this place of torment.' But Abraham saith unto him, 'They have Moses and the prophets; let them hear them.' And he said, 'Nay, Father Abraham; but if one go to them from the dead, they will repent.' And he said 'If they hear not Moses and the prophets, they will not be persuaded, even though one rise from the dead.'"

The Jews spoke of the happy state after death as "Abraham's bosom," for they supposed that because they were the heirs of Abraham, they would be received into the home above, and richly blessed. But Jesus taught them that one man was no better than another in the sight of God, and that the rich Jew was worse off than the poorest beggar at his gate. God would judge a man by his own conduct. It is no sin to be rich; but it is a sin to use our wealth for our own selfish enjoyment, and to neglect opportunities for doing good that are brought to our very doors. While here on earth we must make preparations for heaven, nor leave it until too late. No one can come back to warn those who are going the downward road. Those who do not hear God speak, who do not strive to obey his commands, will not listen to any message from the other world. They are wrapped up in sin and self.

Being asked by the Pharisees when the kingdom of God should come, he answered them and said, "The kingdom of God—the presence of the Messiah—cometh not when men are looking for it. Neither shall they say, 'Lo here! or Lo there?' For lo, the kingdom of God is within you." The king was with them, and his kingdom was in the hearts of men.

And he said to his disciples: "The days will come when ye shall desire to see one of the days of the Son of Man, and ye shall not see it. They would long for the presence of Jesus, but he would

THE RICH MAN AND THE BEGGAR.

not be with them. "And they shall say to you, 'Lo here! or Lo there!' but be not led away by them, nor follow after them. For as sudden and dazzling as the lightning that flashes along the sky, so shall the coming of the Son of Man be."

But first he must suffer many things, and be rejected of this generation. As it was in the days of Noah, even so shall it also be in the days of the Son of Man. They ate, they drank, they married, and were given in marriage until the day that Noah entered into the ark, and the flood came and destroyed them all. After the same manner was it in the days of Lot; they ate, they drank, they bought, they sold, they planted, they builded. But the day that Lot went out of Sodom it rained fire and brimstone from heaven and destroyed them all. Even so shall it be in the day when the Son of Man is revealed. In that day they were to give up all earthly possessions, nor look back with regret upon the pleasures of the world, lest they be punished as was Lot's wife. Christians are to give up all for Christ; to be useful workers, seasoning their words and deeds with Gospel salt. Seek Christ, hold on, and look not back.

"Whosoever shall seek to save his life shall lose it; and whosoever shall lose his life shall preserve it." Whosoever thinks more of himself and of this life than he does of Christ, shall lose the joy of a heavenly life.

Jesus spoke of the separations that would take place between the faithful and the unfaithful at the end of the world, and the Pharisees, anxious to know the time and place, cried out, "Where, Lord?" And he said unto them, "Where the body is, there will the eagles also be gathered together." They were not to be led astray by any false prophets, but to watch for his coming, and be always ready, for over the whole world would the angels wing their flight and bear away those whose names were in the Book of Life.

Jesus spoke a parable to his disciples, to show that they ought always to pray, and not grow faint or discouraged. He said: "There was in a city a judge, who feared not God, and regarded not man. And there was a widow in that city; and she came oft unto him, saying, avenge me of mine adversary." She had been wronged, and asked for justice. The judge paid no attention to her for some time; but afterward he said to himself, "Though I fear not God nor regard man, yet because this widow troubleth me I will avenge her, lest by her continual coming she wear me out."

And the Lord said, "Hear what the unrighteous Judge saith! And if one can plead with such a man and gain their ends, will not God, who is not an unjust Judge, hear and answer his own, who cry to him day and night, though he is long-suffering on their behalf? I say unto you that he will avenge them speedily." All our wrongs will be made right, in God's good time. "Nevertheless when the Son of Man cometh, shall he find faith on earth?" Our faith is shown by our continuance in prayer. Up to the last hour of life we need to pray to him who has promised to be with us always, even unto the end of the world. He will save all those who come unto him.

Jesus spoke another parable, and this was to those who were self-righteous, and thought themselves far superior to other men. They were Pharisees in spirit although they did not belong to that class. And he said to them: "Two men went up into the temple to pray; the one a Pharisee, and the other a publican. The Pharisee stood up in front of every one else, and prayed, "God, I thank thee that I am not as the rest of men, extortioners, unjust, adulterers, or even as this publican. I fast twice in the week, I give tithes of all my gains."

The publican, standing afar off, would not lift up so much as his eyes unto heaven, but smote upon his breast, saying, "God be merciful to me, a sinner!" I say unto you this man went down to his house justified rather than the other; for every one that exalteth himself shall be humbled; but he that humbleth himself shall be exalted." When we come before God, we must come in a reverent mood, not pleading our own merits, for we are sinful creatures, but asking God to forgive us for the sake of his son, Jesus Christ our Lord.

The Pharisees followed Jesus, not from any love to him, but to see if they could not tangle him in his talk, and put a stop to his preaching. Their question "Is it lawful?" had brought forth sharp answers, and in the parable of the Pharisee and the publican they saw their own likeness. Many of the Jews held the marriage bond very lightly, and if they got tired of one wife would put her away and take another, with no thought that they were breaking the seventh commandment. Jesus told them that God meant by this law that men should lead chaste lives, and be true to the wife they had sworn to love and to cherish.

When it became known that Jesus was about to leave Perea, the mothers brought their young children to him that he might lay his hands upon them and bless them. But when the disciples saw it they rebuked them, and tried to turn them away. But Jesus called them unto him, saying, "Suffer little children to come unto me, and forbid them not, for of such is the kingdom of heaven. Verily I say unto you, whosoever shall not receive the kingdom of God as a little child shall in no wise enter therein."

They were not to be harsh in their treatment of each other. Christians were to be as one family, every man and woman being their brother and sister. Jesus said, "If thy brother sin against thee, go and tell him of his fault when you and he are alone. If he listen to thee, thou hast gained thy brother. But if he hear thee not, take with thee one or two more, that by the mouth of two or three witnesses every word may be established. If he refuse to hear them, tell it to the church; and if he refuse to hear the church, look upon him as no Christian, and have no fellowship with him. Verily I say unto you, what things soever ye shall bind on earth shall be bound in heaven; and what things soever ye shall loose on earth, shall be loosed in heaven." Those who made up the church of Christ on earth, were to decide who should be received into their communion, and fellowship. "Again I say unto you," said Jesus, "that if two or three agree on earth as touching anything that they shall ask, it shall be done for them of my Father who is in heaven. For where two or three are gathered together in my name, there am I in the midst of them."

Then came Peter and said to him, "Lord, how oft shall my brother sin against me, and I forgive him? until seven times?" Jesus saith unto him, "I say not unto thee, until seven times, but until seventy times seven.

"Therefore is the kingdom of heaven likened unto a certain king who wished to make a reckoning with his servants. And when he had began to reckon, one was brought him who owed him ten thousand talents. But forasmuch as he had not wherewith to pay, his lord commanded him to be sold, and his wife, and children, and all that he had, and the payment to be made.

"The servant therefore fell down, and worshiped him, saying, lord, have patience with me, and I will pay thee all. And the lord of that servant being

HE PUT HIS HANDS UPON THEM AND BLESSED THEM.

moved with compassion, released him and forgave him the debt. But that same servant went out, and found one of his fellow-servants, who owed him a hundred pence; and he laid hands on him, and took him by the throat, saying, 'Pay me what thou owest me.' And his fellow-servant fell down, and plead with him, saying, 'Have patience with me, and I will pay thee.' And he would not; but went and cast him into prison till he should pay that which was due.

"So when his fellow-servants saw what was done, they were exceeding sorry, and came and told unto their lord all that was done. Then his lord called him unto him, and said, 'Thou wicked servant! I forgive thee all that debt because thou didst beseech me. Shouldest not thou also have had mercy on thy fellow-servant even as I had mercy on thee?' and his lord was wroth and delivered him to the tormentors, till he should pay all that was due. So shall also my heavenly Father do unto you, if every one of you from your hearts forgive not your brother."

CHAPTER XX.

BETHANY—MARTHA AND MARY—"THE GOOD PART" —JESUS GOES AGAIN TO PEREA—THE MASTER CALLETH THEE—LAZARUS IS RAISED FROM THE DEAD—THE HIGH PRIEST PROPHESIES—JESUS RETIRES TO THE CITY OF EPHRAIM.

BETHANY was a small village about three miles from Jerusalem. Sending the disciples on ahead, Jesus stopped at the house of Martha and her sister Mary, who, being people of wealth, were accustomed to entertaining many friends during the various feasts of the year. But this was no ordinary guest, and his coming made a great stir in the house. They felt honored by his presence, and anxious to show their hospitality, yet at the same time were awe-struck, as if they had an angel to entertain.

MARY AND MARTHA.

Martha had charge of the household, and flitted about here and there, through kitchen and courtyard, to see that all was as it should be. Her idea of

BETHANY.

homage was in placing before the guest the best there was in the house. Household cares absorbed her.

Not so with Mary. She forgot everything but that her Lord was in the house, and in his presence was joy and peace. She sat at his feet, and heard his word, and thought not of hunger or thirst, or life's daily cares. But Martha passing back and forth, and seeing Mary still sitting there, and doing nothing to help her, came in suddenly, and said, "Lord dost thou not care that my sister hath left me to do the work alone? Bid her therefore come and help me."

The Lord said unto her, "Martha, Martha, thou art anxious and troubled about many things; but one thing is needful; and Mary hath chosen that good part which shall not be taken away from her."

There are restless Christians, and there are quiet Christians, both intent on doing their Lord's work, and honoring him by their service. But there is such a thing as overdoing. The one thing needful is to have Jesus in the heart; to love him well, and to show our love by doing good in quiet ways.

It was now the Feast of the Dedication, and it was winter; and Jesus walked up and down in the temple courts, and through the colonnade at the eastern end of the temple, which was known as Solomon's Porch. He was alone, and seeing this, his enemies, the Jews, clustered around him and said, "How long wilt thou keep us in doubt? If thou art the Christ, tell us so plainly." Jesus answered them, "I told you, and ye believe not. The works that I do in my Father's name, they bear witness concerning me. But ye believe not, because ye are not of my sheep. My sheep hear my voice, and I know them, and they follow me. And I give unto them eternal life; and they shall never perish, neither shall any one pluck them out of my hand.

"My Father who gave them to me is greater than all; and no one is able to pluck from the Father's hand. I and the Father are one. Then the Jews took up stones again to stone him. Jesus answered them, "Many good works have I showed you from the Father; for which of these works do ye stone me?" The Jews answered him, "For a good work we stone thee not; but for blasphemy; and because that thou, being a man, makest thyself God." Jesus answered them, "Is it not written in your law, 'I said, ye are gods?' If he called them gods, unto whom the word of God came, and the Scripture cannot be broken; say ye of him whom the Father hath consecrated, and sent into the world, 'Thou blasphemest;' because I said I am the Son of God? If I do not the works of my Father, believe me not. But if I do, even though ye believe not me, believe the works; that ye may know and recognize that the Father is in me, and I in the Father." Therefore they sought again to seize him, but he slipped out of their hands, and went away beyond the Jordan to the place where John first baptised, and there he stayed, and many came to him; and they said, "John did no sign; but all things whatsoever John spake of this man were true." And many believed in him there.

Among his hearers was a young man of great wealth. And he, running up to Jesus, threw himself at his feet, saying, "Good Master, what shall I do to inherit eternal life?" Jesus said unto him, "Why callest thou me good? There is none good but one, and that is God. Thou knowest the commandments. Do not commit adultery, Do not kill, Do not steal, Do not bear false witness, Honor thy father and thy mother."

The young ruler said, "All these things have I kept from my youth up." And when Jesus heard it, he said unto him, "One thing thou lackest yet: Sell all that thou hast, and distribute unto the poor, and thou shalt have treasure in heaven; and come, follow me." But when the young ruler heard this he was exceeding sorrowful: for he was very rich. And Jesus seeing him said, "How hardly shall they that have riches enter into the kingdom of God! For it is easier for a camel to go through a needle's eye, than for a rich man to enter into the kingdom of God." And they that heard it, said, "Then who can be saved?" Jesus said, "The things which are impossible with men are possible with God."

The "needle's eye" was the small gate in the wall of the city, through which the people passed to and fro. It would be almost impossible to get a camel through it, even though he knelt very low and was quite free from baggage. But rich men may be good Christians by using their wealth wisely, serving Christ with it, doing all the good they can, and being worthy and humble followers of our Lord. They are to give up all that make them worldly minded. The poor are rich if they have Christ.

Then spoke up Peter, and said, "Lo, we have left all, and followed thee; what then shall we have?" Jesus said unto them, "Verily I say unto you, that ye which followed me, in the New Time, when the Lord shall sit on the throne of his glory, ye also shall sit upon twelve thrones, judging the twelve tribes of Israel." He meant that they were to share in the glories of his kingdom.

"And every one," he said, "that hath left houses, or brethren, or sisters, or parents, or wife, or children, for my name's sake, shall receive a hundredfold in this life, and shall be blest forever in the land above. But many that are first shall be last; and the last shall be first."

And he spoke a parable to them, saying, "The

kingdom of heaven is like unto a man that is a householder, who went out early in the morning to hire laborers to work in his vineyard. And when he had agreed with the laborers for a penny a day, he sent them into his vineyard.

"And he went out at the third hour—about nine o'clock in the morning—and saw others standing in the market-place idle. And to them he said, 'Go ye also into the vineyard, and whatsoever is right I will give you.' And they went their way.

"Again he went out at the sixth and ninth hour, and did likewise. And about the eleventh hour—at five o'clock in the afternoon—he went out, and found others standing about the market-place. And he said unto them, 'Why stand ye here all the day idle?' They say unto him, 'Because no man hired us.' He saith unto them, 'Go ye also into the vineyard.' And when evening was come, the lord of the vineyard said unto his steward, 'Call the laborers and pay them their hire, beginning from the last unto the first.'

"And when they came that were hired about the eleventh hour, they received every man a penny. But when the first came, they supposed that they would receive more; and they likewise received every man a penny. And when they received it, they murmured against the householder, saying, 'These last have worked but one hour, and thou hast made them equal with us who have borne the burden and heat of the day.'

"But he answered, and to one of them said, 'Friend, I did thee no wrong. Didst thou not agree with me for a penny? Take up that which is thine, and go thy way. It is my will to give unto the last, even as unto thee. Is it not lawful for me to do what I will with mine own? Or is thine eye evil, because I am good? So the last shall be first, and the first last; for many be called but few chosen.'"

There is always work to do in Our Lord's vineyard, and we are to toil with unselfish hearts, and without thought of gain. He has promised to give us our day's wages; and whether we begin to serve him in our youth, or in old age, or near the hour of death, we all share in the same reward, and be received into the blessed home above. We are not to be envious of God's kindness to those who seem undeserving. He knows best; and the humble and faithful Christian will have a higher place in heaven, than those who boast of how much they have done for Jesus, and value their services very highly.

Whilst Jesus was living in retirement, and preaching near the fords of the Jordan, Lazarus, the brother of Martha and Mary was taken very sick. The sisters therefore sent unto Jesus, saying, "Lord, behold, he whom thou lovest is sick." When Jesus heard that, he said to the messenger, "This sickness is not unto death, but for the glory of God, that the Son of God may be glorified thereby."

Now Jesus loved Martha, and her sister, and Lazarus, yet when he heard of his sickness, he remained in the place where he was for two days. Then after that he saith to the disciples, "Let us go into Judea again." The disciples say unto him, "Rabbi, the Jews of late sought to stone thee; and goest thou thither again?" Jesus answered, "Are there not twelve hours of the day? If a man walk in the day, he stumbleth not, because he sees the light of the world. But if a man walk in the night, he stumbleth, because there is no light in him." These things said he; and after that he saith unto them, "Our friend Lazarus hath fallen asleep; but I go that I may awake him out of sleep."

The disciples said unto him, "Lord, if he hath fallen asleep he shall do well." Howbeit Jesus had spoken of his death; but they thought that he spoke of taking rest in sleep.

Then therefore Jesus said unto them plainly, "Lazarus is dead. And I am glad for your sakes and for the increase of your faith, that I was not there. Nevertheless let us go unto him." Thomas therefore, who is called Didymus, said to his fellow-disciples, "Let us also go, that we may die with him." They all knew that Jesus went into Judea again at the risk of his life. He must not go alone. They would follow him, and share his faith.

When therefore Jesus came to the home of Martha and Mary, he found that Lazarus was dead, and had lain in the tomb four days already. The rich had tombs of their own in their private gardens. They were usually cut out of the solid rock, and the body after being first anointed with spices, and afterwards with fragrant oils, was wrapped in white clothes and laid in the niche or vault without any coffin.

Now Bethany was but a short distance from Jerusalem, and many of the Jews had come to Martha and Mary to comfort them for the loss of their brother. Martha, therefore as soon as she heard that Jesus was coming, went and met him; but Mary sat still in the house. Martha therefore said unto Jesus, "Lord, if thou hadst been here, my brother had not died. But even now I know that whatsoever things thou shalt ask of God, he will give to thee."

Jesus saith unto her, "Thy brother shall rise again." Martha said unto him, "I know that he shall rise again in the resurrection at the last day." Jesus said unto her, "I am the resurrection, and the life; he that believeth in me, though he were dead, yet shall he live. And whosoever liveth and believeth in me shall never die. Believest thou this?" She saith unto him, "Yes, Lord, I believe that thou art the Christ the Son of God, he that cometh into the world." And when she had spoken thus, she went away, and called Mary, her sister, saying secretly, "The Master has come and calleth thee."

As soon as Mary heard that she arose quickly, and went to where he was. Now Jesus had not come into the village, but was still at at the place where Martha met him. The Jews, therefore, who were with her in the house, comforting her, when they saw that Mary rose up hastily and went out, followed her, supposing that she had gone to weep at the tomb of her brother.

When Mary came where Jesus was, and saw him, she fell at his feet, saying unto him, "Lord, if thou hadst been here, my brother had not died." When Jesus therefore saw her weeping, and the Jews lamenting which came with her, he was moved and troubled in spirit, and he said, "Where have ye laid him?" They said unto him, "Lord, come and see."

Jesus wept.

The Jews therefore said, "Behold how he loved him!" But some of them said, "Could not this man who opened the eyes of him that was blind, have caused that this man also should not die?" Jesus therefore moved with indignation in himself, cometh to the tomb. Now it was a cave, and a stone lay against it. Jesus saith, "Take away the stone." Martha, the sister of him that was dead, said unto him, "Lord, by this time he is not fit to be seen, for he hath been four days here." Jesus saith unto her, "Said I not unto thee, that if thou didst believe, thou shouldst see the glory of God?"

They took away the stone therefore. And Jesus lifted up his eyes and said, "Father, I thank thee that thou didst hear me. I myself knew that thou hearest me always, but because of the multitude standing around, I said it, that they may believe that thou didst send me." And when he had thus spoken, he cried with a loud voice, "Lazarus, come forth!" And he that was dead came forth, bound hand and foot in his grave clothes, and his face was wrapped in a napkin. Jesus said unto them, "Loose him, and let him go."

Many therefore of the Jews, they which came to Mary and beheld the things which Jesus did, believed in him. But some of them went away to the Pharisees and told them what things Jesus had done. The chief priests and Pharisees therefore gathered together and said: "What are we to do? for this man doeth many wonderful things. If we let him thus alone, all men will believe in him, and the Romans will come and take away both our place and our nation."

But a certain one of the Sanhedrin, named Caiaphas, being high priest of that year, said unto them: "Ye know nothing at all, nor consider that it is profitable for you that one man should die for the people, and the whole nation perish not."

How selfish and cruel were these men! The Pharisees said, "If we let him alone, he will bring us to ruin." The high priest answered, "Save yourselves and let him perish!" But this spake he not of himself; but being high priest of that year, he prophesied that Jesus was about to die for the nation and not for the nation only, but that he might gather into one the children of God that were scattered abroad. In spite of himself, this high priest proclaimed God's will, and prophesied against Israel. And it was the last of the high priesthood among the Jews, for he was proved to be a false prophet.

From that day forth, therefore, they took counsel that they might put him to death. Jesus therefore walked no more openly among the Jews; but went away from thence into the country near to the wilderness, unto a city called Ephraim, and there abode

RESURRECTION OF LAZARUS.

with the disciples. And the passover of the Jews was nigh at hand, and many went up to Jerusalem out of the country, before the passover, to purify themselves. If any man had in any way broken the laws of Moses, he would have to go before the priests and perform certain rites, in order to be made fit to take part in the passover feast.

These pilgrims were friends of Jesus and hoped to find him in Jerusalem. They sought him therefore, but failed to see him, and spake among themselves, as they stood in the temple courts, "Do ye think that he will not come to the feast?" Now the chief priests and the Pharisees had given orders that if any man knew where he were, he should let it be known, that they might seize him.

CHAPTER XXI.

ON THE WAY TO JERUSALEM—THE TEN LEPERS—THE SONS OF ZEBEDEE—JERICHO—ZACCHEUS—BLIND BARTIMEUS—PARABLE OF THE TEN POUNDS—THE FEAST AT BETHANY—MARY'S OFFERING—THE RAGE OF JUDAS.

THE time had now come for Jesus to leave his place of retirement, and to join the pilgrim band that wended its way toward Jerusalem, to the passover feast. He passed along the border of Samaria, to a place in Galilee, and as he drew near one of the villages there met him ten men, who were lepers. Shut out from their homes and the haunts of men because of their loathsome disease, they sat in this lonely place outside of the town walls, begging for money with which to buy their daily bread.

They had heard of Jesus, and knew what great things he had done, and when they saw him coming toward them, even while yet he was a great way off, they lifted up their voices, and cried out, "Jesus, Master, have mercy on us!" Attracted by their cry, Jesus turned toward them, and said, "Go and show yourselves unto the priests." This he said to test their faith. And they obeyed him, and as they were going on the way they were cured of the terrible disease.

One of them, when he found that he was healed, turned back, glorifying God, with a heart filled with love and gratitude, and he fell down on his face at the feet of Jesus; and he was a Samaritan. It is supposed that the other nine were Galileans, and as ungrateful as were all the Jews who lived near our Lord's home. Willing to receive all favors at his hands, they yet turned their hearts against him. They had no love for him.

This saddened Jesus, and he said to the grateful leper, "Were there not ten cleansed? Where then are the nine? Were there none found that returned to give glory to God, save this stranger?" And he said to the man, "Arise, and go thy way; thy faith hath saved thee."

Are we thankful for all that Jesus has done for us? or do we take everything as a matter of course, and go on our way without a thought of him.

As Jesus walked on, he led the twelve disciples away from the public road, and said unto them, "Behold, we go up to Jerusalem. And the Son of Man shall be delivered unto the chief priests and Scribes, and they shall condemn him to death, and shall deliver him unto the Gentiles, to mock, and to scourge, and to crucify him, and on the third day he shall be raised up."

Then came to him the mother of Zebedee's children, with her sons, James and John, saluting him with reverence, as she had a great favor to ask him.

He said unto her, "What is thy wish?" She saith unto him, "Grant that these my two sons may sit, the one on thy right hand and the other on thy left, in thy kingdom." But Jesus answered and said, "Ye know not what ye ask. Are ye able to drink the cup that I shall drink of, and to be baptized with the baptism that I am baptized with."

He was on his way to suffering and death. Were they able to endure the agony of soul, and the terrible death that was his portion?

In their ignorance they answered, "We are able." He saith unto them, "The cup that I drink ye shall drink, but to sit on my right hand and on my left hand is not mine to give, but it is for them for whom it hath been prepared by my Father."

Both of these apostles suffered for the cause of Christ, and in this way drank the cup that he drank of.

When the other ten heard of the request they had made of Jesus, they were sore displeased with James and John. Why should they claim any higher place than the rest? They were hot with rage and jealousy. And Jesus called them to him and said, "Ye know that they which are set to rule over the Gentiles exercise lordship over them; and their great ones exercise authority over them. But it is not so with you; but whosoever would become great among you shall be your minister; and whosoever would be first among you shall be servant of all. For even the Son of Man came not to be ministered unto, but to minister, and to give his life a ransom for many."

A ransom was the price paid for the life of a slave, or to redeem a prisoner from captivity. Jesus laid down his life to save the world from the guilt and power of sin. With his precious blood the bond was sealed. He is our Redeemer.

The twelve who were near him were amazed to see how calm and brave Jesus was, leading the multitude all the way, and seemingly eager to reach Jerusalem, whilst those who followed afar off, were afraid, not knowing what might happen.

They had to pass through Jericho, which at this season of the year, the early spring, was a paradise of bloom. It was protected by walls, flanked by four forts. The palace and the royal gardens were gems of beauty, in which nature vied with art. All around were groves of feathery palms, and here and there stretched gardens of roses, and large plantations of sweet-scented shrubs, so that the whole air was filled with perfume. It was at one time known as the "City of Palms," and had always been an important trading-place, standing as it did on the great caravan road from Arabia and Damascus. The streets were filled with a motley crowd of men, women, and children, and when it was noised about that a pilgrim band was passing, and that the Prophet of Nazareth was with them, the road soon was lined with people, and there was much pushing and crowding.

There was a man in Jericho, named Zaccheus. He was a Jew, and at the head of the tax department. He had heard of Jesus, and had a desire to see him, but could not because of the crowd, for he was a short man. This only increased his anxiety, so he ran on ahead of the crowd, and climbed up into a sycamore tree, so that he might see Jesus, for he was to pass that way.

And when Jesus came to the place, he looked up and saw him, and said unto him, "Zaccheus, make haste, and come down: for to-day I must lodge at thy house."

Think of it! The little man so hidden by the crowd that he had to climb a tree, was singled out

JESUS AND ZACCHÆUS.

and spoken to thus publicly! How did Jesus know his name? All a-tremble with a strange joy, Zaccheus did as he was bidden, and came down in great haste, and joyfully led the way to his house. At this the crowd murmured greatly, because Jesus was going to be a guest with a man that was a sinner.

Zaccheus, having Jesus in his house—that is literally, *in his heart*—was sorry for the deeds of his past life. And standing forth, he said unto the Lord: "Behold, Lord, the half of all my goods I will give to the poor; and if I have wrongfully taken anything from any man, I will return it unto him fourfold."

And Jesus said unto him, "To-day is salvation, come to this house, forasmuch as he also is a son of Abraham." His faith was as great as that of Abraham, and he had been brought into the true fold. He was no longer a "lost sheep," for Jesus had found him, and he was safe forever.

In the morning Jesus resumed his journey, and the crowd continued to follow him.

And as they passed out of Jericho, they came near blind Bartimeus, the son of Timeus, who sat by the roadside begging. He could hear the tramp of many feet and the sound of many voices, and when he heard that Jesus of Nazareth was passing by, he cried out, "Jesus, thou son of David, have mercy on me!" Many rebuked him, and told him to hold his peace, but he cried all the more loudly, "Thou son of David, have mercy on me!"

And Jesus stood still, and commanded the blind man to be called. Those who had kept him back were bidden to bring him forward.

And they went to the blind man and said, "Be of good cheer, arise, for he calleth thee." And he, casting away his garment, arose and came to Jesus. And Jesus said unto him, "What wilt thou that I should do unto thee?" And the blind man said, "Lord, that I may receive my sight." And Jesus said unto him, "Go thy way; thy faith hath made thee whole." And straightway he received his sight, and followed Jesus, giving praise to God. And all the people, when they saw the miracle that had been done, gave praise unto God.

The nearer they came to Jerusalem, the nearer the disciples, and those with them, thought they were to the kingdom of God. There in that holy city, he who claimed to be the Christ, and did such wonderful things, would set up his throne and reign as king over Israel. And those who had left all to follow him, would have high rank and favor; for so it was among earthly kings.

Jesus knew their thoughts, and therefore he said to them, "A certain nobleman went into a far country to receive for himself a kingdom, and then to return. And he called his ten servants, and gave them ten pounds, and said unto them, 'Trade with this till I come.' But his fellow-citizens hated him, and sent messengers after him saying, 'We will not have this man rule over us.'

"And it came to pass, when he came back again, having received the kingdom, that he commanded these servants to be called unto him, to whom he had given the money, that he might know what they had gained by trading. And the first came before him, saying, 'Lord, thy pound hath gained ten pounds more.' And he said unto him, 'Well done, thou good servant, because thou hast been faithful in a very little, thou shalt have authority over ten cities.'

"And the second came, saying, 'Lord, thy pound hath made five pounds.' And he said to him, also, 'Be thou over five cities.' And another came, saying, 'Lord, behold, here is thy pound which I kept laid up in a napkin. For I was afraid of thee, because thou art a hard master; thou takest up what thou didst not lay down, and reapest what thou didst not sow.'

"He saith unto him, 'Out of thine own mouth will I judge thee, thou wicked servant. If thou knewest that I was a hard man, why didst thou not put my money in the bank, that at my coming I might have drawn it from there, with interest.' And he said unto those that stood by, 'Take away from him the pound, and give it to him that hath the ten pounds. For I say unto you, that unto every one who hath, more shall be given; and from him who hath not, even what he hath shall be taken away from him. But these, mine enemies, who would not that I should reign over them, bring hither, and slay them before me.'"

Jesus was going away to a far country, and his servants—his disciples—were to spend the time he was away in preaching his gospel, in making his truths better known in the world. Those who did not add to the gift of the Holy Spirit, did not work for the cause of Christ, were not good and faithful servants.

Those who do nothing for Jesus because they are afraid of doing the wrong thing, are wicked cowards, and not worthy the name of Christians. He will forgive our mistakes; and oh, what a blessed reward it will be to hear his voice saying unto us, "Well done, thou good and faithful servant!"

Jesus arrived at Bethany on Friday, six days before the beginning of the Paschal Feast, as it was sometimes called. The lamb used on that occasion was known as the Paschal lamb.

The pilgrim band went on its way to Jerusalem, many of them to visit among friends, while others would build the booths in which they were to lodge during the feast. Jesus parted from them, and went to the house of Martha and Mary to spend a few days in rest and quiet with these beloved friends.

On the evening of the Sabbath they made a feast for him, at which Martha served. It was at the house of one Simon, whom Jesus had cured of leprosy, and Lazarus, whom he had raised from the dead, sat at the same table with him.

What was there for Mary to do? Martha did not need her services, and for awhile she sat lost in thought. In what way should she show her gratitude to him whom she worshiped, and who had saved her brother from death?

She had an alabaster vase of oil made from the genuine spikenard, which was very precious. It could not have been bought for less than thirty dollars, and this was a great sum in those days.

But Mary did not think of the price. It was not too rich a gift for her Lord and Master, the chief guest in the house.

Stepping softly behind him, she broke the alabaster vase and poured the oil on the feet of Jesus, wiping them with the tresses of her hair. And the whole house was filled with the odor of the precious ointment.

Now there was one at the table who thought such a use of costly things was a great waste. This was Judas Iscariot, who was so soon to betray the Lord, whom he pretended to love. And he said aloud, "Why was not this ointment sold for three hundred pence and given to the poor?" This he said, not that he cared for the poor; but because he was a thief, and having the box, could carry off all that was put therein.

Therefore Jesus said, "Let her alone, for against the day of my burying hath she kept this. For the poor ye have always with you; but me ye have not always."

Mary had kept the flask for a long time, and for some special use. The hour had now come. The person worthy of such a gift was here. What better use could she make of the precious oil than to pour it at the feet of Jesus.

The alabaster vase is a symbol of the loving heart. Broken at Jesus's feet, it gives out all its sweetness, and the house is filled with the fragrance of a Christian life.

Jesus said, "Wheresoever this gospel shall be preached in the whole world, that also which this woman did shall be spoken of for a memorial of her."

Judas was in a great rage, and from that hour gave himself over to Satan.

These two, Mary and Judas, are brought together to show the strong contrasts in life. One gives all she has—becomes poor for Jesus's sake—and is made rich forever. Another seeks the wealth of this world, sells his soul to Satan, and walks forever among the spirits of darkness.

What a memorial he has left. Truly "A good name is more to be desired than great riches."

CHAPTER XXII.

BETHPAGE—THE ENTRY INTO JERUSALEM—PALM SUNDAY—HOSSANA—THE BOYS IN THE TEMPLE—THE BARREN FIG-TREE—WHO GAVE THEM AUTHORITY?—THE TWO SONS—THE WICKED HUSBANDMEN—THE CHIEF CORNER STONE—"SHALL WE PAY TRIBUTE TO CAESAR?"—JESUS NEAR THE TREASURY—THE POOR WIDOW—THE SADDUCEES ASK QUESTIONS—JESUS BIDS FAREWELL TO THE TEMPLE.

The time had now come for Jesus to enter Jerusalem as King of the Jews; and on a bright spring day he set out for the last time from Bethany. When he drew near to Bethpage, to the mount that is called the Mount of Olives, he sent two of the disciples, Peter and John, saying, "Go ye into yonder village, and there ye shall find an ass tied, and a colt with her, on which no man has ever sat. Loose the colt and bring him to me; and if any one ask you, 'Why do ye loose him?' say, 'The Lord hath need of him.'"

Then Peter and John went away and as they came to Bethpage, they saw near a doorway the colt tied to its mother. And as they were loosing the colt the owners came, and asked why they were taking the colt away, And they said, "Because the Lord hath need of him." And they brought him to Jesus, and throwing their outer robes upon the colt, they sat Jesus thereon.

Only the rich could afford camels, and horses were only used for going to war; but hardly any man in the East was too poor to keep a mule, on which to ride to visit his friends, or to go into the city. Jesus, riding on the young ass, gave token in this way of his poverty, and that he came on an errand of peace.

Meanwhile, word had been carried into the city

THE MOUNT OF OLIVES.

that Jesus was on his way to Jerusalem to proclaim himself King of the Jews, and a great multitude went out to meet him.

There were those from Galilee and Perea who had heard him preach, and seen his wonderful miracles.

Many of those who had been cured by him, were also among the crowd; and with them came the Pharisees with hearts full of bitter hatred and jealousy.

On the way the crowd cut down the branches of the palm trees, such as were used at the Feast of the Tabernacles, and with shouts of joy, cried out, "Hosanna to the Son of David! Blessed is he that cometh in the name of the Lord! Peace in heaven, and glory in the highest!"

Some of the Pharisees in the crowd said unto Jesus, "Rabbi, rebuke thy disciples." And he said, "I tell you that if these shall hold their peace, the stones will cry out;" meaning that the ruin of Jerusalem would come sooner than it did. And the Pharisees said to one another, "See how ye prevail nothing. The whole world has gone mad after him."

Slowly up the Mount of Olives, from the southward to the northward came the pilgrim band with Jesus at its head. As he drew nigh and beheld the city of Jerusalem, in all its glory of white and gold, his heart was moved with grief, and he gave way to a burst of sobs and tears. And he said, "If in this day even thou hadst known the things which belong to peace! but now are they hid from thine eyes. For days shall come upon thee when thine enemies shall dig a trench about thee, and compass thee round, and shut thee in on every side. And shall dash to the ground thee and thy children; and leave not one stone upon another; because thou knewest not the time of thy visitation."

All through the streets were heard the tramp, tramp of many feet, and the sound of many voices singing songs of praise and welcome as they passed out through the city gates. Men, women, and children thronged the housetops; and some, who saw the excitement, and did not know what it was about inquired "Who is this?" And multitudes said,

THE ENTRY INTO JERUSALEM.

"This is the Prophet Jesus, from Nazareth in Galilee."

As Jesus entered the temple he looked around, thinking sadly of the time, three years before, when he had driven out those who sold oxen and doves in that sacred place. And all in vain. For here was the same state of things, the filth and noise, and buying and selling going on in God's house. The crowd pressed around him, but Jesus would do nothing until these evil things were driven out, and the temple cleansed. Then the sick, the lame, and the blind were brought to him, and he healed them.

Meanwhile the children in the temple kept on singing, "Hosanna to the son of David," which vexed the chief priests and scribes, notwithstanding the miracles they had seen Jesus perform. And they said to him, "Hearest thou what these are saying?" Jesus saith unto them, "Yes; did you never read, 'Out of the mouths of babes and sucklings thou hast perfected praise?' God puts it into the hearts of little children to praise his holy name.'

In the temple were some from Greece that came up to worship at the feast. These came to Philip, who was of Bethsaida, in Galilee, and spoke to him, saying, "Sir, we would see Jesus." Philip cometh and telleth Andrew; and together they go and tell Jesus. And Jesus answereth them, saying, "The hour is come, that the Son of Man should be glorified. Verily, verily, I say unto you except the grain of wheat fall into the ground and die, it has no growth; but if it die it bringeth forth much fruit. He that loveth his life shall lose it; and he that hateth his life in this world, shall keep it unto life eternal. If any one serve me, let him follow me; and where I am there shall also my servant be. If any one serve me, him will the Father honor. Now is my soul troubled; and what shall I say?

Father, save me from this hour? But for this cause came I unto this hour. Father, glorify thy name. Thy will be done."

Then there came a voice out of heaven, saying, "I have both glorified it, and will glorify it again." Those who stood by and heard it, said that it thundered; while others said, "An angel spoke to him." Jesus said, "Not for my sake hath this voice come, but for yours. Now is there judgment of this world; now shall the prince of this world be cast out. And I, if I be lifted up on high, will draw all men unto me." This he said, signifying in what way he was to be put to death.

The multitude therefore said to him, "We have heard out of the law that the Christ abideth forever; how then sayest thou, 'The Son of Man must be lifted up on high? Who is this Son of Man?'" Jesus therefore said to them, "Yet a little while is the light with you. Walk while ye have the light, lest the darkness overtake you; and he that walketh in the darkness knoweth not whither he goeth. As ye have the light, believe in the light, that ye may become the sons of the light."

Jesus himself was the light of the world, and those who walked with him would not stumble because of the darkness.

There was a little while yet in which they might repent of their sins; and after that they would miss the light of his presence, and understand many things that were now hidden from them. It was not safe for Jesus to remain in the city; so, as the shades of evening drew, he and his disciples went off on the Mount of Olives, toward Bethany, and in a quiet place slept peacefully under the trees.

The next day, Monday, early in the morning,

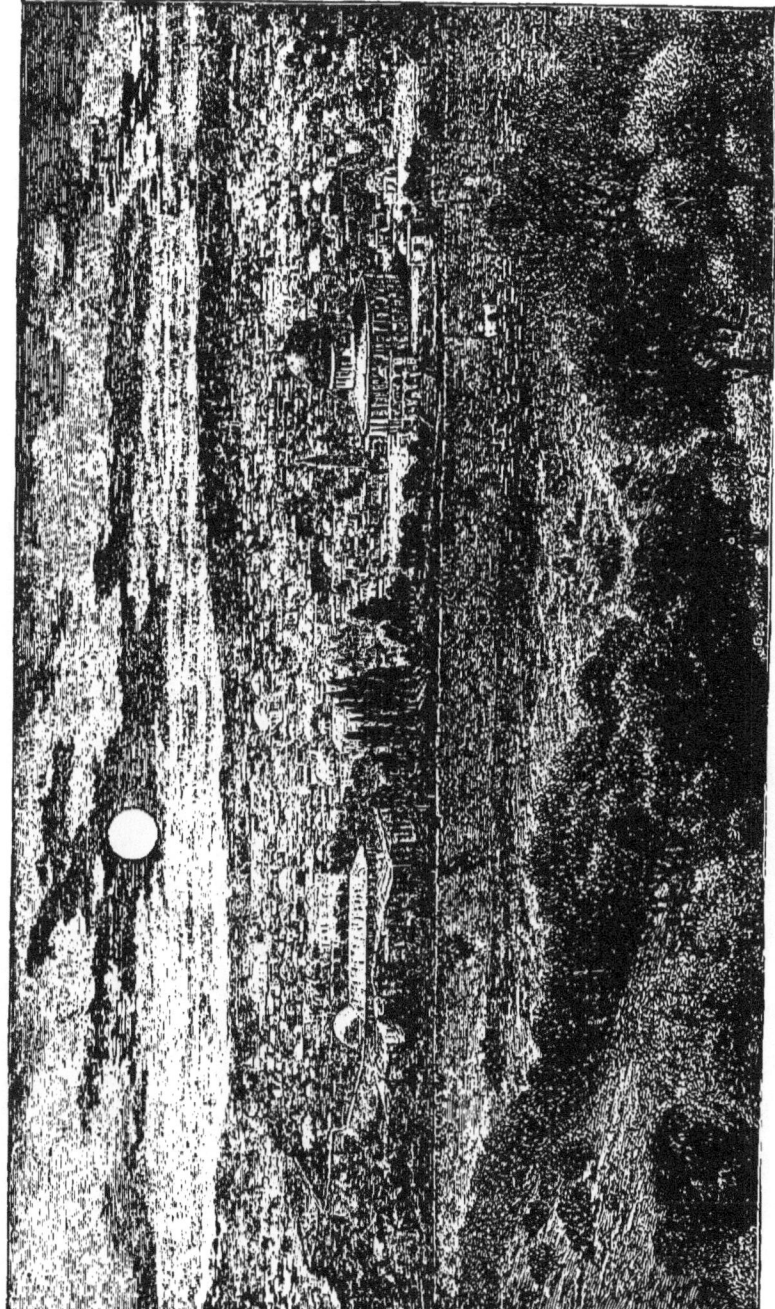

MOONLIGHT ON THE MOUNT OF OLIVES.

Jesus and the twelve set out on their return to Jerusalem. They were in need of food, and seeing a fig-tree from afar with leaves on it, Jesus came to it expecting to find it laden with fruit. But he found neither old nor new fruit on it, nothing but leaves; for it was not the season of figs. Jesus said unto it, "No man shall eat fruit from thee any more forever." And his disciples heard it.

The fig-tree was a type of the Jewish people. They were hypocrites. Their appearance of piety was all a pretence. Their outward ceremonials, were like the leaves that hid the nakedness of the barren fig-tree. They gave the promise of something that was not there. Had their hearts been right they would have felt their need of a Saviour, and would have shown the fruits of Christ's teachings among them.

As the disciples were passing by the next morning, they noticed that the fig-tree was dried up from its very roots. And Peter, remembering, said unto Jesus, "Master, behold the fig-tree which thou didst curse is withered away." Jesus said unto him, "Have faith in God. Verily I say unto you, whosoever shall say unto this mountain, 'Be thou taken up and cast into the sea, and shall not doubt in his heart, but believe that what he saith cometh to pass, it shall be done.

"All things whatsoever ye pray and ask for, believing that God at once answers your requests, ye shall have them." Having faith in God and love for their fellow-men, their prayers would not be selfish, and strength would be given them to do as great miracles as that of the fig-tree.

As Jesus was walking through the porches of the temple on the second day of the passover week, there came unto him a number of the chief priests, Scribes, and elders, and said unto him, "By what authority doest thou these things? Who gave thee this authority?"

The Jews had to go through a regular course of study before they could become teachers, and had to go before the Sanhedrin to be ordained, that is, to receive full orders, and a license to teach, or to judge in courts of law. But this Jesus had not been before the Sanhedrin, and for that reason did they question him. Jesus said: "I will ask you one question. Answer me and I will tell you by what authority I do these things. The baptism of John, whence was it? from heaven or from men? answer me." And they reasoned with themselves, saying, "If we shall say from heaven, he will say, why then did you not believe in him? but if we say from men, we fear the people, for all hold John as a prophet." And they answered Jesus, "We do not know." Jesus, who knew that they could tell if they chose to, said unto them, "Neither tell I you by what authority I do these things." Then in words of love and warning, he said unto them, "There was a man who had two sons. And he came to the first and said, 'Child, go work to-day in the vineyard.' And he answered and said, 'I will not;' but afterward he repented, and went. And he came to the second and said likewise. And he answered, 'I will go sir;' and went not, which of the two did the will of his father?" They said, "The first." Jesus saith, "The publicans and sinners will go before you into the kingdom of God; for John came preaching the way of repentance, and ye believed him not; but the publicans believed, and are saved."

The chief priests and elders, foiled in their attack, began to lay other plans for getting rid of this man. And Jesus, knowing their hearts, spoke to them a parable, saying, "A man planted a vineyard, and set a hedge about it, and dug a pit for the wine-press, and built a tower, and let it out to husbandmen, and then went into another country. When the grapes were ripe, he sent a servant to the husbandmen that he might receive the fruits of the vineyard. And they took him and beat him and sent him away emptyhanded. Again he sent unto them another servant; and at him they cast stones, and wounded him in the head, and turned him out after treating him shamfully. And he sent another, and him they killed, and many others, beating some and killing some outright.

"He had yet one, his well-beloved Son, and at last he sent him unto them, saying, 'They will reverence my Son.' But those husbandmen said among themselves, 'This is the heir; come, let us kill him him, and the inheritance shall be ours.' And they took him, and cast him forth out of the vineyard, and slew him. When therefore the lord of the vineyard shall come, what will he do unto these husbandmen?" They say unto him, "He will destroy those miserable men, and will let out his vineyard unto other husbandmen, who shall render him the fruits in their seasons."

Jesus said, "Did ye never read in the Scriptures,* the stone which the builders rejected, has become the chief corner stone? This is the Lord's doing, and is marvelous in our eyes. Therefore I say unto you, the kingdom of God shall be taken from you and given to a nation bringing forth the fruits thereof. And he that falleth on this stone shall be broken; and on whomsoever it shall fall, it will grind him to powder."

The corner stone is the chief stone of the foundation, joining together two important walls. The spiritual meaning of the parable is this: God is

---

* Psalm cxviii.

Lord of the vineyard, which is the world. The fruits he wishes to gather are the souls of those who have repented of their sins. John the Baptist and others were sent to the Jews, but they had treated them shamefully, and some they had put to death. At last God sent his own Son into the world. Was he treated any better than the others? No, worse. And on that account the whole Jewish nation was to be destroyed, and Christ was to be given to those who would build up the real temple of God—which is built in the hearts of the people. All those who oppose Christ, shall be punished; and those on whom his judgment falls, shall be scattered like chaff before the winds. That is, if they will not repent of their sins.

By this time the chief priests and elders understood that the parable referred to them, and they were more than ever determined to kill him. This they dared not do openly, for they feared the people, but they sent out spies to watch his words, and try to entangle him in his talk. These spies, feigning to be righteous men, came to Jesus with flattering words, thinking to deceive him. And they asked him, saying, "Is it lawful for us to pay tribute unto Cæsar, or not?" This was the same as asking, "Who is Israel's king?"

Jesus perceiving their craftiness, said unto them, "Show me a penny? Whose image and name is upon it?" They answered, "Cæsar's." And he said unto them, "Therefore render unto Cæsar the things that are Cæsar's, and to God the things that are God's." It was right for the Jews to yield to the rule of Rome, and to pay the just tax. Not such wealth did God want. He says unto all of us, "Give me thine heart." It is all that Jesus asks in return for his loving kindness and tender mercy.

Those who had come to entangle Jesus, were caught in their own net, and went away marveling greatly. Leaving those to whom he had been speaking in the porches, Jesus went up the flight of steps which led to the temple, and opened into the court of the women. Here he sat down, watching the crowd. He also had a view of the treasury, a room in which were thirteen chests, with trumpet-shaped

GIVE TO CÆSAR THAT WHICH IS CÆSAR'S.

mouths, into which the people as they passed threw their gifts of money. Each chest, or box, was marked, so that those who put in their money could make it known whether it was to go to the poor, to pay for certain sacrifices, or buy incense, wood, or other things needed in the temple.

Jesus watched the givers, and saw that many of the rich cast in a great deal of money that made a great noise. Presently there came a poor, lone widow, who shrank from the rich ones around her, and seemed ashamed of the small amount she had to give.

It was only two mites that she held in her hand—the smallest Roman coins—each one of which was not equal to one cent of our money. But it was all she had been able to save from her hard earnings, and she would have to go hungry that day for lack of the food this money might buy. Not that she minded this, oh, no. So great was her love that she gave all she had cheerfully.

Jesus saw her, and calling unto him his disciples, said, "This poor widow has cast in more than all they that are casting their gifts into the treasury. For they all did cast in what they could well spare—it cost them nothing; but she, though in want herself, did cast in all the money she had." Then he and his disciples went out of the temple, to spend the night beyond the city wall.

It was now Tuesday, the third day in what is known as Passion Week. And as Jesus entered the temple, there came to him certain of the Sadducees, who believed that when men died that was the end of them. And they asked him if, as the old Jewish law said, it was lawful for a man to marry his brother's widow. And they told a story of a woman who had married seven brothers, and asked, with a sneer, whose wife she was to be in the resurrection.

Jesus said there was no thought of marrying or giving in marriage in heaven, for through the power of God all who entered there were changed, and became as the angels were. They would have no earthly desires, the sins of the bodies would be washed away, but there would be soul-growth, and those whom we had known and loved on earth, with a holy love, we would know and love in heaven.

THE WIDOW'S MITE.

"God," he said, "is not a God of the dead, but of the living, for all live unto him." As the Sadducees did not believe in a life after death, there would be no place in heaven for them.

To the words of Jesus they could make no reply; the crowd itself was amazed at the way in which he had silenced them, and even one of the Scribes spoke out saying: "Teacher, thou hast well said!"

The Pharisees were pleased when they heard how he had silenced the Sadducees but it did not lessen their enmity toward Jesus. And one of the Scribes, a lawyer, asked him a question to test him, saying, "Master, what commandment is great in the law?" And he said unto him, "Thou shalt love the Lord thy God with all thy heart, and with all thy soul, and with all thy mind. This is the first and great commandment. And the second is like unto it, thou shalt love thy neighbor as thyself. On these two commandments hang all the law and the prophets." Love to God and love to man was all the Bible taught from Moses to Malachi.

While the Pharisees were gathered together, Jesus asked them, saying, "What think ye of Christ? Whose son is he?" They say unto him, "The son of David." "How then doth David in the spirit, call him Lord, saying, 'The Lord said unto my Lord, Sit thou upon my right hand till I put thine enemies underneath thy feet?' If David then calleth him Lord, how is he his son?" And no one was able to answer him a word, and they left him, not daring to ask him any more questions.

Then spoke Jesus to the multitude and to his disciples, saying, "The Scribes and the Pharisees sit in Moses's seat, teaching the law. All therefore whatsoever they bid you do, these things do and observe.

"But do not after their works, for they say and do not. All their works are done to be seen of men. They make broad their phylacteries, and enlarge the borders of their garments." Phylacteries were small pieces of parchment on which passages of scripture were written, and were worn at time of prayer on the left arm and the forehead. It is said that the Pharisees wore them constantly for show. The Israelites were bidden to wear fringes around their outer garments fastened with blue ribbon to distinguish them from other nations and to remind them of their duty to obey the law. The Pharisees, believing in the strict observance of the law, made these fringes larger and longer than others.

"They loved the chief place at the feasts, and the chief seats in the synagogues, the salutations in the market-places, and to be called of men, master. But be not ye called master. For one is your Master, and all ye are brethren." They were not to call any one Holy Father, but God, who is the Father of all men. "And whosoever exalteth himself shall be abased; and whosoever humbleth himself shall be exalted." Then, turning toward the Scribes and Pharisees, Jesus pointed out their guilt in doing wrong themselves and leading others astray, and in burning words poured out the divine wrath upon them.

Eight times he pronounced those terrible words, "Woe unto you;" proving by their acts that they were hypocrites. They might appear righteous unto men, but their hearts were full of deceitfulness and sin. They were to blame for all the sins of Jerusalem, and because they were determined to go on in the way their fathers had done they were to be left to do so. And upon them would come the punishment for all the prophets that had been slain since the time of Abel. The Jews by rejecting Christ had brought

JESUS WEEPING OVER JERUSALEM.

the wrath of God upon them, and sorrowfully he lamented over the city he would have saved.

"O, Jerusalem, Jerusalem, that killeth the prophets and stoneth them that are sent unto thee, how often would I have gathered thy children together, even as a hen gathered her chickens under her wings, and ye would not! Behold, your house is left unto you desolate." And he said they should not see him again until they were converted, and welcomed him with hosannas. When he had entered the city three days before, the Jews in Jerusalem had asked "Who is he?" When they had learned to know Christ they would exclaim, "Blessed is he that cometh in the name of the Lord!"

At the end of forty years Jerusalem was in ruins nothing being left of the once handsome city, the pride of the Jews, but the temple, which stood on Mount Zion. Jesus having spoken these farewell words, left the temple courts, and went with the disciples out upon the Mount of Olives.

CHAPTER XXIII.

PARABLE OF THE TEN VIRGINS—TEN TALENTS—PICTURE OF THE LAST DAY—"INASMUCH AS YE DID IT NOT TO ME"—THE PASCHAL FEAST—"LORD IS IT I?"—THE TRAITOR MADE KNOWN.

As Jesus went out of the temple for the last time his disciples drew near to him, and called his attention to the beauty of the holy city, saying unto him, "Master, see what stones and what buildings!" Jesus said unto him, "Seest thou these great buildings? There shall not be left here one stone upon another that shall not be thrown down."

When they reached the Mount of Olives, at a

point opposite the temple, Peter and James, and John and Andrew, spoke to Jesus privately, saying, "Tell us, when shall these things be? and by what sign shall we know that they are about to be done?"

Jesus said unto them, "See that no man deceive you. Many shall come in my name, saying, I am Christ; and he shall deceive many. And when ye shall hear of wars and rumors of wars, be not troubled: these things must needs come to pass, but the end is not yet. For nation shall rise against nation, and kingdom against kingdom; there shall be earthquakes in divers places, and famine and sickness; but these things are only the beginnings of troubles.

Then he warned them of the trials they would have to endure in their efforts to preach the Gospel. They would suffer in many ways, and be the cause of much strife, but those who held out, and stood up for Jesus at all times, and in all places, should have a glorious reward.

They were not to be on the watch for signs, but to watch themselves; to be active in doing the Lord's work. "Lest coming suddenly he find you sleeping. And what I say unto you, I say unto all—WATCH!"

Jesus said, "Learn a parable of the fig-tree. When it is become tender and putteth forth leaves ye know that the summer is nigh. So ye, also, when ye see all these things, know that he is nigh." Jesus told them to be always ready, like faithful servants, "For in an hour when ye think not the Son of Man cometh."

Then he spoke to them another parable, saying, "The kingdom of heaven is like unto ten virgins who took their lamps and went forth to meet the bridegroom. And five of them were wise and five foolish. For the foolish when they took their lamps took no oil in them. But the wise took oil in their vessels with their lamps.

"Now while the bridegroom tarried, they all fell

THE FOOLISH VIRGINS.

asleep, and slept soundly. But at midnight a cry is made, 'Behold, the bridegroom cometh. Go ye forth to meet him.' Then all those virgins arose and trimmed their lamps. And the foolish said unto the wise, 'Give us of your oil; for our lamps are going out.' But the wise answered, saying, 'Not so; lest there be not enough for us and you. Go ye rather to them that sell, and buy for yourselves.' And while they went away to buy the oil, the bridegroom came; and the door was shut.

Afterward came also the foolish virgins, saying, 'Lord, lord, open to us!' But he answered and said, 'Verily I say unto you, I know you not.' Watch, therefore; for ye know not the day nor the hour when the Son of Man cometh." This parable was a word picture of a familiar scene. It was the custom in the East to carry about ten lamps in a bridal procession. These virgins came to the bride's house bringing their own lamps. The meaning of this is that professing Christians were waiting for the coming of Christ, the Bridegroom, who had been far away. The lamps are their hearts, and faith the oil that kept them bright. Five brought their own lamps but no oil to feed them. They may have thought they could get a supply from the other five, but each heart must bear its own light. The faith of others cannot save us. "There is plenty of time," they said, these foolish ones, and so they put off from day to day making any preparation for the marriage-feast.

Then night came on, and they said in their folly, "He will not come now! To-morrow will do." And they fell asleep. Suddenly they were awakened by a cry, "Behold, the Bridegroom cometh! Come ye out to meet him!" Five sprang up with joy and gladness, their hearts burning bright with faith and hope. But five trimmed their wicks in vain. They sought help from others in vain. And when they went out to do the work that should have been done in the daytime, the festive procession had passed in and—the door was shut!

Christ will come when least expected. All our

lives we must make ready for Him. "Without faith it is impossible to please God." Think what a dreadful thing it is to be—too late! We slept when we should have toiled. The day of grace is passed! and forever, forever, will ring through our ears that terrible strain of pitying sadness—"Too late! too late! ye cannot enter now!"

After this parable of the ten virgins—showing the danger of wasting time—Jesus gave the parable of the ten talents. He had been speaking of the kingdom of God, and said, "It is like a man going into a far-off country, who called his servants and delivered to them his goods, and unto one he gave five talents, to another two, and to another one; to each man according to his ability; and he went on his journey.

"Straightway he that received five talents, went and traded with them, and made five other talents, and likewise he that had received the two talents, gained two more. But he that received the one went away, and dug a hole in the ground and hid his lord's money.

"Now, after a long time the lord of those servants cometh to have a reckoning with them, and he that had received five talents came and brought other five talents, saying, 'Lord, thou deliveredst unto me five talents; behold, I have gained other five talents.' His lord said unto him, 'Well done, thou good and faithful servant; thou wast faithful over a few things, I will make the ruler over many things. Enter thou into the joy of thy lord.' He also that received two talents came and said, 'Lord, thou deliveredst unto me two talents; behold, I have gained other two.' His lord said unto him, 'Well done, good and faithful servant; thou wast faithful over a few things, I will make thee ruler over many things; enter thou into the joy of thy lord.'

"Then he who had received the one talent came, and

said, 'Lord, I knew thee, that thou art a hard man, reaping where thou didst not sow, and gathering where thou didst not scatter; and, being afraid, I

THE TALENTS.

went and hid thy talent in the earth; lo, there thou hast thine own.' But his lord answered, and said unto him, 'Thou wicked and slothful servant, thou knewest that I reap where I sowed not, and gather where I did not scatter; thou oughtest therefore to have given my money to the bankers, and then at my coming I should have received back mine own with interest. Take ye away, therefore, the talent from him, and give it unto him that received five talents.' For unto everyone that hath shall be given, and he shall have abundance, but from him that hath not even that which we hath shall be taken away; and cast out the unprofitable servant into outer darkness; there shall be weeping and gnashing of teeth."

We are the Lord's servants, and each one of us has a gift, or talent. Some are more gifted than others, and more is expected of them. If they make it their joy to do their work well, and to add to the wealth of their Master, they will have rich reward. Those who have but few gifts can add to them by putting them to a good use, and if they are faithful to do Christ's work on earth, they will share his joy in heaven.

But what of those who are like the third servant? They do not like their master well enough to work for him. They care only for themselves. They have one gift they might use for the Master's service, but they are idle and ease-loving, and so hide it away under worldly things, fearing, as they say, they might do more harm than good. Christ showed that the excuses of the man with the one talent were false and flimsy. The smallest work for God or for good brings a rich reward.

The talent referred to here was doubtless FAITH, which is given to all. Some have more than others, but, however small our share, we can increase it by prayer and work, and so win the sweet and blessed words of approval, "Well done, thou good and faithful servant!"

Jesus having set forth the danger of waste of time, and waste of talents, now speaks of the glory of his triumph. When the Son of Man shall come in his glory, and all the angels with him, then shall he sit upon the throne of his glory; and before him shall be gathered all the nations. And he shall separate them one from another, as a shepherd divideth the sheep from the goats, and he shall set the sheep on his right hand, but the goats on his left.

Then shall the King say unto them on his right hand, "Come, ye blessed of my Father, inherit the kingdom prepared for you from the foundation of the world. For I was a-hungered, and ye gave me meat. I was thirsty and ye gave me drink. I was a stranger, and ye took me in. Naked, and ye clothed me. I was sick, and ye visited me. I was in prison, and ye came unto me.

Then shall the righteous answer him, saying, "Lord, when saw we thee a-hungered, and fed thee? or thirsty, and gave thee drink? And when saw we thee sick, or in prison, and came unto thee?" And the King shall answer and say unto them, "Verily I say unto you, inasmuch as ye did it unto one of the least of my brethren ye did it unto me."

Then shall he say also unto them on the left hand, "Depart from me, ye accursed ones, into the everlasting fire prepared for the devil and his angels. For I was a-hungered and ye gave me no meat. I was thirsty and ye gave me no drink. I was a stranger, and ye took me not into your homes; naked, and he clothed me not; sick, and in prison, and ye visited me not."

Then shall they also answer, saying, Lord, "When saw we thee a hungered, or athirst, or a stranger, or sick, or in prison, and did not minister unto thee?" Then shall he answer them saying, "Verily I say unto you, inasmuch as ye did it not unto one of the least of these, ye did it not to me." And these shall go away into everlasting punishment; but the righteous into life eternal.

This was a picture of the last day. And when Jesus had finished all these words, he said unto his disciples, "Ye know that after two days the feast of the passover cometh and the Son of Man is to be delivered up and crucified."

Then gathered together the chief priests and elders of the people in the house of Caiaphas, the high priest, and they consulted that they might take Jesus by craft, and put him to death. "Not on the feast day," they said, "lest a tumult should arise among the people."

Now Judas had had hard thoughts in his heart toward Jesus ever since Mary anointed her Lord at Bethany. For Judas was a proud and vain man, and both his pride and vanity were hurt by what Jesus had said at that time. He had hopes that Jesus would set up a throne in Jerusalem, and did not wish to lose his chance of being made one of the chief officers. But as nothing came of the royal entry into the holy city, and Jesus spoke so plainly of his death, the wicked Judas felt that the time had come for him to act. Therefore on Wednesday afternoon he slunk away from the rest of the disciples, and made his way back to Jerusalem, the gates of which were left open during the public feasts.

Arrived there, he went at once to the chief priests and captains to consult with them as to the way in which he should deliver Jesus into their hands.

When the chief priests learned that this man was one of the twelve, who had been with Jesus for the past three years, they were glad, for their way now was safe and clear.

It has been said that "A man's worst foes are those of his own household," and Judas, as well as other false-hearted traitors have proven the truth of these words. Judas need not lay hands on Jesus. He had only to point him out and the officers would seize him.

But was this to be done for nothing? Not by one like Judas. So he put on a bold face and said, "What will you give me?" Now the lowest price of a slave was thirty pieces of silver—less than fifteen dollars—and the chief priests promised to pay this sum to Judas when he delivered his master into their hands.

It was a small sum, but had they offered less Judas would have had to keep to his part of the bargain. And he went back to the Mount of Olives, watching ever for a chance to deliver Jesus into the hands of his enemies.

This was on Wednesday, and all that day Jesus had stayed away from the temple. The people had watched and waited for him in vain. He did not come. The next day, Thursday, was the Passover Feast, when the unleavened bread must be eaten, and the Paschal lamb be killed. The preparation for this feast began shortly after the return of Judas.

Now the Jews, the night before the passover, searched through the house with a lighted candle for any leaven that might be hidden. From ten to twenty persons were gathered as one household.

The lamb was to be kept for four days, and then taken to the temple, and slain by the owner. The priests standing in a row received the blood in silver basins which they passed from hand to hand, until at the foot of the altar it was poured out and flowed through an under-ground channel into the brook Kedron.

The skin and fat of the lamb were then taken off by the householder; the fat being burned on the altar by the priest, and the skin carried home

JUDAS BARGAINING TO BETRAY JESUS.

bound around the lamb. That night the flesh was to be cooked and eaten, and what was left over was to be burned up.

The Jews of olden times were to eat this meal with their loins girded, with shoes on their feet, and staff in hand, as if in haste to start on a journey. But all this had been changed.

Now Jesus was near to Bethany, which is part of Jerusalem, and might have eaten the feast at that place. But Jesus had other plans. Neither he nor his disciples had any home. And where was the Lamb to be killed?

When the day of unleavened bread came, Jesus sent Peter and John, saying, "Go and make ready the passover for us, that we may eat." And they said unto him, "Where wilt thou that we make ready?" And he said unto them, "Behold, when ye enter the city there shall meet you a man with a pitcher of water. Follow him into the house where he enters. And ye shall say unto him, 'The Master saith unto thee, where is the guest-chamber where I shall eat the passover with my disciples?' And he will show you a large upper room furnished. There make ready." And they went, and found everything as he had said. And they made ready the passover.

When the evening was come, Jesus sat down, and the twelve apostles with him. And he said unto them, "With desire have I desired to eat this passover with you before I suffer. For I say unto you I shall not eat it again until the Marriage Supper of the Lamb is made ready."

Then there arose a strife among the disciples as to which should be the greatest in that kingdom. Jesus said, "The kings of the Gentiles exercise authority over them; and they that have authority are looked upon as benefactors. But not so ye."

They were to be kings, but not after the same fashion. "Ye are they," he said, "who have been with me in my temptations, and ye will share in my kingdom." "Simon, Simon," he added, "Behold, Satan hath desired to have you that he might sift you as wheat. But I have prayed that your faith fail not, and when thou hast turned again, strengthen the brethren. For which is the greater, he that sitteth at meat, or he that serveth? Is not he that sitteth at meat? But I am in the midst of you as one who serveth."

Then rising from the table, and laying down his outer garments, Jesus took a towel and girded himself. Then he poured water into the basin, and began to wash the disciples' feet, and to wipe them with the towel which was bound about his waist. This act would usually be done by a servant; but here Jesus, the Master of the feast, puts himself in the servant's place, to teach a lesson in humility.

He cometh therefore to Simon Peter, who saith unto him, "Lord, dost thou wash my feet? It cannot be!" But Jesus said unto him, "What I do thou knowest not now, but thou shalt know hereafter." Peter, shocked at seeing his Lord and Master doing this menial work, saith unto him, "Thou shalt never wash my feet." Jesus answered him, "If I wash thee not, thou hast no part with me." The thought of separation was more than Peter could bear, and feeling in his heart that it was a work of love, he gave up his own will and said unto Jesus, "Lord, not my feet only, but also my hands and my head." He asked for a thorough cleansing, that he might be brought nearer to the one whom he loved. Jesus saith to him, "He that is bathed, needeth only to wash his feet, but is clean every whit. And ye are clean, but not all."

For he knew who had planned to betray him; therefore, said he, "Ye are not all clean."

When therefore he had washed their feet, and had taken his garments, and had sat down again, he said to them, "Do ye know what I have done to you? Ye call me Master and Lord, and ye say well, for so I am. If I, therefore, your Lord and Master, have washed your feet, ye also ought to wash one another's feet. For I have given you an example, that ye also should do even as I did." They were not literally to wash each other's feet, but to be willing to take a lowly position, and to be kind and good to their fellow-men.

"Verily, verily, I say unto you," Jesus continued, "No servant is greater than his lord, neither is one that is sent greater than he that sent him. If ye know these things, happy are ye if ye do them. I speak not of you all. I know whom I have chosen; but that the Scripture may be fulfilled, 'He that eateth of my bread, hath lifted up his heel against me.'* From henceforth I tell you before it comes to pass, that when it is come to pass, ye may believe that I am. Verily, verily, I say unto you, he that receiveth whomsoever I send receiveth me, and he that receiveth me receiveth him that sent me."

When Jesus had thus said he was troubled in spirit, and speaking even more plainly he said, "Verily, verily, I say unto you that one of you shall betray me." The disciples looked at one another, amazed and perplexed, and doubting of whom he spoke, and murmurs of "It is I, Lord?" were heard around the board. As they reclined at table, the head of John, the beloved disciple, was close to the breast of Jesus, and on the left of the Master was Judas, who had no doubt claimed the chief seat at

---

* Psalms xli. 9.

the table, the post of honor. The seats were arranged in the form of a horseshoe, and by this means one end of the table was left free, that the servants might pass back and forth. Peter being opposite John, motioned to him to ask Jesus who it was of whom he spake. John, leaning back on Jesus's breast, said unto him, "Who is it, Lord?" The disciples were still asking "Is it I, Lord? Is it I?" even Judas seeking to veil his guilt, by asking "Is it I, Rabbi?"

Jesus said unto John, "He it is to whom I shall give the sop when I have dipped it in the dish." When therefore he had dipped the sop, he gave it to Judas, the son of Simon Iscariot. And after taking the sop then Satan entered into him. He was as one possessed with a devil. Jesus therefore saith to him, "That thou doest, do more quickly." No one of those reclining at meat understood why he said this to Judas. Some of them thought that as he had the bag Jesus had sent him out to buy something that was needed, or to give something to the poor. But Judas knew what was meant, and having received the sop he immediately rushed out into the darkness of the night.

CHAPTER XXIV.

THE LAST SUPPER—JESUS PRAYS WITH AND FOR HIS DISCIPLES—THE PROMISE OF THE COMFORTER.

JUDAS had gone out, and Jesus was alone with the disciples whom he loved, and from whom he was so soon to part. "Now is the Son of Man glorified," he said, "and God is glorified in him, and God shall glorify him in himself, and that straightway." The Pas-

THE LAST SUPPER.

chal Feast being at an end, Jesus instituted the Lord's Supper, which was to take the place of the Passover Feast and remain as a Holy Communion between Jesus and his disciples.

Jesus took the bread, and having given thanks, he broke it and gave to the disciples, saying, "Take, eat; this is my body, which is given for you. This do in remembrance of me." And he took the cup, and when he had given thanks he gave to them and they all drank of it. And he said to them, "This cup is the new covenant in my blood, which is shed for many for the remission of sins. And I say unto you, I shall not drink henceforth of the fruit of the vine, until that day when I drink it new with you in the Kingdom of God. "Little children," he said, "yet a little while I am with you. Ye shall seek me, and even as I said to the Jews, whither I go, ye cannot come; so now I say it unto you. A new commandment I give unto you, That ye love one another, even as I have loved you. By this shall all men know that ye are disciples of mine, if ye have love toward one another."

Simon Peter saith unto him, "Lord, whither goest thou away?" Jesus answered, "Whither I go, thou canst not follow me now, but thou shalt follow afterwards." Peter saith, "Lord, why cannot I follow thee even now? I will lay down my life for thee." Jesus answereth, "Wilt thou lay down thy life for me? Verily, verily, I say unto thee, the cock shall not crow, till thou hast denied me thrice."

Jesus knew how great would be their grief when he was parted from them, and he longed to comfort them. "Let not your heart be troubled," he said, "ye believe in God, believe also in me. In my Father's house are many mansions; if it were not so I would have told you; because I go to prepare a place for you. And if I go and prepare a place for you, I will come again and receive you unto myself; that where I am there ye may be also. And whither I go ye know, and the way ye know." He was going to his Father's house, and those who knew Christ were on the right road.

Thomas said unto him, "Lord, we know not whither thou goest; and how can we know the way?" Jesus saith unto him, "I am the Way, and the Truth, and the Life. No one cometh unto the Father but through me. If ye had learned to know me, ye would know the Father also. From henceforth ye learn to know him, and have seen him." Soon they would understand many things that seemed dark to them now, for their minds and hearts would be opened.

Philip, being in doubt, saith unto him, "Lord, show us the Father and it sufficeth us." Jesus saith unto him, "Have I been so long time with you, and yet hast thou not learned to know me, Philip? He that hath seen me hath seen the Father. How then sayest thou, show us the Father? Believest thou not that I am in the Father, and the Father in me? The words that I speak unto you I speak not of myself; but the Father abiding in me doeth his works. Believe me that I am in the Father, and the Father in me; or else believe me for his works' sake."

"Verily, verily, I say unto you, he that believeth in me, the works that I do he shall also do; and greater works than these shall he do, because I go to the Father. And whatsoever ye ask in my name, this will I do, that the Father may be glorified in the Son. If ye love me, keep my commandments. And I will pray the Father, and he will give you another comforter, that he may abide with you forever, even the spirit of the truth, whom the world cannot receive, because it seeth him not, neither hath learned to know him. But ye learn to know him, for he dwelleth with you, and is in you.

"I will not leave you comfortless. I will come to you. Yet a little while and the world beholdeth me no more. But ye see me; and because I live ye shall live also. In that day ye shall know that I am in my Father, and ye in me, and I in you. He that hath my commandments and keepeth them, he it is that loveth me; and he that loveth me shall be loved of my Father, and I will love him, and will manifest myself unto him."

Judas saith unto him, not Judas Iscariot, "Lord, how is it that thou wilt manifest thyself unto us, and not unto the world?" Jesus said unto him, "If any one love me he will keep my word, and my Father will love him, and we will come unto him, and make make our abode with him. He that loveth me not, keepeth not my words; and the word which ye hear is not mine, but the Father's which sent me. These things have I spoken unto you while abiding with you. But the comforter, the Holy Spirit, whom the Father will send you in my name, he will teach you all things, and will bring all things to your remembrance that I have said unto you. Peace I leave with you, my peace I give unto you; not as the world giveth give I unto you. Let not your heart be troubled, neither let it be afraid. Ye heard what I said unto you, I go away, and I come unto you again. If ye loved me, ye would be glad that I go unto the Father, because the Father is greater than I. And now I have told you before it come to pass, that when it is come to pass ye may believe. From henceforth I will not talk much with you; for the prince of this world cometh; and he hath nothing in me. But he cometh that the world may perceive that I love the

Father, and that even as the Father gave me commandment, so I do.

"I am the true vine, and my Father is the husbandman. Every branch in me which beareth not fruit he taketh away; and every fruit-bearing branch he cleanseth, that it may bear more fruit. Already are ye clean because of the word which I have spoken unto you. Abide in me, and I in you. As the branch cannot bear fruit of itself, except it abide in the vine; neither can ye except ye abide in me. I am the vine, ye are the branches. He that abideth in me, and I in him, the same beareth much fruit; because, apart from me, ye can do nothing. If any one abide not in me, he is cast forth as the branch, and is withered; and they gather them, and cast them into the fire, and they burn.

"If ye abide in me, and my sayings abide in you, ask whatsoever ye will, and it shall be done unto you. Herein is my Father glorified, that ye might bear much fruit, and become my disciples. Even as the Father loved me, I also loved you; abide ye in my love. If ye keep my commandments, ye shall abide in my love, even as I have kept the Father's commandments, and abide in his love. These things have I spoken unto you, that my joy may be in you, and that your joy may be fulfilled. This is my commandment, that ye love one another, even as I loved you. Greater love hath no man than this, that he lay down his life for his friends. Ye are my friends, if ye do that which I command you.

"If the world hate you, ye know that it hated me before it hated you. If ye were of the world, the world would love its own; but because ye are not of the world, but I chose you out of the world, because of this the world hateth you." Then, after charging them to remember all that he had taught them, he told them of the suffering and persecution they would have to bear in this world, because the world hated both him and his disciples. But they would be strengthened by the Holy Spirit, and have more power among men, because they had been with Jesus from the beginning.

"These things have I spoken unto you," he said, "That ye may not stumble. They shall put you out of the synagogues; yea, the time cometh, that every one that killeth you will think that he doeth God service. And these things will they do, because they know not the Father, nor me.

"A little while, and ye shall not see me; and again a little while, and ye shall see me." Some of the disciples therefore said one to another, "What does he mean by saying a little while, and ye behold me not; and again a little while, and ye shall see me? and of all that he said about going to the Father?"

Jesus, knowing their thoughts, answered them thus: "Verily, verily, I say unto you, that ye shall weep and lament, but the world will rejoice. Ye shall be sorrowful, but your sorrow shall be turned into joy. These things have I spoken unto you in proverbs; but the time cometh when I shall no more speak unto you in proverbs, but will tell you plainly concerning the Father." Hitherto they had not asked anything in his name; but in that day they should ask and receive. "I came forth from the Father," he said, "and am come into the world; again, I leave the world, and go the Father." How well he had read their thoughts! This to them was evidence that he came from God, and they believed in him. Jesus said, "Do ye now believe? Behold an hour cometh, and is even now here, in which ye shall all be scattered—every man to his own home—and will leave me alone. And yet I am not alone, because the Father is with me. These things have I spoken unto you, that in me ye may have peace. In the world ye shall have tribulation ; but be of good courage, for I have overcome the world."

While yet the disciples stood around him, Jesus, acting as their high priest, brought them as an offering to his heavenly Father. Lifting up his eyes toward heaven, he said, "Father, the hour is come ; glorify thy Son, that the Son may glorify thee ; even as thou gavest him power over all flesh, that he might give eternal life to as many as thou didst give unto him. And this is life eternal, that they might know thee, the only true God, and Jesus Christ, whom thou hast sent. I have glorified thee on earth. I have finished the work which thou gavest me to do. And now glorify thou me, O Father, with thine own self, with the glory which I have had with thee before the world was. I manifested thy name unto the men which thou gavest me out of the world ; thine they were, and thou gavest them to me ; and they have kept thy word. Now have they learned that all things thou gavest me are from thee. The words which thou gavest me I have given them, and they received them, and learned to know truly that I came forth from thee, and believed that thou didst send me. I pray for them. I pray not for the world, but for them which thou hast given me ; for they are thine. And all things that are mine are thine, and thine are mine ; and I have been glorified in them. And now I am no longer in the world, but these are in the world, and I pray thee, holy Father, keep, through thine own name, those whom thou hast given me, that they may be one, even as we are one. When I was with them in the world, I kept them in thy name which thou hast given me, and I guarded them, and not one of them perished, but the son of perdition, that the Scriptures might be fulfilled.* But now I come to

---

* Psalms xli. 9.

thee, and these things I speak in the world, that the joy that is mine may be fulfilled in them. I have given them thy word, and the world hated them because they are not of the world, even as I am not of the world. I ask not that thou shouldst take them out of the world, but that thou shouldst keep them away from the evil one. They are not of the world, even as I am not of the world. Consecrate them through the truth; thy word is truth. Even as thou didst send me into the world, I also sent them into the world. For them I consecrate myself, that they themselves may also be consecrated in truth.

"Neither pray I for these alone, but for all those who shall believe in me through their word. That they all may be one, even as thou, Father, art in me, and I in thee; that they themselves may also be in us; that the world may believe that thou didst send me. The glory which thou hast given me I have given them; that they may be one, even as we are one; I in them, and thou in me, that they may be perfected into One; that the world may learn to know that thou didst send me, and lovedst them as thou lovedst me.

"Father, I desire that those whom thou hast given me, be with me, that they may behold my glory which thou hast given me, because thou lovedst me before the foundation of the world. Righteous Father, the world hath not learned to know thee; but I learned to know thee, and these learned to know that thou didst send me. And I made known unto them thy name, and will make it known, that the love wherewith thou lovedst me may be in them, and I in them."

His last thoughts were not of himself, but of those whom he had guided and guarded, and must now leave to carry on the work he had begun.

Our Lord's prayer will not be answered until the

whole world is converted, and united in One Church, and disciples everywhere are One in Christ Jesus. The same spirit must be at work in us, our hope and aim being to grow more like him, and to tell the story of his love so that all the world will be won over to his side, and there will be One Lord, One faith, One baptism. Then there will be joy on earth, and joy in heaven.

CHAPTER XXV.

IN THE UPPER ROOM—GETHSEMANE—THE JUDAS KISS —JESUS ON TRIAL—HE IS SENT TO PILATE—CONDEMNED TO DEATH—CRUELTY OF THE SOLDIERS.

AFTER Jesus had spoken his farewell words, and offered his last prayer in the upper room, a hymn was sung, and then he and his disciples went forth out of the city. It was midnight, and the gates were still open, the streets not yet deserted. Passing down the Temple-mount, on the eastern side, they crossed the valley of the Kedron, the brook being at this time of the year a roaring torrent, and made their way toward the Mount of Olives.

On this mount was a small garden, or orchard, called Gethsemane—a Greek word signifying "Oil-press"—which contained fruit trees, and flowering shrubs, and a place for storing the olives and pressing out the oil. Here in this quiet nook Jesus had been wont to meet with his disciples, and to talk with them; and the place was known to Judas.

As they drew near the garden at this time, Jesus said to the disciples, "All ye shall turn away from me this night." Judas had left him, and so would they. "For it is written," he said, "I will smite the shepherd, and the sheep shall be scattered

IN THE GARDEN OF GETHSEMANE.

abroad. But after I am raised up I will go before you into Galilee."

Peter said, "If all be offended with thee, yet will not I." Jesus saith unto him, "Verily I say unto thee, that this night before the cock crow, thou shalt thrice deny me." Peter spoke even more decidedly, and said "Even if I die with thee, I will not deny thee." And the rest of the disciples said the same.

Soon they came to the Garden of Gethsemane, and Jesus said to the disciples, "Sit ye here, while I go yonder and pray." And he began to be sorrowful, and in sore trouble. He felt as God had left him to meet his foes alone. He was in need of human sympathy, and he said to Peter, James, and John, "Stay here, and watch with me." And he went forward a little, and knelt down and prayed, "If it is possible let this cup pass away from me; nevertheless, not as I will, but as thou wilt." And he cometh to his disciples, and findeth them sleeping, and saith unto Peter, "What, could ye not watch with me one hour? Watch and pray, that ye enter not into temptation. The spirit indeed is willing, but the flesh is weak."

Peter loved the Lord, and promised to stand by him. But alas! being weary, he fell asleep. But Jesus forgave him.

And going away a second time he prayed, saying, "O my Father, if this cup cannot pass away except I drink it, thy will be done." And he came again, and found them still sleeping, for their eyes were heavy. And he left them, and went away a third time, saying again the same words.

And there appeared unto him an angel, strengthening him. And being in an agony, he prayed more earnestly, and his sweat became as it were great drops of blood falling upon the ground. And when he arose from his prayer, he came to the disciples, and found them still sleeping. And he said unto them, "Sleep on now, and take your rest. It is enough, the hour is come. Behold, the Son of Man is betrayed into the hands of sinners." There was no more need of watching. The conflict was over. "Arise, and let us be going, for he that betrayeth me is at hand."

While he yet spake, there came Judas, one of the twelve, and with him a multitude with swords and clubs, whom the chief priests, Scribes, and elders, had sent out to do his bidding. Judas had said to these soldiers, "Whomsoever I kiss, that is he. Take him, and lead him away safely."

When he came unto the garden, he went straightway to Jesus, saying, "Rabbi, rabbi," and drew near to kiss him. Jesus saith unto him, "Judas, betrayeth thou the Son of Man with a kiss?" Then as the men came near with their lanterns and torches, Jesus said unto them, "Whom seek ye?" And they said, "Jesus of Nazareth." Jesus said unto them, "I am he." And Judas was standing with them. When therefore he said unto them, "I am he," they went backward, and fell to the ground.

Again, therefore, he asked them, "Whom seek ye?" And they said, "Jesus of Nazareth." Jesus answered, "I told you I am he. If, therefore, ye seek me, let these go their way. Let no harm come to them." The disciples were wide awake now, and as the soldiers drew near to take Jesus, they said: "Lord, shall we smite them with the sword?" Peter, not waiting for an answer, but acting on the impulse of the moment, drew his sword, and struck one of the servants of the high priests, and cut off his right ear. The man's name was Malchus. Jesus said unto Peter, "Put thy sword back in its place; for all they that take the sword shall perish by the sword. Thinkest

JUDAS BETRAYS CHRIST.

thou that I cannot pray to my Father, and even now he would send me twelve legions of angels? How then should the Scriptures be fulfilled that say these things must be? Suffer ye thus far," he said. And he touched the wounded man's ear and healed him. So kind and forgiving is he even to his worst enemies!

Then turning to the company of soldiers sent out by the chief priests, and the officers of the temple, he said unto them: "Are ye come out as against a robber, with swords and clubs, to seize me? When I was daily with you teaching in the temple, ye stretched not forth your hands to take me. But all this has come to pass that the words spoken by the prophets might be fulfilled. This is your hour, and the power of darkness."

As the armed men closed around Jesus, the disciples drew back, fearing to stay by him lest they also should be seized and put in prison. So they all forsook him and fled. But among those who had joined the crowd was a young man, who had sprung out of bed in great haste, throwing around him only a loose linen wrapper. As the armed men moved off with Jesus, he followed at the rear, not thinking that he was in any danger. But the soldiers attempted to lay hold of him, and slipping from their grasp, he left in their hands the linen garment, and fled, naked.

The armed men led the bound Christ back through the same gate by which he and his disciples had gone forth, and took him first to the palace of Annas. Annas had once been high priest, and was much thought of by the Jews. He was as much bent upon the death of Jesus as was his son-in-law, Caiaphas, but was a calmer and a craftier man. Caiaphas was the high priest of that year, and it was he who had told the members of the Sanhedrin that it was well that one man should die for the people. We are not told what took place before Annas, but he must have decided to take no part in this plot, as he sent Jesus bound to Caiaphas.

The disciples, in their fear, had forsaken him and fled; but Peter and John soon came to their senses, and, turning back, joined the crowd that was now on its way to the high priest. The palace of Caiaphas was built up on four sides, leaving an open court in the middle. John was well known by the servants of the high priest, and he went in with Jesus into the court. But Peter was stopped at the door, and Jesus was lost to his view.

John, as soon as he missed his companion, went out to the waiting-maid and told her that a friend of his was outside, and she opened the door and let Peter in. The maid therefore said unto Peter, "Art thou also one of his disciples?" He answered, "I am not." Now the soldiers and the servants were standing around a fire of charcoal warming themselves, and talking of what had taken place during the night. And Peter also was with them warming himself, for the air was chilly. Presently one of the housemaids drew near, and as the light from the fire fell on Peter's face she saw he was a stranger, and said, "This man was with Jesus of Nazareth." Peter had already told one falsehood, and must tell another to make that good. Therefore he said so that all could hear him, "I know not the man." And at that moment a cock crew.

In the meantime, Jesus had been brought before Caiaphas, who asked him about his disciples and his teachings. Jesus answered him, "I have spoken boldly to the world. I even taught in synagogues, and in temple-courts where the Jews assemble, and in secret I spoke nothing. Why askest thou me? Ask those who have heard me what I said unto them. Behold, they know the things that I have said."

And when he had thus spoken, one of the soldiers

who stood near struck Jesus with his hand, saying, "Answereth thou the high priest so?" Jesus said unto him, "If I have spoken evil, bear witness of the evil; but if well, why smitest thou me?"

Now the chief priests and the whole council sought witness against Jesus to put him to death; but found it not. For many told falsehoods about him, and their stories did not agree. And one stood up and spoke falsely against him, saying, "We heard him say, I will destroy this temple that is made with hands, and in three days I will build another made without hands."

And the high priest stood up in their midst, and asked Jesus, "Hast thou nothing to say? What is it that these men charge thee with?" But he held his peace, and made no reply. Again the high priest spoke, and said unto him, "Art thou the Christ, the Son of God?" And Jesus said, "I am. And ye shall see the Son of Man sitting at the right hand of Power, and coming with the clouds of heaven." Then the high priest rent his clothes, as though mad with rage, saying, "He hath spoken blasphemy; what further need have we of witnesses? Behold, now ye yourselves have heard him blaspheme. What think ye, gentlemen?" And they all declared him guilty unto death.

The Sanhedrin could only try those who were brought before them. They had not the power to put any one to death, but those guilty of a crime deserving this punishment, were sent to Pilate, the Governor. Jesus was therefore given into the hands of the soldiers, who blindfolded him, and did spit in his face, and strike him with their fists. And some struck him with the palms of their hands, saying, "Prophesy unto us, thou Christ. Tell who it was that struck thee!" But Jesus bore all their taunts without a word.

About an hour had passed after the first cock-crowing, and Peter now stood near the gateway leading out to the street. The bystanders had been busy talking of the trial, and Peter had for awhile been forgotten. But now the light from the fire fell more directly on his face, and one of the men, a kinsman of Malchus, whose ear Peter had cut off, said, "Truly this one was with Jesus, the Nazarene, for he is from Galilee." Peter, calling down curses on himself, and calling God to witness that he spoke the truth, said boldly, "I know not the man." Scarcely had he finished speaking when loud and shrill the cock crowed for the second time.

At the same moment Jesus passed by with the armed men, on his way to the halls of Pilate. And the Lord turned and looked upon Peter. Oh, what a look of pity and of love! In the light of that look he knew his dreadful sin. He remembered the word of the Lord, how that he said "This day thou shalt deny me thrice." And, overcome with grief and shame, he went out and wept bitterly.

It was on Friday morning, in the early dawn of a spring day, that the armed men led Jesus unto Pilate, who dwelt in a palace near the temple. Among those who saw the procession was Judas, who knew by this that Jesus had been condemned to death. His soul was moved. The full force of his guilt came up before him. He had not meant to bring about bloodshed! The Jews were going to put an innocent man to death, and he was to blame for this awful deed!

Judas went in hot haste to the chief priests and elders, who were then in the temple, bringing back with him the thirty pieces of silver, he had been paid that night. And he said, "I have sinned, in that I have delivered up an innocent man." And they said, "What is that to us? See thou to it." He had been a tool in their hands, and they had no further use for him.

Judas flung down the thirty pieces of silver in the holy place, and then rushed out of the temple, and went off to a solitary place, where he afterwards hanged himself.

And the chief priests took the pieces of silver, and said: "It is not lawful for us to put them into the treasury, since they are the price of blood." And they took counsel together, and bought with them the Potter's Field, to bury strangers in. Wherefore that field was called "the field of blood" unto this day. Then was brought to pass that which was spoken by Jeremiah the prophet: "And they took the thirty pieces of silver, the value of him whom they priced, on behalf of the sons of Israel. And they gave them for the Potter's Field, as the Lord commanded me." *

It was still early in the morning when the Jews led Jesus into the judgment hall. But they went not in themselves, lest they should lose the Passover Feast, which had been sadly interrupted. The night was flying fast. Jerusalem was filled with people, and many of the Jews had rushed to the garden, hoping to return and finish their meal at daybreak. They had hurried to the house of Annas, hoping to deliver Jesus into his hands. Failing in this they made haste to Caiaphas, and now they had come to Pilate's house. Already had they wasted too much time, and with every appearance of haste they brought Jesus before Pilate.

Pilate, therefore, saith unto them, "What accusation bring ye against this man?" They answered him, "If this man were not an evildoer we should not

---

* Zach. xi. 13.

have delivered him up unto thee. We found this man giving false directions to our people, forbidding them to pay tribute to Cæsar, and saying that he himself is the Christ, and a king."

Then said Pilate unto them: "Take him yourselves and judge him." The Jews said: "It is not lawful for us to put any man to death." The Jewish mode of putting to death was by stoning; but it had been foretold that Christ should be lifted up on high," which meant that he should be put to death on the cross. And this mode of punishment could be inflicted by the Roman power alone. Pilate, therefore, entered again into the palace, and calling Jesus, said unto him: "Art thou the King of the Jews?" Jesus answered: "Sayest thou this of thyself, or did others speak concerning me?" Pilate answered, "Am I a Jew? Thine own nation and the chief priests delivered thee unto me. What hast thou done?"

Jesus answered: "My kingdom is not of this world; if it were of this world then would my servants strive that I should not be delivered up unto the Jews." Pilate said unto him, "Art thou then a king?" Jesus said, "Thou sayest it. To this end have I been born, and for this cause came I into the world, that I should bear witness of the truth. Every one that is of the truth heareth my voice."

Pilate said unto him, "What is truth?" And when he had thus spoken, he went out to the chief priests and the multitudes, and said unto them, "I find no fault in this man." This only made them the more fierce; and they cried out, "He stirreth up the people, teaching throughout all Judea, and beginning from Galilee even unto this place."

When Pilate heard the name of Galilee, he asked whether the man were a Galilean. Learning that he came from that part of the country, which was under

Herod's authority, he sent him unto Herod, who was also in Jerusalem in these days.

When Herod saw Jesus, he was exceeding glad; for he had been for a long time anxious to see him, because he had heard many things concerning him, and hoped to see some miracle done by him. And he questioned him with many words, but Jesus answered him nothing. And all the while the chief priests and Scribes stood by, loudly accusing him.

And Herod with his attending bodyguard treated him with scorn and contempt, and mocked at him with sneering words and gestures. And Herod had him arrayed in a scarlet robe, in mockery of his claim to royalty, and sent him back to Pilate. And that very day Pilate and Herod became friends with each other, for before they were at enmity, having had a serious quarrel.

Pilate, when he had called together the rulers and the people, said unto them, "Ye have brought unto me this man as one that stirreth up the people, and behold, I, having examined him before you, find no fault in him concerning the things whereof ye accuse him."

Now it was customary at this feast, for the Governor to set free any prisoner that the people desired. And there was in prison at that time, a wicked man named Barabbas, who was guilty of murder. When therefore the elders were gathered together, Pilate said unto them, "Whom will ye that I release unto you; Barabbas or Jesus who is called the Christ?" For he knew that for envy because of his popularity with the common people, they had delivered him up on a false charge.

While Pilate was sitting on the judgment seat, his wife sent unto him, saying, "Have thou nothing to do with that just man; for I have suffered much this day in a dream because of him." This was a warning sent from God, but Pilate paid no heed to it. While he was listening to the messenger, however, the chief priests and the elders had persuaded the multitudes to ask for the release of Barabbas. And when the Governor said unto them, "Which of the two will I release unto you?" they shouted "Barabbas!"

Pilate saith unto them, "What then shall I do with Jesus, who is called Christ?" They cried out, "Crucify him! Crucify him!" Pilate willing to release him, spoke to them again, but they cried the more, "Crucify him! Crucify him!" And he said unto them the third time, "Why, what evil hath this man done? I have found no cause of death in him. I will therefore scourge him and let him go." But the mob cried out even more loudly, "Crucify him! Crucify him!"

When Pilate saw that his words were of no avail, and that there was danger of a disturbance, he took water and washed his hands before the multitude, saying, "I am innocent of the blood of this righteous man; see ye to it." Then answered all the people, and said, "His blood be on us, and our children." Then Barabbas was set free, and sentence of death was passed upon Jesus. Did washing of his hands free Pilate from the guilt of having shed innocent blood? Would water cleanse his soul from so great a sin? No. And his crime was the greater because he knew Jesus to be an innocent man. And this thought still disturbed him.

Jesus was first scourged, and this Roman scourging was a fearful punishment, and only inflicted upon slaves. The prisoner was stripped to the waist, and bound to a post in a stooping posture, so that the skin of the back was tightly stretched. The whips were leather straps with bits of lead or of bone

CHRIST BEFORE THE PEOPLE.

made fast to them. These cut into the back, and caused such agony that the poor victims frequently fainted, and sometimes died. The soldiers who had Jesus in charge were not likely to be mild in this case, and, oh, what must his sufferings have been when under the lash in such cruel hands?

But this was not all. The soldiers then took him into the room where prisoners were confined, and here they amused themselves. They plaited a crown of thorns and put it on his head, and they put on him a purple robe. And they came unto him with mock ceremony, saying, "Hail, King of the Jews!" and giving him blows with their hands. And Pilate went out again, and saith unto the crowd, "Behold, I bring him out unto you, that ye may perceive that I find no crime in him."

Jesus therefore came forth, wearing the crown of thorns, and the purple robe, and Pilot saith unto them, "Behold the man!" When therefore the chief priests and elders saw him, they cried out, "Crucify him! Crucify him!"

Pilate said, "Take him yourselves and crucify him; for I find no crime in him." The Jews answered, "We have a law, and by the law he ought to die because he made himself Son of God." When Pilate heard that, he was more afraid. And he went again into the judgment hall, and saith unto Jesus, "Whence art thou?" But Jesus made him no answer. Then said Pilate, "Wilt thou not speak to me? Dost thou not know that I have power to release thee, and power to crucify thee?" Jesus answered, "Thou wouldst have no power against me unless it were given thee from above."

Upon this Pilate sought even yet to release him; but the Jews cried out, saying, "If thou let this man go thou art not Cæsar's friend. Every one who maketh himself a king speaketh against Cæsar."

362   THE LIFE OF JESUS CHRIST.

These words had weight with Pilate, for it was his ambition to be on good terms with the Emperor of Rome, to be regarded with friendship by the great Cæsar Augustus. Rather for him the glories of this

THE WHIPPING POST.

world, than the honor of being a friend of Jesus. And won over by his pride and vanity, he sat down once more on the judgment seat at a place called the PAVEMENT, where the floor was beautifully laid out in mosaic work of small colored stones.

Day was already dawning, when Pilate said unto the Jews, "Behold, your King!" But they cried

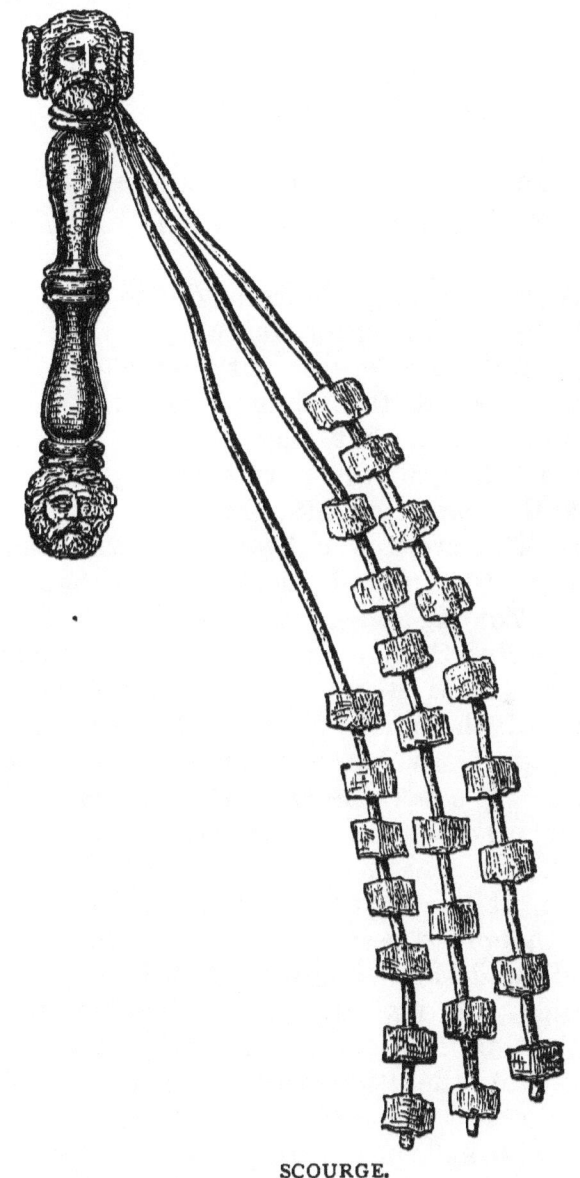

SCOURGE.

out, "Away with him! Away with him! Crucify him!" Pilate saith, "Shall I crucify your King?"

The chief priests answered, "We have no King but Cæsar." Then therefore he delivered Jesus up to them to be crucified.

CHAPTER XXVI.

THE WAY TO THE CROSS—THE CRUCIFIXION—THE BURIAL—THE ASCENSION—"HE IS RISEN!"

The chief priests and elders made no delay, but hurried Jesus to his cruel death. The place of execution was outside of the city, on a small rise of ground, called at that time Golgotha, because it was shaped somewhat like a skull. The soldiers having taken off the purple robe, put on him his own clothes, and led him forth, he bearing his own cross. The cross was heavy and the end of it dragged on the ground; so, looking around, the soldiers saw coming across the field a black man named Simon, of Cyrene, and him they compelled to help Jesus bear the cross. But it was the lighter end of the cross he carried, Jesus bearing the heavier part on his own shoulders. And so it is always. We may be sure that Jesus is helping us bear all our crosses and trials.

Heavy though they seem we shall not faint under them, if we put our trust in him. The weight of the cross rests on his shoulders.

There followed him a great crowd of women, who bewailed and lamented him. Not because of any affection or friendship they had for Jesus, but because of the sympathy of their sex, with all those who are afflicted. Some few there may have been who had heard Jesus speak at various times, and wept and wailed over his cruel fate. Jesus, turning to them said, "Daughters of Jerusalem, weep not for me, but weep for yourselves and your children." And he warned them of the ruin that was to come upon Jerusalem, when it would be a curse rather than a blessing to be a mother. For in that great day of God's wrath, they would say to the mountains, "Fall on us," and to the hills, "Cover us." This literally took place at the destruction of Jerusalem, forty years after

JESUS CROWNED WITH THORNS.

the crucifixion, when the Jews hid themselves in the underground passages and the sewers of the city.

"If they do these things in the green tree," said our Lord, "what shall be done in the dry?" If he, the "green tree" and the fruitful vine, could be made to suffer thus for sins of which he was innocent, how ought they, the dry and unfruitful trees, to suffer for the sins of which they themselves were guilty.

When they reached Golgotha Jesus was made fast to the cross by nails, which were driven through the hands and feet. Then the cross was lifted and let fall into the hole dug for it, and this gave to the sufferer another and more violent shock. Even in the midst of his agony, Jesus thought of the

CARRYING THE CROSS.

sinners who nailed him to the cross, and full of forgiving love and pity he prayed aloud, "Father, forgive them; for they know not what they do." The crowd kept moving about, gazing upon the scene, and wagging their heads as they passed by. And the chief priests, Scribes, and elders scoffed at him, saying, "He saved others; let him save himself, if he be the Christ, the chosen one of God."

THE CRUCIFIXION.

And the soldiers also mocked him, coming to him and offering him the vinegar, or sour wine, they used at their midday meal. For it was now the hour of noon. And they said, "If thou art the King of the Jews save thyself."

Now, there were two thieves crucified with Jesus, one on his right hand, the other on his left. Over the head of each one was written the crime for which he suffered; and Pilate had had put on the cross of Jesus, in large letters, JESUS OF NAZARETH, KING OF THE JEWS. And this was in Hebrew, Latin, and Greek, so that all who passed by might be able to read it.

The chief priests of the Jews, therefore, said to Pilate: "Write not 'The King of the Jews,' but 'The man that said I am king of the Jews.'" Pilate, whose sole aim was to mock at them, and their desire for a kingdom of their own, answered them: "What I have written, I have written."

One of the thieves, hearing the mob mock at Jesus, joined in their taunts, saying: "If thou art the King of the Jews, save thyself and us." But the other rebuked him, saying: "Dost thou not even fear God, seeing thou art suffering the same punishment as this one? We, indeed, suffer justly, for we receive the due reward of our deeds; but this man has done no wrong." And, repenting of his sins, at this the eleventh hour, he said unto Jesus: "Lord, remember me when thou comest into thy kingdom!" And Jesus said unto him: "Verily, I say unto thee, *to-day* shalt thou be with me in paradise."

Near the cross of Jesus stood his mother, and his mother's sister, Mary, the wife of Cleophas, and Mary Magdalene. When Jesus saw his mother and the disciple whom he loved standing by her, he saith to his mother, "Woman, behold thy son!" And he saith to John, "Behold thy mother!" And from that hour the disciple took her into his own home, and cared for her all the rest of her life.

Jesus was crucified at nine o'clock in the morning, and at noon, when the sun should have shone the brightest, a thick cloud began to gather over the sky, and the darkness kept increasing until three o'clock in the afternoon, and not a sigh or a groan was heard from the sufferer on the cross. He had hung there for six long hours, and his sufferings were great. The woes of the flesh forced him to cry out, "My God, my God, why hast thou forsaken me?" He felt in his misery as if God had deserted him. He spoke in Hebrew, saying, "Eli, Eli, lama sabacthani?" And some of those that stood there said: "This man calleth for Elijah."

There was a bowl there containing the vinegar, and straightway one of the soldiers took a sponge, and, dipping it into the vinegar, put it on the end of a reed, and brought it to his mouth so that he could drink. The others tried to stop him, saying, "Let him be. Let us see if Elijah cometh to save him." But Jesus said with a loud voice, "I thirst;" and when he received the vinegar, he drank it, and said: "It is finished."

The victory was won! The work he had come to do was finished! And he bowed his head, and yielded up his spirit!

And there was darkness all over Jerusalem. Deep midnight darkness, for there was no light of the sun. The veil of the temple was torn in two from the top to the bottom. The earth quaked, and the rocks were broken. The tombs were opened, and the bodies of the saints were raised and appeared unto many after the resurrection of our Lord. The centurion, who stood with his soldiers under the cross, had witnessed many scenes of horror, but none like this. And when he saw and heard what took place

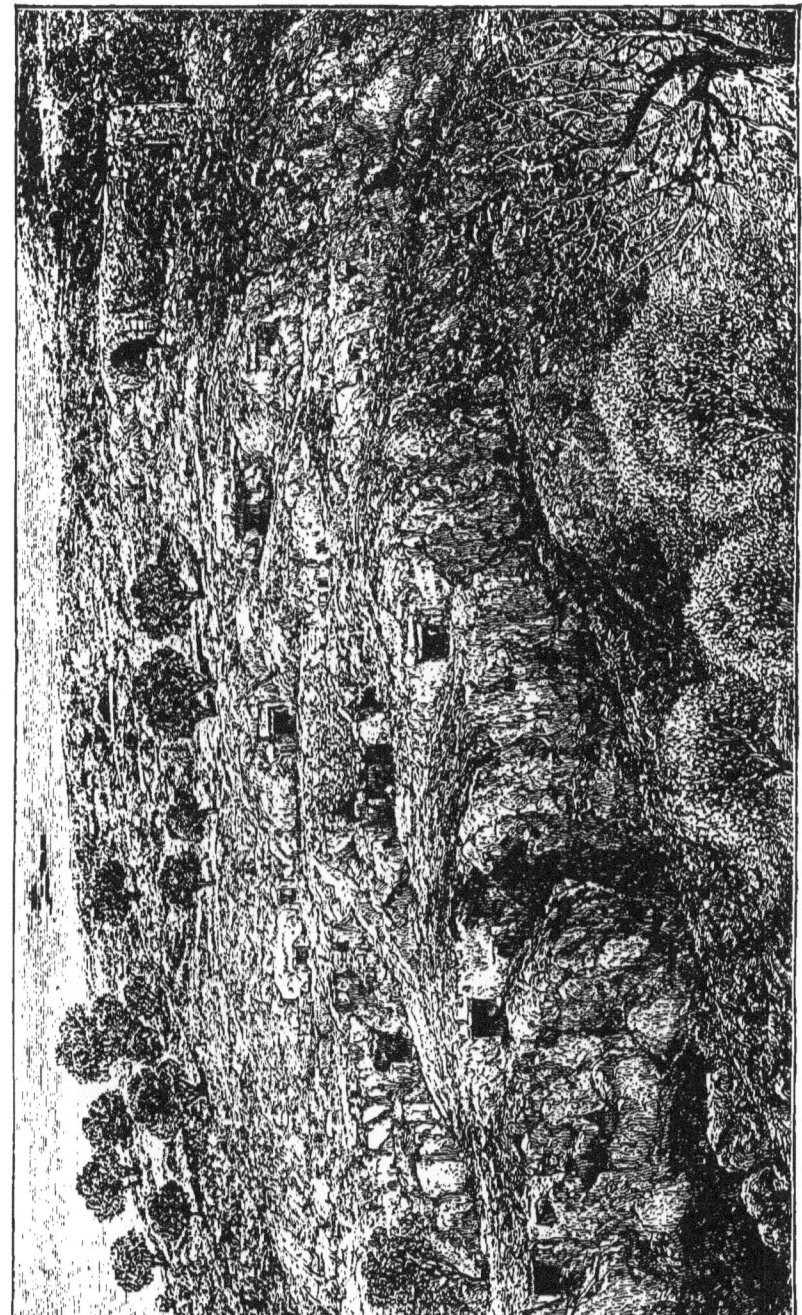

ACELDAMA, OR THE FIELD OF BLOOD.

it was forced upon his mind and heart that the Jews had made a grave mistake. They had not only punished an innocent man; they had done worse. And repenting of his own sins, and obeying God's command by believing in Jesus, he exclaimed, "Truly this was the Son of God!"

Nor was the Jewish law that no dead bodies should remain unburied over night, nor should any hang upon the cross on the Sabbath day. The Jews' Sabbath began on Friday evening, at sunset, and lasted until sunset of the next day, and there were special reasons why they were anxious to bury the dead out of their sight. For it was a "high day," a holy day in the church, and a sacred part of the Passover Feast. Therefore the chief priests and elders went to Pilate and begged that the legs of those on the cross might be broken and the bodies taken away.

It was slow death to die on the cross, the sufferings often lasting, not only for hours, but for days. The breaking of the legs, which was done with a club or hammer, would not cause death, but would hasten it. Pilate consented that this should be done, and the soldiers therefore came and broke the legs of the two thieves, who hung on either side of Jesus. But when they came to Jesus and found that he was dead already, they broke none of his bones.

One of the soldiers, fearing that Jesus might not be dead, thrust the iron point of his spear into the side of him who hung upon the cross, and straightway there came forth blood and water. The *blood* was a sign of the life laid down for the sins of the world. The *water* of the baptism, or gift, of the Holy Spirit.

John must have seen this, for he says in his Gospel: "He that saw it bare witness, and his witness is true; and he knoweth that he saith true, that ye also may believe. For these things were done that the Scripture might be fulfilled. 'A bone of him shall not be broken.' * And elsewhere it saith, 'They shall look on him whom they pierced.' " †

Now, there was in Jerusalem a certain rich man named Joseph, whose birthplace was at Arimathea. Although a member of the Sanhedrin, he was at heart a disciple of Jesus, and took no part in his murder. Fearing that some harm might be done to the body of his Lord by his cruel enemies, he went boldly to Pilate, and asked that he might take the body away.

Pilate wondered if Jesus were already dead ; and calling the centurion to him, asked him whether he had been dead for any length of time. Finding that he had, Pilate gave his consent that Joseph should take charge of the body.

Joseph, and those with him, took the sacred body from the cross. After removing from the hands and feet those dreadful nails, and wrapping it in fine linen cloth, they bore it to the rock-hewn tomb in a garden near by. The tomb was new, and no one had ever been buried there ; and as Joseph was a rich man he had doubtless spent much money in adorning this resting-place for the dead. For the garden, or cemetery, was quite near the city.

Afterwards came Nicodemus—he who came to Jesus by night—and he brought with him about a hundred pounds of myrrh and aloes, and they embalmed the body, wrapping it in linen clothes after the manner in which the Jews prepare their dead for burial.

Then they laid the body inside the tomb, and as they went out they rolled the large stone to close the entrance, and fixed it so it would not

---

* Psalms xxxiv. 20.
† Zach. xii. 10. Rev. i. 7.

THE DESCENT FROM THE CROSS.

fall. For the next day, Sunday though it was, the Jews would place their seal upon the tomb so that the door could not be opened without their knowing it.

LAYING JESUS IN THE TOMB.

The crowd who had watched the crucifixion had gone to their several homes, all except the few faithful women who had come with Jesus of Galilee. These watched to see what was done with

Jesus, and when they saw where his body was laid, and with what haste it had been buried, they went away to prepare spices and ointments to still further anoint it.

The next day, which was the Jewish Sabbath, the chief priests and Pharisees came to Pilate, saying, "Sir, we remember that that deceiver said while he was yet alive, 'After three days I rise again.' Command therefore that the sepulchre be made sure until the third day, lest his disciples come and steal him away, and say unto the people, 'He is risen from the dead.' The last deceit then will be worse than the first."

Pilate said unto them, "Take a guard of soldiers, and make it as sure as ye know how." So they went, and stretching a string across the great stone they sealed it to the rock at either end with wax, and left the soldiers there to watch the tomb.

Early the next morning, while it was yet dark, the women set out for the tomb in the garden with their spices to anoint the body of Jesus. And while they were on the way there came a great earthquake; for an angel of the Lord descended from heaven and came and rolled away the great stone and sat upon it. His appearance was dazzling, and his garments as white as snow; and at sight of him the watchers quaked with fear, and became as dead men.

Mary Magdalene, in her haste, was first at the tomb; and seeing the stone rolled away, she stopped not to ask questions, but ran at once to Peter and John, and said unto them, "They have taken the Lord out of the tomb, and we know not where they have laid him."

Meanwhile the other women on reaching the tomb, and seeing the stone rolled away, and the angel seated upon it, were in great terror. But the angel said to them, "Be not afraid, for I know that ye seek Jesus, who hath been crucified: He is not here; for he is risen even as he said. Come, see the place where the Lord lay, and go tell his

HE IS RISEN.

disciples that he is risen from the dead, and lo, he goeth before you into Galilee. There shall ye see him; lo, I have told you." And they departed from the tomb with fear and great joy, and ran to tell his disciples. And as they went, Jesus met them, and saluted them, saying, "All hail!" And they came and took hold of his feet, and worshiped him. Then saith Jesus to them, "Fear not; go and tell my brethren, that they depart into Galilee, and there they shall see me."

When Mary Magdalene told Peter and John that the Lord had been taken away, both of the disciples set out to the tomb to see if her words were true. They ran all the way, but John, being a younger man, outran Peter, and came first to the place. And stooping down and looking in, and seeing the linen clothes lying about, he was filled with awe and dared not enter.

Not so Peter, however. As soon as he came up, he went at once into the tomb, and seeth the linen clothes lying there. And he saw also, what John had not seen, that the napkin which had been bound upon his head was laid carefully in a place by itself. Peter's boldness gave courage to John, and he went into the tomb, and saw that Jesus had not been taken away by human hands. All doubts and fears were at rest, and John believed now more fully than ever that he was indeed the Son of God. For not even yet had they learned that he must rise again from the dead. Therefore, believing that it was of no use to search for him, the two disciples left the garden and went back to their own homes.

Mary had followed them when they first ran to the tomb, but failing to keep up with them, did not reach there until after they had left. And she stood weeping and lamenting, and as she wiped the tears from her eyes, she stooped down, and looking into the tomb, beheld two angels in white sitting there, one at the head

JESUS APPEARING TO MARY MAGDALEN.

and the other at the feet, where the body of Jesus had lain. And they said unto her, "Woman, why weepest thou?" She said, "They have taken away my Lord, and I know not where they have laid him." When she had thus said, she turned around, and beheld Jesus standing near, but did not know that it was Jesus.

Jesus saith unto her, "Woman, why weepest thou? Whom seekest thou?" She, supposing him to be the gardener, saith unto him, "Sir, if thou didst bear him hence, tell me where thou hast laid him, and I will take him away." Jesus saith unto her, "Mary." She turneth herself, and with the glad cry of "Rabboni!—Master!"—would fain have fallen at his feet and held him fast in her grasp. Jesus said unto her, "Touch me not; for I am not yet ascended to the Father; but go to my brethren, and say unto them, I ascend unto my Father and your Father; and my God and your God." And Mary Magdalene came and said to the disciples, "I have seen the Lord!" and told them what he had said unto her.

In the meantime some of the soldiers who had been on guard came into the city, and told the chief priests all that had taken place. And they called a meeting of the Sanhedrin, and took counsel together, and gave a large sum of money to the soldiers, telling them to say that the disciples of Jesus came by night and stole him away while they slept.

But it is a crime punished with death for a soldier to fall asleep at his post, and the soldiers were unwilling to run any such risk. But the chief priests and elders said that if Pilate took any notice of the matter they would make it all right with him, and no harm whatever should come to the soldiers. So they took the money that was given them, and did as they were told. And for a long time the Jews believed that the body of Jesus had been taken away by his disciples, and that he had not risen from the dead.

CHAPTER XXVII.

EASTER SUNDAY—THE WOMEN AT THE TOMB—PETER AND JOHN—WHY WEEPEST THOU?—THE WALK TO EMMAUS—JESUS SHOWS HIMSELF TO HIS DISCIPLES—DOUBTING THOMAS—THE HEAVY NET—"FEED MY LAMBS"—THE DAY OF PENTECOST.

On the afternoon of that Easter Sunday, on which Jesus rose from the dead, two of the disciples left the circle of friends, and went out of the city. Passing out through the western gate, and turning to the north, they wandered along by the quiet nooks, the lovely gardens, enjoying the sweet fragrance in the air, and talking over the events of the day. They were on their way to Emmaus, a village about eight miles from Jerusalem; and as they walked they spoke of the report sent out by the soldiers—that the grave had been robbed of its dead—and they wondered what effect this would have, and who was to lead them in their work.

While they thus talked, Jesus drew near and went along with them for some time before he spoke. But they did not know him. He is often near us, and we do not know him. Doubts and fears dim our sight. And he said to them, "What disputes are ye having with one another? and why are ye so sad?" And one of them, named Cleophas, said unto him: "Art thou so much of a stranger in Jerusalem that thou dost not not know the things that are taking place there?" Jesus said: "What things?"

And they said unto him, "The things concerning Jesus of Nazareth, who was a prophet, mighty in deed and word before God and all the people. And how the chief priests and our rulers delivered him up to death, and crucified him. But we hoped that it was he who should redeem Israel. Yea, and beside all this, it is now the third day since these things came to pass. Moreover, certain women of our company amazed us, having been early to the tomb, and not finding his body, they came, saying that they had seen a vision of angels, who said that he was alive. And certain of them that were with us went to the tomb, and found it even as the women had said. But they saw not Jesus.

Then Jesus spoke to the two with whom he was walking, saying: "Foolish men, and slow to believe in all that the prophets have spoken. Ought not Christ to have suffered these things, and enter into his glory?" And beginning with Moses and all the prophets, he explained every passage of Scripture that bore any relation to himself. How clear they seemed with this light thrown upon them!

All too soon they drew near to the village of Emmaus, and the stranger made as if he would go on further. But Cleophas and Luke could not part with him. They urged him to stay and spend the night with them. "Abide with us," they said, "for it is toward evening, and the day is even now far spent." And he consented, and went into the house to be their guest. And as they sat down to supper, the stranger taking the loaf of bread, he blessed, and breaking it, he gave to them. And their eyes were opened, and they knew him; and he vanished out of their sight. But there was no trace of sadness on their faces now. All was light and joy. He had risen, indeed! And they said to one another, "Did not our hearts burn within us while he talked with us, and opened to us the Scriptures?" And that very hour they returned to Jerusalem to tell the glad tidings to the rest of the disciples.

On account of their fear of the Jews, the disciples met secretly in a room in a quiet part of the city. And on this Easter Sunday evening, they were gathered together, when the two from Emmaus arrived. The doors were shut to prevent any surprise, when suddenly Jesus came and stood among the disciples, and said unto them, "Peace be unto you." But they were terrified, and thought that they beheld a spirit. And he said unto them, "Why are ye troubled? and wherefore do doubts arise in your heart? Behold my hands and my feet. Handle me and see for yourselves; for a spirit hath not flesh and bones." And when he had said this he showed them his hands and his feet. And while they were still unbelieving for joy and wonder, he said unto them, "Have ye here anything to eat?" And they gave him a piece of broiled fish, and he took it and did eat before them.

Then were the disciples glad when they saw it was their Lord. Jesus therefore said unto them again, "Peace be unto you. As the Father hath sent me, so I also send you." And when he had said this he breathed on them, and saith unto them, "Receive the Holy Spirit. Whosoever sins ye forgive they shall be forgiven, and whosoever sins ye do not forgive they shall not be forgiven."

This was the power given unto the Church of Christ on earth, a promise that Jesus would be with them to strengthen their own souls, and to help them do his work.

Now Thomas, one of the twelve, was not with them when Jesus came. The other disciples therefore said unto him, "We have seen the Lord." But Thomas said, "Except I shall see in his hands the print of the nails, and put my finger into the print of the nails, and put my hand into his side, I will not believe."

The next Sunday the disciples met together in the same room, and Thomas was with them. When the doors were shut, Jesus appeared in the midst of his disciples, with the well-known salutation, "Peace

THE INCREDULITY OF THOMAS.

be unto you!" Then saith he to Thomas, "Reach hither thy finger, and see my hands; and reach out thy hand and put it into my side; and be not faithless, but believing."

Thomas, fully convinced, cried out in the rapture of his soul, "My Lord and my God!" Jesus saith unto him, "Because thou hast seen me thou hast believed; happy are they that have not seen, and yet have believed."

After these things the eleven disciples went into Galilee, unto the mountain where Jesus had said he would meet them. And when he came they worshiped him. But there was still some among those whom Jesus had taught, who doubted that he had risen from the dead. And he came near to them, and spoke unto them, saying, "All power is given unto me in heaven and on earth. Go ye therefore, and make disciples of all the nations, baptizing them in the name of the Father, and of the Son, and of the Holy Ghost. Teaching them all things whatsoever I commanded you." And to give his disciples fresh strength and courage, he said, "Lo, I am with you always, even unto the end of the world!"

Many other signs did Jesus in the presence of his disciples, which are not written down in the New Testament. "The half has not been told." But these are written that ye may believe that Jesus is the Christ, the Son of God; and that believing ye may have life in his name.

One morning seven of the disciples went down to the Sea of Galilee near which they made their home. There were together, Simon Peter, Thomas called Didymus, Nathaniel, of Cana, in Galilee, James and John, the two sons of Zebedee, and two other disciples. It was at night, and there had been some talk as to what they should do.

Peter settled the case for himself, by saying, "I go a-fishing." The others say, "We will come with thee." They went into the boat, and pulled out from shore, and though they spent the whole night on the lake they caught nothing.

As the day began to break Jesus stood on the shore; but the disciples did not recognize him.

JESUS SHOWS HIMSELF TO HIS DISCIPLES.

They might have seen the figure of a man, but did not know that it was Jesus. Jesus therefore said, unto them, "Children, have ye anything to eat!" They answered, "No." And he said to them, "Cast the net on the right side of the boat, and ye shall find." They cast, therefore, and had not strength to draw it in for the multitude of fishes.

That disciple whom Jesus loved, saith unto Peter, "It is the Lord!" When Peter heard this, he tied his fisher's coat about him, for he was naked, and did cast himself at once into the sea. The others followed in the little boat, for they were not far from land, dragging the net full of fishes. As soon as they came to shore, they saw there a fire of charcoal, and a fish laid thereon and a loaf of bread.

Jesus said unto them, "Bring the fishes which ye have now caught. Peter, therefore, went up to help them, and they drew the net to the land full of great fishes, to the number of a hundred and fifty-three. And for all there were so many, yet the net was not broken.

This net is a type of the Gospel net which is to be cast out into the world to catch sinners. There are many meshes in a net, each one strengthened by cords and knots, so that the fish cannot break through. And there are also many churches in the world for the gathering in of saints and sinners. And as all these meshes in the net are held together by one great cord of love which strengthens it, so is it with the churches, where Christ is worshiped. The more sinners that are brought in, the stronger is the net.

If we do not catch men as we ought, we may be sure that we are not on the right side of the boat, and we must not only wait for orders, but ask for them in prayer. We must make our wants known, and God will surely give us all we need.

Jesus saith unto them, "Come and break your fast." With reverent awe they accepted the invitation, not daring to inquire, "Who art thou?" so well did they know it was the Lord. Jesus then came, and taking the loaf, gave to each one a portion of the bread and a piece of the fish. And this is the third time that Jesus appeared to the disciples, after he was raised from the dead.

After they had breakfasted, Jesus saith to Simon Peter, "Simon, son of Jonas, lovest thou me more than these?" He saith unto him, "Yea, Lord; thou knowest that I love thee." Jesus saith unto him, "Feed my lambs." He saith to him a second time, "Simon, son of Jonas, lovest thou me?" Peter answered, "Yea, Lord; thou knowest that I love thee." Jesus said unto him, "Feed my sheep." He saith unto him the third time, "Simon, son of Jonas, lovest thou me?" Peter was grieved because he said unto him the third time, "Lovest thou me?" And he answered, "Lord, thou knowest all things; thou knowest that I love thee." Jesus said unto him, "Feed my sheep. Verily, verily, I say unto thee, when thou wert younger thou didst gird thyself, and wert free to walk wherever thou didst choose. But when thou shalt be old, thou shalt stretch forth thy hands, and another shall gird thee, and bear thee where thou wouldst not choose to go." This he said signifying by what manner of death he should glorify God. And when he had thus spoken, he said unto Peter, "Follow me."

Peter rose to do so, but turning around saw another following. This was John the disciple whom Jesus loved, and who leaned back at the Lord's Supper, and asked who was to betray him.

Peter seeing John following, saith unto Jesus, "Lord, what of this man? What is to be his fate?" Jesus answered, "If I will that he wait until I come,

THE COMING OF THE HOLY GHOST.

what is that to thee? Follow thou me." This word therefore went forth among the brethren that John was not to die, but was to wait patiently for the Second Coming of the Lord, when he would be borne upward as were Enoch and Elijah, to the land of rest above. Yet Jesus said not unto him, "He dieth not; but, if I will that he wait till I come, what is that to thee?"

Peter loved the Lord. Three times had he denied him, and three times was he forced to answer the question "Lovest thou me?" His after life was one of struggle and endeavor to walk in the footsteps of his Master, and to win souls for Christ. Feed my sheep, Feed my lambs, and Follow me, was his threefold order, and he taught with great power throughout the land, and old and young were brought into the Church of Christ. The date of his death is not known, but is supposed to have been at the same time and place as that of St. Paul. He was sentenced to be crucified; and in his humility he prayed that he might be nailed to the cross with his head downward, that his death might exceed in shame that of his dear Lord and Master. John also had his life-work, and suffered many trials which he bore with Christian patience and resignation. Because of his preaching he was banished by the Roman Emperor, Domitian, to the lonely Isle of Patmos; and there he had a vision of the glory prepared for those who love the Lord. This Revelation he wrote down and sent out, that all believers everywhere might be comforted and strengthened thereby.

Jesus rose from the dead on Easter Sunday, and for forty days thereafter showed himself to the apostles at various times and places. And on one occasion he said to them, "These are my words which I spake unto you while I was yet with you, that all things must come to pass which are written in the Law of Moses, and in the Prophets and Psalms, concerning me. Then opened he their minds that they might understand the Scriptures. And he said unto them, "Thus it is written, that Christ should suffer death, and rise again on the third day. And that repentance and forgiveness of sins should be preached in his name throughout the whole world, beginning at Jerusalem. Ye are witnesses of these things. And behold I send forth the promise of my Father upon you; but tarry ye in the city until ye be gifted with the power from on high."

And when he had said these words, he led them out upon the Mount of Olives and over the brow of the hill, towards Bethany. Then lifting up his hands he blessed them, and while he blessed them, he parted from them, and was carried up into heaven. And they fell down and worshiped him, and returned to Jerusalem with great joy. They spent much time in prayer, blessing God for the promise of the Holy Spirit, and this promise was granted them not long after Jesus appeared to them for the last time.

The disciples to the number of one hundred and twenty, were in the room where they were wont to meet, and with them were the women who were "last at the cross and first at the grave." And suddenly there was the sound of a rushing wind, that seemed to fill all the house. And at the same time were seen forked tongues of flame that settled like a crown of fire on the head of each one present. And they were all filled with the Holy Spirit, for each one felt in himself new strength and love, and with a wild outburst of joy gave thanks and praise to God. This day was called PENTECOST, which meant the fiftieth day, and from that time began the first preaching with a view to building up the Church of Christ. In some of the churches at

THE ASCENSION.

this present day, it is known as Whitsunday, or White Sunday, because of the white dresses worn by the young girls who come to be baptized.

Ten years after the Crucifixion, a church was established at Antioch, where the Gospel was preached with great success. And to distinguish them from the other Jews, who still held to the old faith and the old forms, the people of Antioch gave the name of Christians to these followers of the Lord.

Jesus, though not in sight, is still very near to all those who put their trust in him. He says unto all those weary of the sins of the world, "Come unto me, and I will give you rest."

To those who are lonely and sad, he says, "Lo, I am with you alway; even unto the end of the world, I will not leave thee nor forsake thee." There is always a chance for us to do loving service; but we must be willing to do it in the Lord's way, and not in our own way. It is when we work against him that we get into trouble.

Always at the door of your heart is one who stands knocking, saying, "Come, Open, Let me in." Everywhere, if we listen, we will hear the loving call; in the night time, in the dark hours, in the midst of sorrow and pain. The winds say it, the tides say it, as they bring the word from heathen lands, "Come over and help us!" The vineyards and the harvest fields cry, "Come, gather us in! Gather us in!"

It is a call to work, to suffering maybe, to daily cross-bearing and hardships; but when we think of all that Jesus did for us, how poor seems any return we can make. All he asks is that we pay the debt with love. More love for Christ, more love for our fellow-men, and less love for self, will make earth seem a little heaven below;" and happy are they who early give their hearts to him, and FOLLOW JESUS all their lives.

INDEX.

Ænon, John the Baptist at, 71
Amen, meaning of word, 188
Andrew becomes a disciple of Jesus, 58
   chosen an Apostle by Jesus, 96
   feeds the multitude, 170
   informs Jesus some Greeks seek him, 303
   asks Jesus for a sign of his second advent, 320
Angel (An) foretells to Mary birth of Jesus, 5
   announces birth of Jesus to shepherds, 9
   warns Joseph to take Jesus to Egypt, 17
   bids Joseph bring back Jesus to Judea, 21
   foretells to Zachariah birth of John, 45–46
   appears to Jesus in Gethsemane, 347
   removes stone from entrance to sepulchre of Jesus, 378
   tells the women that Jesus is risen, 379
Anna, a witness to Simeon's words, 14
Annas, Jesus taken before, 351
Antioch, church established at, 399
Antipas. *See* Herod Antipas
Antonia, Tower of, 38
Apostles, names of, 96, 152
   power given to, 152
   sent to preach to the Jews, 152
   instructions to, 152–156
   return from their mission, 168
   go with Jesus to Bethsaida, 169
   asked by Jesus if they would leave him, 181
   jealous of Peter, James and John, 209
   displeased with James and John, 239
   strife among them as to which would be greatest, 331
   at the Last Supper, 331
   Jesus washes feet of, 332
   Jesus foretells their desertion, 344
   their desertion of him, 351
   Jesus appears before them after his death, 380, 386, 388, 395
Archelaus, son of Herod, 21, 163
Ark containing the Law and the Prophets, 81
Ascension of Jesus, 396
Ashes strewn on the head to denote sorrow, 120
Ass, Jesus enters Jerusalem on, 298
Augustus (Emperor) takes census of Jews, 5
   Herod seeks to please, 14

Baptism of Jesus by John, 50
   Jesus commands, 388
Barabbas released by Pilate, 358
Barley raised in the East, 183
Bartholomew chosen an Apostle by Jesus, 96
Bartimeus, Jesus restores sight of, 293
Bathing frequent among the Jews, 50
Beatitudes. *See* Sermon on the Mount
Beelzebub, the prince of devils, 154
Bethany, Jesus goes to, 295
   situation of, 273
Bethesda, pool of, 158
Bethlehem, Jesus born at, 6
   brought back to, 14
   murder of boys by Herod in, 18
Bethpage, Jesus draws near, 298
Bethsaida upbraided for its sins, 120, 220
   Jesus goes with his Apostles to, 169
Bible, verses of it learned by Jewish children, 25
   their principal text-book when young, 26
Blasphemy, Jesus discourses on, 190
Blind made to see. *See* Miracles
Bottles, leathern, 144
Burial customs, 373
Burying-ground. *See* Potter's Field

Cæsarea Philippi, Jesus goes to, 203
Caiaphas urges Jews to kill Jesus, 284
   plots death of Jesus, 327
   Jesus taken before, 352
   questions Jesus, 352–353
Camel's hair, clothes made of, 49
Camels used only by the rich, 298
Cana, the marriage at, 62
Capernaum, Jesus heals boy at, 79
   Jesus teaches at, 88
   upbraided by Jesus for its sins, 120, 221
   Jesus teaches in synagogue of, 180
Census of Jews, 5

INDEX.

Centurion's servant healed by Jesus, 114-116
Cephas, Peter so called by Jesus, 58
Chest. See Holy Chest
Children blessed by Jesus, 209, 269
Chorazin upbraided by Jesus for its sins, 120, 220
Christ. See Jesus
Cities upbraided by Jesus for their sins, 120, 220-221
Cleophas, Jesus appears before, 384
Commandments repeated by Jesus, 278
   Jesus gives the two great, 315
   Jesus gives a new one, 340
Communion instituted by Jesus at the Last Supper, 337
Corn not raised in the East, 183
Courts, the Sanhedrim, 70
Covetousness, Jesus discourses on, 194
Creed of Jews, 83
Crucifixion, slowness of death by, 373
Crucifixion of Jesus, 364-370
   foretold by him, 327
Crucifixion of Peter, 395

Dalmanutha, Jesus goes to, 202
Damascus Gate of the Temple, 38
David, building of Temple planned by, 30
   shew-bread eaten by him, 183-184
Dead restored to life, 117-118, 148, 281-284
Deaf made to hear. See Miracles
Death. See Crucifixion
Decapolis, 140
   Jesus passes through, 200
Dedication of the Temple, Feast of, 245, 277
Devil. See Satan
Dinner customs in the East, 123
Disciples, Jesus chooses twelve Apostles from, 96, 152
   he sends forth seventy of them on a mission, 216-219
   the seventy given power over evil spirits, 244
Dives and Lazarus, parable of, 263
Domitian banishes John the Apostle to Patmos, 395
Dove, Spirit of God takes form of, 50

East. See Orientals
Easter Sunday, 384
Education of Jewish children, 22-30
Egypt, Jesus taken to, 17-18
Elijah sent to Zarephath, 86
   declared by Jesus to be John the Baptist, 119, 207
   seen with Jesus at the transfiguration, 206
Elizabeth, mother of John the Baptist, 45-46

Emmaus, situation of, 384
Ephraim, Jesus goes to, 284
Esther, Queen, 157
Eucharist. See Communion

Fasting, teaching of Jesus about, 105
Feasts of the Jews, boys required to attend, 29
   See also Dedication, Marriage, Passover, Purim, Tabernacles
Feet. See Washing
Fig-tree withered by Jesus, 307
   parable of, 245
Fishes, miraculous draughts of, 95, 391
Flood (The), 267
Forgiveness, Jesus commands, 270
   of sin, Jesus grants Apostles power of, 387

Gabriel, the angel who foretold birth of John, 46
Gadara, Jesus visits, 138
Galileans quarrel with Pilate's soldiers, 244
   ingratitude of, 288
Galilee divided from Judea by Jordan, 5
Galilee, Sea of, 92
   its width, 138
   Jesus cures sick at, 175
   Same as Lake Gennesaret
Gennesaret, Lake. See Galilee, Sea of
Gentiles, blessings bestowed upon, 87
   meaning of word, 198
Gergesa, 140
Gerizim (Mt.), temple on, 73
Gethsemane, Jesus goes to, 344
Ghost. See Holy Ghost
Golden rule, 109
Golgotha, scene of the crucifixion, 364

Hallel, Psalms of David, 226
Haman, 158
Hands. See Washing
Harvest time in Palestine, 78
Hearing restored to the deaf. See Miracles
Hebrews. See Jews
Hermon (Mt.), Jesus ascends, 206
Herod the Great made governor of the Jews, 1
   his iron rule, 14
   seeks to destroy Jesus, 17
   slays all the young boys in Bethlehem, 18
   rebuilds the Temple, 34
Herod Antipas (his son) imprisons John the Baptist, 118, 163
   marries Herodias, 164
   beheads John, 167
   wishes to see Jesus, 168
   Jesus led before, 357

INDEX. 403

Herod Antipas mocks Jesus and sends him back to Pilate, 357
  his death, 169
Herod Philip, husband of Herodias, 163
  made governor of Cæsarea Philippi, 203
Herodias, wife of Philip, 163
  marries Antipas, 164
  causes death of John, 167
Hiram assists Solomon to build the Temple, 33
Holy Chest, depository of the Law and the Prophets, 81
Holy Ghost, coming of, 396
  typified by pouring water on the altar, 226
  foretold by Jesus, 339
Holy Land. *See* Palestine
Horses used only in war, 208
Hospitality in the East, 123
Houses in the East, 2
Hypocrisy, Jesus discourses on, 194

Immortality, disbelief of Sadducees in, 315
Isaiah, his prophecy of John the Baptist, 49
  his prophecies read by Jesus in the synagogue, 84
  his prophecy as to sympathy of Jesus, 91
  a praise song from, 226
Israelites. *See* Jews

Jacob's well, Jesus rests at, 73
Jaffa Gate of the Temple, 38
Jairus, his daughter restored to life, 147-148
James (son of Alpheus) chosen an Apostle by Jesus, 96
James (son of Zebedee) becomes a disciple of Jesus, 61
  chosen an Apostle by Jesus, 96
  beholds transfiguration of Jesus, 206
  disciples jealous of, 209
  his anger when shelter and food are refused Jesus, 219
  his sufferings for cause of Jesus, 289
  asks Jesus for a sign, 320
  Jesus bids him watch with him, 347
  Jesus after his death appears before, 388
Jericho, distance from Jerusalem to, 249
  description of, 290
Jerusalem as first seen by Jesus, 30
  at Feast of Tabernacles, 223
  Jesus foresees his death in, 247
  entry of Jesus into, 299
  its destruction foretold by Jesus, 247, 300, 319, 364
  See also Temple

Jesus, his birth foretold to Mary by an angel, 5
  his birth at Bethlehem, 6
  shepherds informed of it by an angel, 9
  taken to Jerusalem for presentation at the Temple, 10
  visited by Simeon, 10-13
  brought back to Bethlehem, 14
  visited by the wise men, 17
  taken into Egypt to avoid Herod, 17-18
  brought to Nazareth by Joseph, 21-22
  his boyhood, 22-30
  taken to the Passover feast, 30
  questions the Rabbis in the Temple, 38-41
  his probable aid to Joseph in carpentry, 41
  studies nature and men, 41-42
  baptized by John, 50
  spends forty days in wilderness, 53
  tempted by Satan, 53-54
  returns to the Jordan, 57
  John the Baptist bears witness to him, 58
  chooses some of his disciples, 58-61
  changes water into wine, 62
  drives the money-changers out of the Temple, 64-66
  tells Nicodemus how to be saved, 69-70
  jealousy of John's disciples towards, 71
  labors in Samaria, 73-78
  heals boy at Capernaum, 79
  attends the synagogue at Nazareth, 81
  conducts the service, 83-86
  driven from Nazareth, 87
  teaches in Capernaum, 88
  casts out evil spirits, 91
  cures Simon's wife's mother, 91
  miraculous draught of fishes, 95
  names of his Apostles, 96
  Sermon on the Mount, 96-113
  heals a leper, 114
  heals centurion's servant, 114-116
  restores the dead to life, 117-118
  preaches concerning John the Baptist, 118-119
  upbraids unrepentant cities, 120, 220-221
  visits Simon the Pharisee, 123
  his feet washed by Mary Magdalene, 124
  his parable of money-lender, 127
  forgives the sins of Mary Magdalene, 128
  his parable of the sower, 129
  that of the wheat and tares, 131
  that of the mustard seed, 132
  that of the leaven, 132
  that of the hidden treasure, 135

404 INDEX

Jesus, his parable of the pearl, 135
  that of the net, 135
  calms the sea, 138
  casts out evil spirits, 134-140
  heals the paralytic, 142
  eats with publicans, 143
  his parable of new wine and old bottles, 144
  heals the sick woman, 144
  restores the dead to life, 148
  restores sight to the blind, 151
  restores speech to the dumb, 151
  gives Apostles power over evil spirits, 152
  instructs Apostles, 152-156
  at the pool of Bethesda, 158
  declares that he is equal with God, 160-162
  goes with his Apostles to Bethsaida, 169
  feeds the multitude, 170
  walks on the sea, 172
  cures the sick at Gennesaret, 175
  preaches faith to the Jews, 176-180
  foretells treachery of Judas, 181
  accuses Jews of hypocrisy, 183
  on Sabbath-keeping, 183-184
  restores a withered hand, 186
  teaches the Lord's Prayer, 187-188
  heals a demoniac, 189
  discourses on blasphemy, 190
  foretells his resurrection, 191, 205, 288
  rebukes the Pharisees, 192
  rebukes lawyers, 193
  discourses on hypocrisy and covetousness, 194
  his parable of the rich man, 195
  warns his disciples to be always ready, 196
  shows that faithfulness will be rewarded, 197
  goes to Tyre and Sidon, 198
  heals daughter of Syro-Phœnician woman, 200
  restores speech to the dumb, 201
  feeds the multitude, 201
  enmity of Pharisees and Sadducees to, 202
  restores sight to the blind, 203
  declares that upon Peter he would build his church, 204
  rebukes Peter, 205
  his transfiguration, 206
  declares John the Baptist to be Elijah, 207
  drives out evil spirits, 208
  blesses little children, 209, 269
  declares his disciples must become as little children, 209-212
  bids them cut off hand or foot if it offends, 213
  on paying taxes, 214-215
  sends forth seventy disciples, 216-219

Jesus refused food and shelter, 219
  declares he came to save, not to destroy, 220
  declares he has no place to lay his head, 222
  goes to Jerusalem, 223
  teaches in the Temple, 224
  priests order him to be seized, 225, 230
  accuses Jews of keeping the letter and not the spirit of the law, 225
  calls upon all who thirst to come unto him, 229
  again teaches in the Temple, 231-235
  Jews seek to stone him, 235
  restores sight to the blind, 236
  accused by Jews of breaking Sabbath, 239
  parable of the sheep-fold, 242
  leaves Jerusalem, 244
  parable of the fig-tree, 245
  foretells destruction of Jerusalem, 247, 300, 319, 364
  parable of good Samaritan, 248
  heals man with the dropsy, 250
  parable of the marriage feast, 250
  parable of the great supper, 253
  parable of the lost sheep, 254
  parable of lost piece of silver, 256
  parable of prodigal son, 257
  parable of unjust steward, 260
  rebukes the Pharisees, 262
  parable of Dives and Lazarus 263
  declares the kingdom of God is in the heart, 264
  parable of the unrighteous judge, 268
  parable of the Pharisee and publican, 268
  parable of the king and servant, 270
  visits Martha and Mary, 273
  reproves Martha, 277
  repeats the commandments, 278
  tells how to be saved, 279
  parable of the vineyard, 280
  restores Lazarus to life, 281-284
  goes to Ephraim, 284
  heals the lepers, 287-288
  declares that he came to ransom others, 289
  passes through Jericho, 290
  lodges with Zaccheus, 293
  restores sight of Bartimeus, 293
  parable of the pounds, 294
  reaches Bethany, 295
  anointed with precious oil by Mary, 296
  sends Peter and John for a wild ass, 298
  enters Jerusalem on the ass, 299
  again cleanses the Temple, 303
  a voice from heaven declares that he will be glorified, 303
  returns to Mt. of Olives, 304

Jesus withers the fig-tree, 307
  Jews question his authority to teach, 308
  parable of the vineyard, 308
  declares the kingdom of God shall be taken from the Jews, 309
  declares it is right to pay just taxes, 310
  the widow's mite, 311
  declares there will be no marriage in the resurrection, 312
  the two great commandments, 315
  condemns the Scribes and Pharisees, 316
  warns Apostles of their coming trials, 320
  parable of the virgins, 320
  parable of the talents, 323
  speaks of the glory of his triumph, 325
  condemns the uncharitable, 326
  foretells his crucifixion, 327
  Judas agrees to betray him, 327–328
  sends Peter and John to prepare the Passover, 331
  sits down to the Last Supper, 331
  washes feet of Apostles, 332
  tells them that Judas will betray him, 333
  institutes communion, 337
  tells Peter he will deny him, 337, 347
  bids his disciples keep his commandments, 338
  foretells the coming of the Holy Ghost, 339
  parable of the vine, 340
  gives a new commandment, 340
  foretells persecutions of his disciples, 341
  his prayer to God, 342–343
  a hymn is sung, 344
  goes to Gethsemane, 344
  tells his disciples they will forsake him, 344
  prays apart at Gethsemane, 347
  an angel appears to him, 347
  betrayed by Judas, 348
  heals wound of servant, 351
  forsaken by his disciples, 351
  taken before Annas, 351
  sent bound to Caiaphas, 352
  questioned by Caiaphas, 352
  denied by Peter thrice, 352, 354
  struck by a soldier, 353
  declares he is the Son of God, 353
  blindfolded and spit upon by soldiers, 353
  led before Pilate, 354
  Pilate questions his accusers, 355
  questioned by Pilate, 356
  sent by Pilate to Herod, 357
  mocked by Herod and sent back to Pilate, 357
  sentenced by Pilate, 357
  scourged by the Romans, 358
  Jesus crowned with thorns and mocked, 361
  Pilate seeks to release him, 361
  delivered to the Jews, 364
  bears his own cross, 364
  taken to Golgotha, 366
  his crucifixion, 366
  offered vinegar for drink, 369
  placed between two thieves, 369
  inscription over his head, 369
  pardons the penitent thief, 369
  commends his mother to John, 369
  his thirst assuaged with vinegar, 370
  his last words, 370
  his death, 370
  phenomena at time of his death, 370
  spear thrust in his side, 373.
  his body placed in a sepulchre, 374
  angel removes stone from entrance to sepulchre, 378
  his resurrection, 379
  appears to his disciples, 380
  appears to Mary Magdalene, 383
  Jews believed his body stolen by his disciples, 384
  appears before Cleophas and Luke, 384
  appears before the Apostles and grants them power to forgive sins, 386
  convinces Thomas he is Christ, 387
  appears again before the Apostles and commands them to baptize all disciples, 388
  appears before seven Apostles, 388
  the draught of fishes, 391
  bids Peter follow him, 392
  shows himself at various places, 395
  his ascension, 396
Jews, their condition at birth of Christ, 1–5
  their fear of Herod, 17
  education of their children, 22–30
  commanded to bathe often, 50
  their hatred of Samaritans, 73, 234
  religious service of, 80–82
  creed of, 83
  drive Jesus from synagogue, 87
  their hatred of taxes, 95
  Jesus bids Apostles preach to, 152
  their custom of washing their hands before meals, 182
  their strictness in keeping the Sabbath, 183
  pour water on the altar, 226
  attempt to seize Jesus, 225–230
  seek to stone Jesus, 235, 278
  accuse Jesus of breaking the Sabbath, 239
  expulsion from synagogue a punishment among, 240
  forbidden to eat flesh of swine, 259
  ask Jesus if he is Christ, 277

Jews, theological studies of, 308
  Jesus declares kingdom of God shall be taken from, 309
  Paschal lamb, how eaten by, 331
  believed the disciples took away body of Jesus, 384
  See also Pharisees, Sadducees
John (the Apostle) becomes a disciple of Jesus, 61
  chosen an Apostle by Jesus, 96
  beholds transfiguration of Jesus, 206
  other disciples jealous of, 209
  questions Jesus, 210
  his anger when shelter and food are refused Jesus, 219
  sent by Jesus for wild ass, 298
  asks Jesus for a sign of his second advent, 320
  sent by Jesus to prepare Passover, 331
  called the beloved disciple, 333
  asks Jesus who is to betray him, 334
  Jesus bids him watch with him, 347
  accompanies Jesus before Caiaphas, 352
  takes care of mother of Jesus, 369-370
  finds Jesus risen from the dead, 380
  Jesus appears before, 388
  recognizes Jesus, 391
  Apostles believed he was not to die, 395
  Revelation written by him, 395
John the Baptist, his birth as foretold by an angel, 45-46
  begins preaching in the wilderness of Judea, 49
  baptizes Jesus, 50
  bears witness to Jesus, 57-58, 101
  his disciples jealous of Jesus, 71
  declares himself only the messenger of Jesus, 72
  Pharisees compare his teaching with that of Jesus, 73
  imprisoned by Herod, 118, 103
  Jesus preaches about him, 118-119
  offends Herodias, 164
  for brief time doubts divinity of Christ, 164
  is beheaded, 167
  declared by Jesus to be Elijah, 207
  Jesus questions Jews on baptism of, 308
Jonah, a prophecy of Jesus, 191
Jordan (river) separates Galilee from Judea, 5
  John baptizes sinners in, 50
Joseph (patriarch), place of burial of, 73
Joseph (husband of Virgin Mary), 5
  goes to Bethlehem, 6
  warned by angel to take Jesus to Egypt. 17
  an angel tells him to return to Judea with Jesus, 21

Joseph (husband of Virgin Mary) takes Jesus to Nazareth, 22
  a carpenter by trade, 23
  finds Jesus in the Temple questioning the Rabbis, 38-41
  probably assisted by Jesus in carpentry, 41
Joseph (of Arimathea) helps place body of Jesus in sepulchre, 374
Jot, definition of, 100
Judas (son of James) chosen an Apostle by Jesus, 96
  questions Jesus, 339
Judas Iscariot chosen an Apostle by Jesus, 96
  his betrayal foretold by Jesus, 181
  reproves Mary for anointing Jesus, 296
  agrees to deliver Jesus to the Jews for thirty pieces of silver, 327-328
  designated by Jesus as his betrayer, 333
  departs from the Last Supper, 334
  betrays Jesus with a kiss, 348
  repents his crime, 354
  hangs himself, 355
Judea divided from Galilee by Jordan, 5
Judge, parable of unrighteous, 268
Julias, Jesus restores sight of, 203

Kedron (brook), 328
  valley of, 344

Labor, wages of, 248
Lamb. See Paschal lamb
Last Supper (The), 331-344
Lawyer (A) questions Jesus, 247
Lawyers rebuked by Jesus, 193
Lazarus and Dives, parable of, 263
Lazarus (brother of Martha) restored to life, 281-284
  sits at table with Jesus, 296
Leather, bottles made of, 144
Leaven, parable of, 132
  sought for by Jews on eve of Passover, 328
Lectern in synagogues, 81
Leprosy in the East, 113
  healed by Elijah, 86
  healed by Jesus, 114, 287-288
Levi tribe, priests taken from, 45
Levites, Jewish name for priests, 45
Leviticus first studied by Jewish children, 29
Locusts used as food by the poor in the East, 49
Lord's Prayer, 187-188
Lot and destruction of Sodom, 267
Luke, Jesus appears before, 384

Magdala, Jesus goes to, 202

INDEX. 407

Magi. *See* Wise men
Magicians foretell future by stars, 1
Malchus wounded in ear by Peter, 348
  wound healed by Jesus. 351
Mammon, meaning of, 262
Manna sent to the Jews, 179
Marriage (The) at Cana, 62
  Jesus declares there will be none in the resurrection, 312
Marriage-feast, parable of, 250
Martha, Jesus visits, 273
  reproved by Jesus. 277
  her brother restored to life, 281–284
  Jesus goes to house of, 296
Mary (mother of Jesus), angel foretells birth of Jesus to her, 5
  gives birth to Jesus, 6
  presents Jesus at Temple, 10
  Simeon foretells manner of Jesus's death to her, 10–13
  finds Jesus in the Temple questioning the Rabbis, 38–41
  at the marriage at Cana, 62
  her anxiety for Jesus, 191
  commended to care of John by Jesus, 369
Mary (sister of Martha), Jesus visits, 273
  sits at feet of Jesus, 277
  her brother restored to life, 281–284
  anoints Jesus with precious ointment, 296
Mary (wife of Cleophas) present at crucifixion, 369
Mary Magdalene and Jesus, 124–128
  present at the crucifixion, 369
  at sepulchre of Jesus, 378
  finds two angels where Jesus had lain, 380
  Jesus appears before her and speaks to her, 383
Matthew testifies to sympathy of Jesus, 91
  becomes a disciple of Jesus, 95
  chosen an Apostle, 96
  Jesus goes to house of, 143
Messiah. *See* Jesus
Micah foretells place of Jesus's birth, 17
Mint, tithing of, 192
Miracles of Jesus: changing the water into wine, 62
  healing boy at Capernaum, 79
  casting out evil spirits, 91, 207–208
  healing Simon's wife's mother, 91
  the draught of fishes, 95, 391
  healing lepers, 114, 287–288
  healing centurion's servant, 114–116
  restoring the dead to life, 117–118, 148, 281–284
  making the blind see, 118, 151, 203, 236, 293
  healing the paralytic, 142
  curing the sick woman, 147

Miracles of Jesus: making the dumb speak, 151, 201
  healing sick at pool of Bethesda, 158
  feeding the multitude, 170, 201
  walking on the sea, 172
  healing the sick at Gennesaret, 175
  making whole a withered hand, 186
  healing the demoniac, 189
  curing daughter of Syro-Phœnician woman, 200
  healing man with the dropsy, 250
  withering the fig-tree, 307
  healing wound of Malchus, 351
Mite, value of, 312
Money-changers driven from the Temple, 65–66
Money-lender, parable of, 127
Mordecai. 158
Moriah (Mt.) the site of the Temple, 30
Moses, his commandment to lepers, 114
  a witness to Jesus, 162
  his prophecy of Jesus, 171–172
  seen with Jesus at the transfiguration, 206
Mount. *See* names of mounts
Mules used by the poor, 298
Murder, commandment against, 278
Mustard seed, parable of, 132

Naaman, the Syrian, 86
Nain, Jesus goes to, 116
Nathaniel becomes a disciple of Jesus, 61
  Jesus appears before, 388
Nazareth, situation of, 5
  Jesus taken by Joseph to, 22
  life of Jesus at, 42
Needle's eye, 279
Net, parable of the, 135
Nicodemus told by Jesus how to be saved, 69–70
  defends Jesus, 230
  helps embalm body of Jesus, 374
Nineveh a witness against the Jews, 191
Noah and the flood, 267

Ointment, Jesus anointed with precious, 296
Olives (Mt. of), Jesus ascends, 300
  Jesus returns to, 304
Orientals, dress of, 195–196

Palestine, its division into two parts by the Jordan, 5
Palms borne by spectators of entry of Jesus into Jerusalem, 300
Palms (City of), name given to Jericho, 290
Pan, the god of woods, 203
Paneas, ancient name of Cæsarea Philippi, 203

408 INDEX.

Parables, their use among the Jews, 128
Parables of Jesus: the money-lender, 127
  the sower, 129
  the wheat and tares, 131
  the mustard seed, 132
  the leaven, 132
  the hidden treasure, 135
  the pearl, 135
  the net, 135
  new wine in old bottles, 144
  the rich man, 195
  the sheep-fold, 242
  the barren fig-tree, 245
  the good Samaritan, 248
  the marriage-feast, 250
  the great supper, 253
  the lost sheep, 254
  the lost piece of silver, 256
  the prodigal son, 257
  the unjust steward, 260
  Dives and Lazarus, 263
  the unrighteous judge, 268
  the Pharisee and the publican, 268
  the king and his servant, 270
  the vineyard, 280
  the pounds, 294
  the virgins, 320
  the talents, 323
  the vine, 340
Parents, honoring, 182
Paschal lamb, 295
  how prepared for Passover, 328-331
Passover, Feast of, 29, 65, 287, 331
Patmos, John banished to, 395
Paul, a witness to the help of Jesus, 209
Pearl, parable of, 135
Penny, value of, 248
Pentateuch studied by young Jewish children, 29
Pentecost, 396
Perea, Jesus teaches in, 247
Perfumes in the East, 124
Peter becomes a disciple of Jesus, 58
  seeks Jesus, 91
  healing of his wife's mother by Jesus, 91
  his amazement at draught of fishes, 95
  chosen an Apostle by Jesus, 96
  Jesus goes to house of, 141
  walks on the waters, 172
  asserts belief of Apostles in Jesus, 181
  asks explanation of parable, 182
  questions Jesus, 196, 270, 279
  meaning of his name, 204
  declares Jesus to be the Son of God, 204
  rebuked by Jesus, 205
  beholds transfiguration of Jesus, 206
  disciples jealous of, 209
  and the Temple tax, 214-215

Peter sent by Jesus for a wild ass, 298
  speaks of the withered fig-tree, 307
  asks Jesus for a sign of his second advent, 320
  sent by Jesus to prepare Passover, 331
  demurs at Jesus washing his feet, 332
  asks Jesus who is to betray him, 334
  his denial of Jesus foretold by him, 337, 347
  watches with Jesus, 347
  wounds servant's ear, 348
  reproved by Jesus, 348-351
  denies Jesus, 352
  a third time denies him, 354
  finds that Jesus is risen from the dead, 380
  Jesus appears before, 388
  thrice declares he loves Jesus, 392
  his death by crucifixion, 395
Pharisee and publican, parable of, 268
Pharisees wish John to baptize them, 50
  their strictness, 57-58
  compare Jesus with John, 73
  teachings of Jesus against, 104
  jealous of Jesus, 128
  declare Jesus the prince of devils, 151
  plot death of Jesus, 163, 186
  accuse Apostles of Sabbath-breaking, 183
  claim Jesus to be in league with Satan, 189
  their jealousy of publicans and sinners, 259
  mock Jesus, 262
  their hypocrisy exposed by Jesus, 315
  See also Jews
Philip becomes a disciple of Jesus, 61
  chosen an Apostle by Jesus, 96
  asked by Jesus how to feed the multitude, 170
  asked by Greeks who Jesus is, 303
  asks Jesus to show the Father, 338
Phylacteries, meaning of, 316
Pilate, Galileans quarrel with soldiers of, 244
  Jesus led before, 354
  questions his accusers, 355
  questions Jesus, 356
  sends him to Herod, 357
  Jesus brought back to, 357
  releases Barabbas and sentences Jesus, 358
  seeks to free Jesus, 361
  delivers him over for crucifixion, 364
  refuses to alter inscription on cross of Jesus, 369
  orders legs of crucified broken, 373
  consents that Joseph take charge of body of Jesus, 374
  orders soldiers to guard tomb of Jesus, 378

INDEX. 409

Pilgrimages to Passover Feast, 30
Pool. *See* Bethesda, Siloam
Pork, Jews forbidden to eat, 259
Potter's Field bought with the thirty pieces of silver, 355
Prayer, necessity of secret, 105
  answered by God, 189
  See also Lord's Prayer
Prodigal son, parable of, 257
Prophets studied by Jewish children, 29
Psalms learned by young Jews, 25
Publican and Pharisee, parable of, 268
Publicans, tax-collectors, 95
Purim, Feast of, 157

Rabbis questioned by Jesus in the Temple, 38–41
  allowed to dwell in synagogues, 83
Ransom, meaning of, 289
Redeemer, Jesus our, 289
Resurrection of Jesus, 379
Revelation written by John, 395
Riches, uselessness of, 195
  a hindrance to salvation, 279
Roman dominion over the Jews, 1
Royal Porch to the Temple, 37
Rue, tithing, 192

Sabbath, Mosaic law forbidding work on, 159
  how kept by Jews, 183
  Jesus discourses on, 184
  Jews accuse Jesus of breaking, 239
  healing sick on, 249
  duration of, 373
Sack-cloth worn to denote sorrow, 120
Sacraments. *See* Baptism, Communion
Sacrifices, Jewish, 108
Sadducees wish John to baptize them, 50
  their enmity to Jesus, 202
  disbelieve in a life after death, 315
Salome demands head of John, 167
Samaria, Jesus refused food and shelter in, 219
Samaritan, parable of good, 248
  woman, Jesus reveals himself to, 74–77
Samaritans, hatred of Jews to, 73, 234
  Jesus labors among, 74–78
  gratitude of, 288
Sandals worn in the East, 123
Sanhedrin (The), 70
  a court of law, 230
  power of, 353
  declares the disciples stole body of Jesus, 383
Satan tempts Jesus, 53–54
Schools among the Jews, 26
Scourging, mode of, 358

Scribes. *See* Pharisees
Sermon on the Mount, 96–113
Shechem, Joseph buried at, 73
Sheep, parable of lost, 254
Sheep-fold, parable of, 242
Shekel, its value, 65
Shepherds told by angel of birth of Jesus, 6–9
  visit Jesus and repeat words of shepherds, 9–10
Sidon, wicked cities likened to, 120, 221
  Jesus goes to, 198
Sight restored to the blind. *See* Miracles
Siloam (pool of), water brought from, 226
  Jesus bids blind wash in, 236
Siloam, tower of, 245
Silver, parable of lost piece of, 256
  value of thirty pieces of, 328
Simeon visits Jesus, 10
  foretells the manner of his death to Mary, 10–13
Simon Peter. *See* Peter
Simon of Cyrene helps Jesus bear his cross, 364
Simon the leper, Jesus goes to house of, 296
Simon the Pharisee visited by Jesus, 123–127
Simon (the zealot) chosen an Apostle by Jesus, 96
Sin compared to leprosy, 114
Sodom, destruction of, 267
Solomon, Temple built by, 30–33
Solomon's Porch to the Temple, 37
Sower, parable of, 129
Speech restored to the dumb. *See* Miracles
Spikenard, oil made from, 296
Spirit. *See* Holy Ghost
Star of Bethlehem, its mention in the Old Testament, 1
  seen by the wise men, 14
  guides the wise men to Jesus, 17
Stephen's Gate of the Temple, 38
Steward, parable of unjust, 260
Swine, Jesus drives evil spirit into, 140
  Jews forbidden to eat flesh of, 259
Sychar, Jesus goes to, 73
Synagogues, description of, 80–82
  Jews punished by expulsion from, 240
Syro-Phœnician woman, Jesus heals daughter of, 200

Tabernacle suggests plan of the Temple, 33
Tabernacles, Feast of, 216, 223–229
Talents, parable of, 323
Tares, parable of, 131–134
Taxation, Jewish hatred of, 95
  among Jews, 214

Taxes, Jesus declares it right to pay, 310
Tetrarch, office of, 163
Temple, Jesus presented at, 10
  building of, 30-38
  Jesus questions Rabbis in, 38-41
  Jesus drives money-changers from, 65-66
  service in, 82
  See also Dedication
Thieves crucified with Jesus, 369
Thomas chosen an Apostle by Jesus, 96
  accompanies Jesus to Judea, 282
  asks Jesus the way, 338
  convinced by Jesus he is risen, 387
  Jesus appears before, 388
Tishri, a Jewish date, 223
Tithes, payment of, 192
Tittle, definition of, 100
Tombs for the dead, 282
Transfiguration of Jesus, 206
Tribute-money paid to the Temple, 65
Tyre, wicked cities likened to, 120, 221
  Jesus goes to, 198

Vine, parable of, 340
Vinegar offered Jesus on the cross, 369
Vineyard, parables of, 280, 308

Virgins, parable of, 320
Wages of laborers at time of Jesus, 248
Washing of hands, 181, 192
Washing of feet in the East, 123, 127
  those of the Apostles washed by Jesus, 332
Water changed into wine, 62
Wealth. *See* Riches
Wedding. *See* Marriage
Wheat and tares, parable of, 131-134
  raised in the East, 183
Whit-Sunday, 399
Widow's mite, 311-312
Wilderness, John dwells in, 49
  Jesus spends forty days in. 53
Wine, water changed into, 62
  parable of, 144
Wise men from the East visit Jesus, 14-15
Women required to attend Passover, 29
  (court of), in the Temple, 230

Zaccheus becomes a disciple of Jesus, 290-293
Zachariah, the birth of his son John foretold him by an angel, 45-46
Zarephath, Elijah sent to, 86
Zebedee's children, mother of, 288
Zerubbabel builds new Temple, 33
Zion Gate of the Temple, 33

www.ingramcontent.com/pod-product-compliance
Lightning Source LLC
Chambersburg PA
CBHW030545300426
44111CB00009B/869